HASIDISM
IN ISRAEL

HASIDISM IN ISRAEL

A History of the Hasidic Movement
and Its Masters in the Holy Land

TZVI RABINOWICZ

with a foreword by
Dr. Jonathan Sacks
Chief Rabbi of the United Hebrew Congregation
of the British Commonwealth

JASON ARONSON INC.
Northvale, New Jersey
Jerusalem

This book was set in 11 pt. Garamond by Hightech Data Inc., of Bangalore, India, and printed and bound by Book-mart Press, Inc. of North Bergen, NJ.

Library of Congress Cataloging-in-Publication Data

Rabinowicz, Tzvi, 1919–
    Hasidism in Israel: a history of the Hasidic movement and its masters in the holy land/by Tzvi Rabinowicz.
        p. cm.
    Includes bibliographical references and index.
    ISBN 0-7657-6068-1
    1. Hasidism—Israel—History. 2. Israel—Religion. 3. Hasidim—
Israel. I. Title.
BM198.4.I7R33 2000
296.8'332'095694—dc21   98–46952

Printed in the United States of America on acid-free paper. For information and catalog write to Jason Aronson Inc., 230 Livingston Street, Northvale, NJ 07647-1726, or visit our website: www.aronson.com

To my wife
Bella

Proverbs 31:1–10

Contents

Foreword

Rabbi Harry Rabinowicz is one of Anglo-Jewry's outstanding scholars, whose works, particularly on the hasidic movement, have enriched Jewish scholarship and contributed greatly to our understanding of Judaism's ever-lively spiritual world. His latest work, a study of the great hasidic Rebbes active in the reborn State of Israel, is no exception. It is a book to lift the spirit and delight the mind.

The hasidic movement was no mere passing moment in the history of the Jewish spirit. Coming to birth in the second half of the nineteenth century, it spoke to the vast masses of East European Jewry, giving new life to Judaism's three ancient loves: God, the Torah, and the Jewish people. What was new about it was less the substance than the form of its message. The early *hasidim*, disciples of the great Israel Baal Shem, the Baal Shem Tov, spoke in simple ways of simple things—what Rabbi Rabinowicz rightly describes as the "sublimely simple principles" of the joy of life, love of God and of His creations, and of religious deeds made luminous by the power of devotion. In an age when, to many, Judaism was in danger of becoming over-intellectualized through the high scholarship of its leading sages, it restored the dignity of ordinary lives dedicated to the service of God.

Hasidism has often been seen as a revolutionary turn in Jewish spirituality. To some degree it was. It took many of Judaism's more mystical doctrines, especially those of Lurianic Kabbalah, and turned them from esoteric wisdom into a way of life and belief accessible to many. It popularized what had hitherto been regarded as the "secrets of the Torah." But in a very real sense, Hasidism was a return to that most ancient of rubrics of Jewish life—the call, at Mount Sinai, to become a "kingdom of priests and a holy nation," meaning a kingdom for everyone, whose members are priests, and a nation whose citizens are holy.

It was this profoundly democratic ideal of spirituality to which Hasidism gave new drama and energy. Not only the great rabbinic sages, but every Jew, has within him or her the power to relate to the invisible Thou at the heart of reality. Simple deeds of piety and kindness could affect the highest spiritual worlds. The heroes of Judaism, like the angels who visited Abraham and Sarah, might appear as ordinary, even anonymous people, the thirty-six "hidden righteous individuals" of mystical doctrine. Time and again hasidic teaching brought the reverberations of infinity into the here-and-now of ordinary life. As Rabbi Rabinowicz points out, the great legacy of the Baal Shem Tov was to bring people close to God by bringing God close to the people, through songs, stories, and sayings that spoke directly to the heart.

The historian Paul Johnson once described rabbinic Judaism as a "highly efficient social machine for the production of intellectuals," and there is some truth in what he says. Judaism is a religion of study, interpretation, commentary, and "argument for the sake of heaven." But when Judaism speaks, not in the language of the mind but of the soul, the intellectual virtues fall away, to be replaced by an altogether more direct and intimate relationship with God, spanning the spectrum between exuberance and awe. It was this that the hasidic masters communicated with such consummate skill, and in doing so re-energized large parts of the Jewish world.

The popular image of Hasidism is of a movement whose setting is Eastern Europe of the eighteenth and nineteenth centuries. Less well known is the deep attachment many of its leading figures had for the land of Israel and for the project of re-establishing a strong Jewish presence there. They were not Zionists in the conventional sense of the word. Theirs was not the world of political action but of personal pilgrimage and deep faith that Providence would bring about the return to Zion. More than most, perhaps, they understood the dangers in secularizing the terms of Jewish history. Israel the land was, for them, not a place like others, any more than the Jewish people was a secular nation like others. They saw Zion as the setting of the great love affair between God and the Jewish people, and they brought to Israel a religious presence that, far from being extinguished, has grown and flourished into the present age.

The *hasidim* have much to teach us all, and our thanks are due to Rabbi Rabinowicz for a wholly fascinating insight into the lives of the great hasidic Rebbes and their followers, each one a vivid universe of the spirit, each a living counterweight to a secular age that is in danger of mastering creation while forgetting the Creator. In these several songs of the soul we hear the astonishingly varied music of the Jewish people, undefeated by the Holocaust, still singing the old-new words in the old-new land in the great duet between a people and their God. This is a lovely book by a fine writer, a fitting tribute to the masters of the Jewish spirit and to the faith that inspired them and continues to inspire us.

—Chief Rabbi Jonathan Sacks

Preface

So many people have helped me that it is impossible to list them all, and I am deeply indebted to many rebbes and *hasidim* in Israel and in Britain, who have taken the trouble to provide me with information and of sharing their memories with me. In addition, I would like to thank a number of friends for reading the various drafts of the chapters and making helpful and constructive suggestions, and for carefully scrutinizing the typescript: Miss Miriam Bloom; Messrs Alex Kaminsky, Simon Kritz, David Shepherd, and M. L. Weiser; Reverend Bernd Koschland, B.A.; Rabbi Yisrael Moshe Friedman; and Rabbi Avraham Moshe Kraus. I alone, of course, remain responsible for all comments and assessments.

I would like to take this opportunity of expressing my sincere thanks to the Chief Rabbi Professor Jonathan Sacks for his appreciative foreword.

Mr. Arthur Kurzweil deserves special mention for his enthusiastic support of the project. His personal and professional help is gratefully acknowledged.

I would like to express my warm appreciation to my friend Mr. Cyril Shack and his brother Mr. J. Shack, who have provided generous support for this project in memory of their parents, Avigdor and Hannah Shakowitz, early pioneers of Hasidism in England; to Mr. Marcus J. Margulies on behalf of the Stella and Alexander Margulies Charitable Trust; and to Mr. and Mrs. Heinoch Bronstein.

Above all, I owe an enormous debt to my wife, Bella, for her support throughout the year of research and writing. Without her constant interest and creative participation, this work could not have been finished.

—Tzvi Rabinowicz

Introduction

In the mid-eighteenth century Eastern Europe gave birth to the greatest revivalist movement in the history of the Jewish people. This movement was Hasidism, the cataclysmic force that wiped away the narrow intellectualism that had estranged the Jewish masses from their heritage. Hasidism focused upon fundamental Judaism, on sublimely simple principles that stressed the joy of life, love of man, and sincerity in word and deed, qualities that the common people potentially possessed in full measure. This mystical, almost miraculous movement brought comfort, courage, and a form of otherworldly ecstasy to the suffering stepchildren of humanity.

Around no other figure in Jewish history, ancient or modern, have there evolved so many legends as around the founder of Hasidism, R. Israel Baal Shem Tov (1700–1760), the "Master of the Good Name," popularly known as the Besht. As has recently been pointed out by Moshe Rosman in his book *The Founder of*

Hasidism—A Quest for the Historical Baal Shem Tov,[1] based on Polish archival sources, the founder, far from being a "revolutionary," faithfully conformed to the establishment. "I have come into the world," he said, "to show man how to make the observance of three principles his aim in life, namely: love of God, love of Israel, and love of the Torah."

He transferred abstractions into living reality, speaking directly to the masses in a language they understood. His aim was not to bring man close to God but to bring God closer to man. He rejected asceticism and self-affliction. As a child of the Kabbalah, he was heir to the doctrines of Lurian mysticism and to the yearnings for redemption. According to him, exile from the Holy Land was the cause of Israel's spiritual degeneration, and every individual could therefore help to hasten the advent of the Messiah. A national redemption could be achieved only as the result of individual effort.

Like drowning men, the Jews of Eastern Europe clutched at this rejuvenated Judaism. The movement was not a new form of Judaism but a revival of quintessential Judaism. Its objective was to establish the Kingdom of God. Boldly, it proclaimed that every human being has a rightful place in the world—and that every human being has in him a spark of the soul of the Messiah.

From the Ukraine the movement spread across borders, "converting" a high proportion of Eastern European Jewry. Soon it was no longer confined to the *shtiebl* but began to exert considerable influence on every phase of Jewish life. Many tiny far-flung Polish hamlets, even today, owe their immortality to the hasidic rebbes who once lived there and adopted the names as their title, as with Ger, Belz, Vizhnitz, and Alexander.

Luminous personalities arose. Men of vision, of vitality, who molded and remade the lives of men. Here was Judaism, fundamentally opposed to the cult of personality yet giving rise to a generation of charismatic leaders, each inspiring intense loyalty and dedication, and engendering, as must be admitted, some fac-

---

1. Moshe Rosman, *Founder of Hasidism* (Berkeley: University of California Press, 1996), pp. 11–27.

tional strife among its passionately partisan adherents. Many-faceted was the role of the rebbe. He was an attorney (*melitz yosher*), who pleaded for his clients. He was the *guter Yid*, the friend to whom his followers could pour out their hearts.

Whether they needed spiritual strengthening or *gezund* and *parnossa* (health and sustenance), the rebbe's blessing and his assurance that "the Almighty will help" was like manna on the parched lips of the afflicted Jew. The power of the rebbe was far-reaching. His most casual utterances were invested with layers of mystical meaning, and his considered judgments were counsels beyond fathom. The hasidic rebbe was a guide and spiritual mentor. Unlike the rabbi (*rav*) he required no ordination, but like the High Priest, he inherited his office.

The six years between 1939 and 1945 saw the catastrophic climax of a millennium of East European Jewish culture. Poland became the graveyard of six million Jews, and over two million *hasidim* perished. Rebbes by the score died, with holy Scrolls in their hands and holy words on their lips. They died the death of martyrs, closely following Jewish heroism in the days of the Maccabees and Chmielnicki. On the road to Treblinka and Auschwitz they heard the footsteps of the Messiah. They met their death with dignity and thus personified the indestructible soul of Polish Jewry.

Hasidism today is not, despite all prognostications, a spent force. Out of the ashes—phoenix-like—a new generation of *hasidim* has arisen. Pietists, in long silken *capotes* and streaming sidecurls, add color and character to Jewish life in Israel and elsewhere. Proudly, they identify themselves as *hasidim* of Ger, Belz, Lubavitch, Satmar, and Vizhnitz. These are the contemporary defenders of the Jewish tradition, who have replanted the faith of their fathers in the Land of Israel. There seems to be today a religious renaissance. It marks a re-emphasis on the Torah, and the re-emergence of a *Shulhan Aruch* Jew, for whom the Torah is all-embracing and all-sufficient. It may be "hard to be a Jew," but it is also "good to be a Jew." Many young and bright stars illuminate today's hasidic constellation. For this is not *Dor Yatom*, an orphaned generation.

The hasidic link with the Land of Israel is strong indeed. Before the kindling of the Sabbath candles, it used to be the custom of the mistress of the house to drop a few coins in a collection box, known as *Kupat Rabbi Meir Baal Hanes*. Even the poorest of the poor felt the need to make a contribution. It was regarded a *mitzvah*, a religious obligation, and, in this way, everyone identified himself with the Holy Land. Supporting the *Yishuv*, moreover, was tantamount to the "ransoming of prisoners" (*pidyon shevuyim*), a sacred duty that takes precedence over all other obligations. In the 1830s the *kollelim* (groups in the Holy Land supported by communities in their countries of origin) came into being. By the middle of the nineteenth century, the *kollelim* were split and splintered into twenty-five sections. Among the most prominent *kollelim* were Habad, Karlin, Koidanov, Kosov, and Vizhnitz. Each *kollel* had its own president, as well its own hasidic rebbe who acted as its guardian angel, and each devised its own method of distribution of funds.

The Besht's abortive journey to the Holy Land is described in *Shivhe HaBesht*.[2] Writing to his brother-in-law, R. Gershon, he stated: "If God wills it, I shall be with you. But this is not the proper time for it."[3] As early as 1777, the first major *Aliyah* of more than three hundred people under R. Menahem Mendel of Vitebsk and R. Abraham of Kalisk, took place. R. Menahem Mendel did not underestimate the sacrifices that resettlement in the Holy Land would involve.

This was followed by the journey of R. Nahman of Braclav, Hasidism's strongest Zionist, who yearned for the Holy Land. His thoughts on this subject are gathered in a book called *Zimrat HaAretz*, "Song of the Land." He stressed that only in the Holy Land can a man pray with true ardor. The Holy Land is the foundation of the world, the center of spiritual life, the wellspring of

---

2. *Shivhe HaBesht*, ed. S. A. Horodetzky (Tel Aviv: Dvir, 1947), p. 486.

3. Yaakov Yosef of Polonnoye, at the end of his book *Ben Porat Yosef* (Koretz, 1781).

joy, and the perfection of faith. If we abuse *Eretz Yisrael*, we go down into exile. The motive for making the journey to the Holy Land should be purely spiritual, to draw closer to God. Genuine wisdom comes only in the Land of Israel, where "the air I breathe and my very being and whatever holiness I possess, comes from it." He continually relived every detail of his memorable visit of 1779.[4]

In the nineteenth century, however, only individuals and a few hasidic families made the arduous journey to the Holy Land. While the Jewish world at large was growing increasingly enthusiastic over the activities of Dr. Theodor Herzl (1860–1904), the father of Political Zionism, whose activities were directed toward the possible restoration of a Jewish home in Palestine through political means, the *hasidim* did not generally share this enthusiasm, for the battle still raged between Hasidism and *Haskalah*. The *hasidim* associated *Haskalah* with assimilation, which often led to apostasy, and many of the *Maskilim* carried the flag of Zionism.

It is well-known that Herzl was anxious to enlist the support of the *hasidim*. Though his knowledge of Eastern European Jewry was limited, he soon grasped the great potential of this vast, untapped reservoir. He was, however, a free-thinker and refused to be bound by traditional Judaism. To the *hasidim*, he was not "a king in Jerusalem" or "the great eagle." They had no affinity with Herzl, as he had been brought up in an assimilationist milieu with a superficial knowledge of Jewish culture. Even the Mizrachi, whose motto was "The Land of Israel for the people of Israel according to the Torah of Israel," did not win the support of all religious Jews, and few hasidic rebbes were won over.

The Agudat Yisrael was born on 27 May 1912. Its leaders felt that only a Torah-entrenched citadel could hold back the triple tidal waves of assimilation, the militant anti-religious ideology of the secularists, and the arid nationalism of the Zionists. Admit-

---

4. *Advice (Likkute Etzot)*, trans. Avraham Greenbaum (Jerusalem: The Breslov Research Institute, 1983), pp. 27–31; see also Arthur Green, *Tormented Master* (University of Alabama Press, 1979), pp. 63–93.

tedly anti-Zionist, the Aguda paradoxically was passionately pro Zion. Its constitution stated that "it shall be the purpose of the Aguda to resolve all Jewish problems in the spirit of the Torah, both in the Galut and in Eretz Yisrael." It was the first international political movement among Orthodox Jews and the largest political movement among the Jews in Poland. The Aguda did not participate in the negotiations that led to the Balfour Declaration. Regrettably, for most Agudists the love of Zion remained a purely spiritual passion, and only a few translated these ideals into action. The Aguda played party politics, though Isaac Breuer (1883–1946) believed "that political Zionism seeks to exchange the *Galut* of Israel for the *Galut* of the nation."

While the Zionists in the interwar years were building up the National Home, the Aguda was mainly diaspora-orientated. Their achievements in the Holy Land were negligible. Vociferous in the political arena, they were almost invisible in the area of colonization. True, in August 1923, the first World Conference (*Kenesiyah*) in Vienna resolved to support the Jewish people spiritually and physically in holy undertakings and reconstruction work in Palestine. It even set up a *Hachsharah* camp in Poland, and many *hasidim*, regrettably all too few, were among the Jews who emigrated to Palestine between 1919 and 1936.

The Rebbe of Ger visited the Holy Land on six occasions and urged his followers to support the *Yishuv*, but few Agudists translated the ancient yearnings into practical actions. R. Yosef Hayyim Sonnenfeld, who settled in the Holy Land, was very antagonistic toward the Zionists. There were, however, a number of exceptions. R. Hayyim Meir Yehiel Shapira of Drohobycz, together with R. Shlomo Friedman, formed a *Yishuv Eretz Yisrael* Society in 1918 and issued an appeal to fellow *hasidim*: "Our aims are the aims of Ezra and Nehemia. We are anxious to establish a settlement in the Holy Land in the spirit of the Torah."

The first hasidic effort to establish an agricultural settlement in the interwar years was made by R. Yehezkel Taub of Yablonov in 1923. He emigrated to the Holy Land and the Jewish National Fund supported his settlement. He was not the only one. R. Yeshayahu Shapira, the youngest son of the Rabbi of Grodzisk, settled in Israel and became the head of the Mizrachi Immigration and Labour Department. Another active hasidic lover of Israel was R. Yisrael Eliezer Hofstein of Kozienice, who in 1925 established a colony that later became known as *Kfar Hasidim*. In 1925, Eliyahu Kirshbaum, a leading Aguda politician, founded the society *Nahlat Lublin* and purchased 5,700 *dunam* of land in Palestine to build an Orthodox Jewish colony.

Apart from the United States of America, Israel now has the largest number of *hasidim*, probably numbering more than two hundred thousand. They live in a world of their own. They are known by the dress they wear, by the way they speak, and by the melodies they hum. While most tourists visit the *Mea Shearim* quarter of Jerusalem, many miss the nearby bustling hasidic district of Geula. Tourists dally in the popular resort of Netanya, but few ever bother to visit *Kiryat Zanz*, just outside it. Similarly, few who visit Tel Aviv ever find their way to Bene Berak.

Israel is no melting pot. The hasidic community retains its Eastern European dress. *Hasidim* wear the kind of clothes that kept their grandparents warm during the bitter Russian winters. Women wear long-sleeved and high-necked dresses, thick stockings, and no cosmetics. Little girls wear thick, white stockings. Though most of them were born in Israel, they all speak Yiddish, for *a Yid red Yiddish* ("a Jew speaks Yiddish"). A small number of *hasidim* live on Aguda and Poale Aguda settlements. They work efficiently on their own farms and observe such Torah injunctions as to the nonmixture of plants and the prohibition against seed grafting. Work is carried out by hydroponics (growing plants without soil) in a manner that is permissible in the *Shemitah* year. R. Yitzhak Meir Levine served in the Israeli Provisional Government as minister of social welfare; R. Moshe Zeev Feldman (1931–1997) represented the Aguda in the Knesset and was deputy minister of labour and chairman of the Knesset Finance Committee. In the 1996 elections, the religious parties combined elected twenty-three members—more than it had achieved at any other time in the history of the State of Israel. In the local election in November 1998, the religious parties gained fifteen representatives and held almost half of the thirty-one seats on the Jerusalem Council.

There have, however, been demographic changes in the first three decades of the State of Israel. Tel Aviv, the all-Jewish city, was the home of many prominent rebbes, such as, R. Shalom Friedman, his son-in-law R. Yaakov of Husyatin, R. Mordecai Shalom Yosef of Sadagora, R. Tzvi Arye Twersky of Zlatapol, R. Yitzhak Friedman of Bohush, R. Yaakov Yosef Halpern of Vaslui, R. Yaakov David of Pascani, and the Rebbes of Sochaczev and Belz. Of late, Tel Aviv, theater-land, fashion-center, sophisticated city with concert halls, espresso bars, and cinemas, no longer offers the right environment for the rebbes. Bene Berak, is now the home of 50 hasidic rebbes.

In Jerusalem, there are now over 30 hasidic rebbes, 130 junior yeshivot, over 134 Talmud Torah centers, 240 yeshivot, and 34 ritual baths. Many hasidic families now reside in the Har Nof, Bayit Vegan, Mattersdorf, Mekor Baruch, Ezrat Torah, Ramot, and Tel Arza districts.

"Studies," said Francis Bacon, "serve for delight, for ornament, and for ability." For *hasidim*, however, learning is more than a means to an end; it is a way of life. Most *hasidim* send their children to *Hinuch Atzmai* (Torah schools), which now control 239 schools and 410 kindergartens, with an enrollment of over 60,000 children. The *Bet Yaakov* schools, founded in Poland by Sarah Schenierer, dressmaker turned educator, have been transplanted to Israel. "The *Bet Yaakov* schools," acknowledged the *Kenesiyah Gedolah* of the Aguda, "are the best solution for the education of girls." Many girls attend these schools. To supply the teachers for this mushrooming movement, there are now a number of *Bet Yaakov* Teachers' Seminaries.

Graduating from the elementary schools, the boys attend junior yeshivot, which prepare them for a yeshivah education. The growth of the yeshivot in Israel has been phenomenal. Almost every rebbe now has his own yeshivah. The voice of the Torah is heard by day and by night, not only in Israel's mitnaggedic yeshivot of Mir, Brisk, and Slabodka, but also in hasidic citadels. The hasidic yeshivot in Israel, like their forerunners in Eastern Europe, are not training schools for professional rabbis, and students have no immediate vocational objectives. Apart from

Lubavitch, the hasidic yeshivot frown upon yeshivah-cum-technical instruction.

The humiliating system that prevailed in Eastern Europe of *essen teg* (literally, "eating days"), when local residents undertook to feed at least one yeshivah student one day each week, so that a student had to go to seven houses each week, has died out in Israel. Most yeshivot now provide adequate dormitories and kitchens. In the last three decades there has been an extensive growth of *kollelim* in Israel, where students continue their studies for five to ten years after marriage. To maintain their ever growing families, a number of students attend two *kollelim*, one in the morning and the other in the afternoon or evening, to qualify for two stipends. Aid from in-laws, salaries from working wives, and supplementary social services benefits enable them, with difficulty, to support their growing families.

The birthrate among the *hasidim* is high. The average hasidic family has six children, and ten is not unusual. They reject birth control as contrary to *halachah*, and in the aftermath of the Holocaust, they also consider it the sacred duty of every Jew to increase the birthrate. Apart from the students in the *kollelim*, the *hasidim* are no longer an unproductive element, depending on *halukah* (charity), but are for the most part integrated into the economy of the country. They are highly organized and participate in the municipal and national elections. They are represented on the town councils, including those of Jerusalem, Tel Aviv, Haifa, and Bene Berak. Poverty, too, hits large hasidic families. Almost one-quarter of all the children in the country, that is, 328,000 children, live below the poverty line.

The dastardly assassination, two years ago, of the then prime minister Yitzhak Rabin by an Orthodox *kippa*-wearing killer, Yigal Amir, and the murderous attacks of Dr. Baruch Goldstein and Noam Friedman have accentuated the gulf between the *Haredi* and the secular community. The leftist groups, aided by the secular media and a number of decisions by courts of law, allege that the *hasidim* discriminate against the Reform and Conservative movements in Judaism. There is great tension over the draft Knesset law that would deny recognition to non-Orthodox conversions in Israel. They are criticized for being fundamentalists, religious fanatics, and extremists who wish to set up a theocratic state in Israel. They are, moreover, accused of avoiding military service, of intolerance, and of trying to impose their way of life on the community as a whole, and it is said that they are not making an equitable contribution to the general economy of the country.

A group of overzealous Orthodox extremists physically attacked a number of Reform women who wore *talleisim* and were holding a *Shavuot* prayer service near the Western Wall in 1997. Thousands gathered in an anti-Orthodox demonstration in June 1997 at the Tel Aviv Museum Plaza under the banner of "Stop the Haredim."

Non-Orthodox rabbis have no legal status in Israel, and there are no provisions for civil marriages between Jews. Under the threat of a collision crisis, the religious parties extorted from Prime Minister Benjamin Netanyahu a promise to support two legislative innovations: conversion law and the religious council law. The former finance minister, Yaakov Neeman, was in charge of a committee of five members representing the Orthodox camp, and one representative each from the Reform and Conservative movements. The committee proposed the establishment of a central conversion institute under the auspices of the Jewish Agency, to be run jointly by the three streams of Judaism. The would-be converts would go there for classes, but the actual conversions would be carried out by Orthodox representatives. The committee also developed a formula whereby the rabbis of the Conservative and Reform movements could perform marriages if assisted by supervisers from the Chief Rabbinate.

The twenty-three members of the religious lobby, made up of the representatives of *Shas*, the *United Religious Party*, and the *United Torah Judaism Party*, rejected the proposals out of hand. They do not realize that a rift between Israel and the diaspora Jews would be a detrimental development and will increase the already wide gulf between Orthodox and non-Orthodox.

True, many *hasidim* are involved in public protest demonstrations against the desecration of the Sabbath, as was reflected in the recent incidents in Bar Ilan Street, Jerusalem, and against certain archaeological excavations of alleged ancient burial sites. They naturally do not endorse the view expressed by Ben Gurion that Israel is a state based upon the rule of law and not ruled by *halachah*. The *hasidim* involve themselves in politics. They feel that they have to safeguard their rights and that their streets should be free from Sabbath desecration, that no sports stadium should be built in their neighborhood, and that they should receive allocations from public funds. But under no circumstances must they, as an entity, be identified with the *Neture Karta*, a tiny, highly vocal group of militant followers of the late R. Yoel Teitelbaum of Satmar and his successor, R. Moshe, who regard Zionism "as a product of false messianism" founded on assimilationist ideology. The *Neture Karta* regard the Zionist ideal of an independent Jewish State as a threefold denial of God, of Israel, and of the Torah. The vast majority of *hasidim* totally reject the ideas of those few active zealots and are repelled by their activities. "The *hasidim*," commented a hasidic rebbe, "are incapable of harboring such poisonous hatred."

In recent years, scholars have been increasingly attracted to the vast storehouse of wisdom and lore of the movement. The public appetite for books on the subject seems insatiable. Israel is now a thriving center of hasidic publishing, and most of the hasidic works have been reprinted. Many rebbes have their own publishing facilities. The mantles of Gershom Scholem, Rivka Schatz Uffenheimer, and Isaiah Tishby have fallen on Moshe Idel, Rachel Elior, and Adin Steinsaltz. Also important are the thirty works by the prolific writer Yitzhak Alfasi and the publications of R. Shalom Hayyim Porush, Meir Wunder, and Gedalia Nigal. In Israel great interest focuses on recordings of songs with hasidic themes. The proliferation of long-playing albums and compact discs of hasidic songs and dance music is tangible evidence of the timelessness of hasidic melodies, which poignantly express the strivings of the Jewish soul.

Although many books have been published on Hasidism in Israel, not a single English-language work has thus far appeared in Israel or elsewhere that deals with the rebbes in Israel. In 1982, the Littman Library of Jewish Civilization published my book

Hasidism in the State of Israel, which has been out of print for many years. The hasidic scene in the Holy Land has since undergone a transformation. Many rebbes, then living, have, alas, passed away, and others have taken their places. This work does not, in any way, claim to be comprehensive; only a number of rebbes are herein described. A number of dynasties that became extinct for lack of male successors have now been revived by grandsons, many of them American-born, who maintain and even expand their domain.

It is not an easy task to deal with contemporary events. *Hasidim*, apart from Lubavitch and Kalev, are not publicity-minded. It is particularly difficult to obtain the curricula vitae of the contemporary rebbes. A compiler of a *Who's Who in Hasidism* would receive little cooperation. The *hasidim* are not historically conscious and regard biography as a chronicle of geneaology. The day on which a rebbe dies, his *Yahrzeit*, is cherished and observed, but the date of his birth is rarely known. The publication of an updated version of my original work—at the approach of another millennium—is in itself an indication of the vigor and vitality of Hasidism.

1

Ger
A Kingdom of Torah

Ger is the largest dynasty in Israel, numerically claiming the allegiance of over four thousand families. It controls the Aguda, the *Bet Yaakov* movement, and *Hinuch Atzmai*, the ultra-Orthodox Hebrew education system. Eight thousand *hasidim* attend its services on the High Holy Days, and a new $13-million place of worship to accommodate even larger numbers is now being built in the Geula area. The *hasidim* of Ger place Torah-study at the center of their spiritual life and are continuously striving for self-perfection.

When the rabbis of Vizhnitz, Belz, and Lubavitch were establishing networks of educational institutions, Ger did not lag behind. Sixty-five institutions, scattered throughout the country from Hazor in the north, Emanuel in the center, and Ashdod and Arad in the south, have an annual budget of over $20 million. In Bene Berak alone there are twenty-one *shtieblech* of Ger. Over 10,000 students are enrolled in Ger institutions. Arad used to be a completely secular town, until, in 1981 a Ger community was established with a Talmud Torah, a high school, a yeshivah with fifty students, and a *kollel, Nahlat Yitzhak,* for young married men. Over 130 hasidic families now live there.

A similar picture emerges in Ashdod, where a hasidic community was founded in 1978 to alleviate the acute housing problems in the large cities, where apartment prices are very high. Nearly 1,000 young hasidic families have settled there in apartments that are considerably cheaper. The Talmud Torah has over 600 children in twenty-three classes, and a yeshivah, *Bet Yisrael,* has over twō hundred and fifty students.

In Jerusalem, the Yeshivah *Sefat Emet,* founded in 1926 with fifteen students, now has over three hundred, and this is supplemented by the Yeshivah *LeZeirim,* with five hundred students and a network of primary schools. The *kollel Avreichim* has two hundred young men devoting themselves to higher Torah studies.

In Bene Berak, the Yeshivah *Imre Emet,* under the guidance of Rabbi Moshe Zeev Feldman, and the nearby Yeshivah *Meor Yisrael,* named in memory of Rabbi Yisrael Alter, are bursting at the seams. The Talmud Torah *Masoret Avot* is housed in three large buildings with over one thousand students, and *Bet Talmud Lehoraah* is an institution for advanced Torah scholars.

Tel Aviv, in the 1950s, was not equipped with many hasidic centers of learning, for most of the *hasidim* settled in nearby Bene Berak. To fill this gap, Ger *hasidim* established·in Iyar 1954 a *Bet Hamidrash Lehoraah* at Nahalat Binyamin. By 1972, it had nearly fifty students and moved to more spacious accommodations in the *Bet HaKnesset* of Yavne. One of the aims of the Institute is to publish the second volume of the letters of R. Avraham Mordecai, as well as the work *Hiddushe Ha-Rim* on *Yoreh Deah* by R. Yitzhak Meir, a manuscript that was rescued from the Holocaust.

In Tel Aviv, where hardly any hasidic rebbes now reside, Ger has established deep roots. The *Ha-Rim Levin Campus* houses the *Yeshivah Hiddushe Ha-Rim,* established fifty years ago. Its five-floor edifice on a five-*dunam* site in Ramat Hayil, a garden suburb of Tel Aviv, now accommodates over five hundred students. Its synagogue, seating one hundred worshipers, entailed a capital expenditure of three million Israeli pounds. The foundation stone was laid in Elul 1952 and the building consecrated on 9 Sivan 1969. Apart from the Yeshivah of Ponovezh in Bene Berak, this is the most ambitious hasidic yeshivah project in Israel.

The Ger hasidic settlement in Hazor, in the hills of Gallilee, established only eighteen years ago, is already a large Torah center with a yeshivah, *Sifte Tzaddik*.

Ger has a central fund for interest-free loans, making large amounts of money available to institutions and individuals in need. The present Rabbi of Ger is Rabbi Yaakov Arye Alter, who succeeded his uncle Rabbi Pinhas Menahem, who died in 1996.

The son of R. Simha Bunem and Yuta Henni (the daughter of R. Nehemia Alter), he was born in Lodz on 29 Iyar 1939 and named after R. Yaacov Arye Guterman of Radzymin. In Nisan 1940, he, together with his grandfather, reached the Holy Land. On 21 Kislev 1960, he married Shoshanah, the daughter of R. Menahem Weitz, the principal of the Yeshivah *Hiddushe Ha-Rim* in Tel Aviv, a former disciple of the Yeshivah *Hachme Lublin*. The Rebbe is an inordinately modest man, an exceptionally private individual. Shy, retiring, unassuming, he is always ready to advise and help. He remains free of self-importance and prefers to achieve his goals by consensus and friendly persuasion. He is a man of great presence, with a warm and compassionate nature.

He studied in the Ger Yeshivah in Tel Aviv and for one year under R. Hayyim Milikovsky. He twice visited the Rabbi of Lubavitch in New York and, for a time, lived with his father in London, Antwerp, and Marienbad. A man of great personal integrity, he is conscientious to a fault. He is soft-spoken and shuns the limelight. It is doubtful whether he ever nursed dreams of high office. Until he became Rebbe, he made the journey to Jerusalem by bus. His manifold investments in real estate, inherited from his father, are controlled and administered by his hasid Meir Glusman.

In May 1998, the Rebbe together with R. Aaron Leib Steinman visited New York and briefly London. He stressed again and again that the greatest blessing is unity and peace. Over ten thousand *hasidim* participated in the marriage of his son Yisrael Menahem in Jerusalem on 12 Kislev 1998 who married Esther, the grand-daughter of the Lubliner Rebbe, R. Avraham Eiger of Bene Berak. The Rabbi encouraged all his Yeshivah Bachurim to participate in the festivities. "You are all my *Machutanim*," he said.

In interwar Poland, the most powerful hasidic "court" was that of the Rebbe of Ger (Gora Kalwaria), a small town nineteen miles southwest of Warsaw. Although the town's population before the Second World War consisted of barely three thousand five hundred Jews, it became the home of a tremendous dynasty. How did this small town on the river Vistula achieve such fame and immortality? At one time, more than 100,000 Jews owed allegiance to the Rebbe and there was hardly a town or village in Poland that did not have a *shtiebl* of Ger. The Rebbe's influence was far-reaching. A word from him could decide a communal election, and any cause he favored was assured of success. His followers included outstanding rabbinical scholars and leaders of Polish Jewry. In 1898, a special narrow gauge railway was built, known as a *koleika*, or colloquially as the "Rebbe's railway," in order to bring his followers to him. The Poles called Ger the "New Jerusalem" (Nowy Jerusalem).

The founder of the dynasty was R. Yitzhak Meir Rotenburg (Alter), better known as the *Hiddushe Ha-Rim* (Novellae of R. Yitzhak Meir), after the title of his works. He was born in 1799 and was a devoted follower of R. Yisrael Hofstein the Maggid of Kozienice, and his son R. Moshe, R. Yaakov Yitzhak Horowitz, the "Seer of Lublin"; of R. Yaakov Yitzhak, the "Holy Jew" of Przysucha; and of R. Simha Bunem of Przysucha.

His personal life was beset by tragedy. He had thirteen children and outlived them all. In 1834, his sole surviving son, R. Avraham Mordecai, died at the age of forty, and reluctantly, R. Yitzhak Meir became a hasidic rebbe, first in Warsaw and later in Ger. Like his teachers, R. Yisrael of Kozienice, R. Menahem Mendel Morgenstern of Kotsk, and R. Simha Bunem of Przysucha, he felt that Jews should be active in promoting a return to Zion. During the Polish Rebellion of 1863, he commented pointedly, "We see how the Poles are sacrificing themselves to liberate their country from foreigners. What are we doing to liberate our Land?"

After seven years of leadership, R. Yitzhak Meir was succeeded by his grandson R. Yehuda Leib (1847–1904), known as the *Sefat Emet* from the verse in Proverbs (12:19): "The lip of truth shall be established for ever," which became his literary pseudonym. In a letter to R. Hayyim Morgenstern of Pulawy (1870–1906), the author of a booklet, *Shalom Yerushalayim* (1891), in which he demonstrated that every Jew was duty-bound to participate in the rebuilding of the Holy Land, R. Yehuda Leib wrote: "Certainly, it will be reckoned as a *mitzvah* to settle in the Holy Land." Like R. Hayyim Eliezer Waks of Kalish, the Rabbi urged the *hasidim* to import Palestinian *etrogim*.

Dr. Theodor Herzl, the Zionist leader, strove to enlist the support of the *hasidim* in Poland. Writing to the third Rebbe of Ger in 1899, Herzl insisted that Zionism was not opposed to religion. "Our main aim is to work for the welfare of our people . . . . In the name of tens of thousands of Jews whose conditions are continually deteriorating, in the name of those who are fleeing from Russia, Romania, Galicia, to America, whose destiny is assimilation and disintegration, I beseech your Honor to support us." [1]

Herzl's moving appeal remained unanswered. To the editor of the *Jewish Chronicle*, Asher Meyers, Herzl remarked: "I am a freethinker, and our principle in the Jewish State will be: Let everyone seek salvation in his own way." [2] Equally unsuccessful in eliciting hasidic support was Nahum Sokolow (1859–1936), whose grandfather, Ephraim Yitzhak, was a follower of Rabbi Elimelech of Lejask. He visited the Court of Ger but was unable to evoke any positive response. The Rebbe of Ger could not be persuaded that Zionism would not weaken Orthodoxy.

The son and successor of the *Sefat Emet* was R. Avraham Mordecai Alter, born on 7 Tevet 1866 and married on 17 Adar 1881 to Hayyah Rada, the daughter of R. Noah Shahor of Biala Podolski. They had four sons (Meir, Yitzhak, Yisrael, and Simha

---

1. A. Y. Bromberg, *Sefat Emet* (Jerusalem, 1957), p. 108; S. Federbush, *HaHasidim VeZion* (Jerusalem, 1953), p. 52.

2. Raphael Patai, ed., *The Complete Diaries of Theodor Herzl*, vol. 1 (New York, 1960), p. 283.

Bunem) and four daughters (Feiga, Breindel, Esther, and Devorah Matil). When his wife died on 13 Shevat 1922, he married Feiga Mintza, the daughter of R. Yitzhak Biderman. They had one son, Pinhas Menahem.

The Rebbe participated in the Conference under the leadership of Dr. Yitzhok Breuer in Bad Homburg (a German summer resort), which paved the way to the founding of the Aguda. He also attended Agudist World Conferences (*Kenesiyah Gedolah*) in Vienna in 1923 and 1929, and in Marienbad in 1937.

The Aguda Conference in Marienbad in 1937 discussed the proposal of the Peel Commission (set up by the British government under Viscount Peel in 1936) that the Holy Land be partitioned into two sovereign states, one Jewish and the other Arab, with historic and strategic sites remaining under British jurisdiction. In forceful opposition, R. Avraham Mordecai quoted the Prophet Joel:[3] "I will gather all nations, and will bring them down to the valley of Jehoshaphat, and I will enter into judgment with them there, for my people and my heritage Israel, whom they have scattered among the nations and divided my land."

When the Rabbi of Ger came to a town, it was in the nature of a state visit, full of pomp and ceremony. Mr. (later Judge) Neville Laski, then president of the Board of Deputies of British Jews (1933–1940), gives an eyewitness account:

> I heard much talk of the wonder-working Rabbi, who is almost worshipped by a section of the population, and I managed to obtain ocular demonstration of his popularity. I went to see his arrival from his cure at Carlsbad and was presented with a spectacle such as I had never imagined. Hundreds and hundreds of, to me, medieval-looking Jews wearing strange hats and kaftans, crowded on the platform, alongside which steamed a train of the latest type, composed of wagons-lits. Excitement reigned supreme. I stood on a railway truck against a fence to obtain a better view, but soon repented, as the surging crowd, marching step by step with the Rabbi, nearly turned me and my truck into the roadway. Four policemen in front, four behind and two on either side,

---

3. Joel 4:2.

pushed a way through a seething and excited mob, for a very small old man who took not the slightest notice of the crowd of admirers who had come specially to see him, and went to a motor car, in which he was whisked away preparatory to his going to his *nachkur* (rest after treatment).[4]

"Just as a hasid must visit his Rabbi from time to time," said R. Avraham Mordecai, "so must I visit the Land of Israel periodically." His first visit took place in 1921 and lasted twenty-eight days. Accompanied by his wife and a number of wealthy *hasidim*, he left Poland on *Shushan Purim* and traveled via Vienna, Trieste, and Jaffa. When he arrived in Jerusalem in Adar, he made his way to the Western Wall, where he tore his coat as a sign of mourning. He had great admiration for the Chief Rabbi of the Holy Land, R. Avraham Yitzhak Kook (1865–1935), whom he described in the rabbinic idiom as *Ish Ha-Eshkolot*, "a man in whom all is contained." When the Rabbi mentioned to him his concern over the irreligious pioneers, R. Kook told him: "The Holy of Holies was very sacred. Only the High Priest was permitted to enter there once a year, and this annual visit was preceded by special preparations. But when the Holy of Holies was being built, all kinds of workmen went casually in and out. Similarly, at this stage, the Land of Israel is being rebuilt and we should not worry about the practices of those who are engaged in the rebuilding."

On board ship on his homeward journey, on 7 Iyar, R. Avraham Mordecai wrote down his impressions:[5]

I visited the institutions, the yeshivot and the Talmud Torah schools, and I was very pleased with what I saw. However, they all need financial help from the diaspora. It reassured me to observe that it is possible to conduct oneself in the ways of our fathers and forefathers. Those whom God favours can undoubtedly make a living there and lead a true Torah life without difficulty

4. Neville Laski, *Jewish Rights and Jewish Wrongs* (London: Soncino Press, 1939), p. 73.

5. Binyamin Mintz, *Rabbenu MiGur* (Tel Aviv: Shearim, 1950), pp. 57–71.

or restraint. Those who are either unwilling or unable to settle
there, should support those who go. They should set aside a fixed
sum of money for investment there. It will yield rich dividends.
I myself have acquired land in Jaffa for commercial development. . . . I visited the High Commissioner, Eliezer Samuel [later
Viscount Samuel, 1870–1963] and he assured me that he would
give every assistance to religious settlers.

The Rebbe was convinced that a friendly relationship could be
established with the Arabs. "I noticed that the Arabs, riding their
camels, cleared the way for our entourage. If only our neighbors
in Europe showed a little of this respect! It is my opinion that we
can live together with the Arabs in brotherhood." He was in contact with the Agudist leaders, Rabbis Sonnenfeld and Yitzhak
Yeruham Diskin, head of the Jerusalem rabbinate, and tried to
make peace between them.

Three years later in Shevat 1924, he again visited the Holy Land,
accompanied by R. Yitzhak Zelig Morgenstern, Rabbi of Sokolov;
his own brother-in-law R. Zvi Hanoch Hakohen Levin, Rabbi of
Bendin; the Rebbe's son-in-law R. Yitzhak Meir Levin; and a
number of followers from Lodz. This time, he stayed six weeks.
"If five hundred wealthy *hasidim* would emigrate to the Holy
Land," he said on his return to Poland, "they could take over the
country economically and spiritually."

In 1925, a delegation of Ger *hasidim* purchased four hundred
dunams in Hadar Ramatayin. That year the Yeshivah *Sefat Emet*
was established in Jerusalem. The Rebbe believed that the existing yeshivot were inadequate and their methods unsuitable for
Polish *hasidim*. On his third visit in the summer of 1927, the
Rebbe traveled via Trieste and Alexandria, accompanied by his
brother-in-law R. Tzvi Hanoch Hakohen Levin and his son Pinhas
Levin. At the Cave of Machpelah, the Arab guard was willing to
allow the venerable visitor to descend to the cave (at that time
Jews were allowed no farther than the first few steps), but the
Rebbe declined to take advantage of this concession. "All the children of Israel are the children of the King. I do not desire special
privileges." The Rebbe's friendship with R. Kook aroused the
antagonism of the Orthodox extremists, who wrote scurrilous

pamphlets and pasted placards full of abuse. The Rabbinic Association of Poland excommunicated both the authors and the printers.

The Rebbe's fourth visit took place five years later in the winter of 1932, and this time he traveled overland through Vienna, Sofia, Istanbul, Syria, and Lebanon, an itinerary that aroused the interest of hasidic Jewry. "I want to explore the different ways that lead to the Holy Land," he explained to his followers. On his return journey there was a violent storm at sea. "This is because we are leaving the Holy Land," commented the Rabbi. When Hitler came to power in January 1933, the Rabbi said: "For one hundred fifty years our German brethren have not known the meaning of the word *exile*. Now they will probably find refuge in the Holy Land. I am afraid of one thing: They will take with them their assimilated customs and will adversely influence the vitality of religious life."

His fifth pilgrimage, the longest and the last, took place before Rosh Hashanah 1936 and lasted eight months. By then the Rabbi regarded himself as a resident of the Holy Land and no longer observed Yom Tov Sheni (the second day of a festival that is observed in the diaspora). He even took a walk carrying a stick. He was reluctant to return home, but a special *Bet Din*, consisting of Rabbis Yaakov Meir Biderman, Heinoch Levin, and Avraham David Eisner, counseled him not to desert his great multitude in Poland.

With the outbreak of World War Two on 1 September 1939, the fate of Polish Jewry was sealed. After twenty-seven days of bombing, Warsaw capitulated on 27 September. The Rebbe moved to Warsaw and lived at first at the home of his brother-in-law R. Yitzhak David Biderman, on *Twarda* 29, and then kept changing his residence to evade the Nazis, who spared no efforts to locate the *wonder rabbi*.

An energetic committee in the United States, headed by R. Menaham Mendel Kasher and Eliezer Silver, and supported by Justice Louis Dembitz Brandeis (1865–1941) and Congressman Sol Bloom (1870–1949), managed to get him an entry visa to Palestine. The Rebbe, accompanied by his wife; his sons Pinhas Mena-

hem, Yisroel, and Simha Bunem; and his sons-in-law R. Yitzhak
Meir Levin, R. Shlomo Yoskowitz, and R. Yitzhak Fishel Heine,
left Poland for Italy in Adar 1940, eventually reaching the Holy
Land.

He participated in a special service of intercession for Polish
Jewry, held in the *Hurva* Synagogue of R. Yehuda HaHasid in
Kislev 1942. "It is a time of trouble for Yaacov," he lamented. "We
must pray that wickedness may pass from the world and evil will
be consumed like smoke." He was always aware of his tragic role
as the only surviving leader of the remnant of a once-great hasidic house. His son R. Meir, his two brothers, R. Moshe Bezalel
and R. Menahem, and all their families perished in the Holocaust.

The Rabbi died on Shavuot (Pentecost) 1948, and Chief Rabbi
Yitzhak Herzog declared in his eulogy: "On Shavuot the Torah
was given and on Shavuot the Torah was taken away." He was
buried in the courtyard of the Yeshivah *Sefat Emet* in Jerusalem.

He was succeeded by his third son, R. Yisrael, known as the
Bet Yisrael. He was born in Ger on 24 Tishri 1895 and was named
after the father of the *Hiddushe Ha-Rim*. He married Hayyah Sa-
rah, the daughter of his uncle R. Yaacov Meir Biderman (the son-
in-law of the *Sefat Emet*) in Ger on 24 Adar II 1914. During World
War One, he lived in Warsaw. He had an only daughter, Rebecca
Yocheved, who married R. Aaron Rapport in 1928, and one son,
R. Yehuda Arye Leib, whose wife and children perished in the
Holocaust. R. Yehuda Arye Leib managed to escape from Poland
with his father and reach the Holy Land.

There, eight years later, in 1948, he married Perl, the daughter
of R. David Weidenfeld and sister-in-law of R. Avraham Weinberg
of Slonim who lived in Tel Aviv. They had no children. In accordance with the "Last Will and Testament" of R. Avraham
Mordecai, R. Yisrael succeeded his father as Rebbe of Ger in 1948.
It was said of R. Yisrael that although time was precious to him,
he had time for everybody. Twice daily he would receive people
in private audience. He was able to grasp the most complicated
problems with almost lightning speed. People of all shades of religious observance sought his advice on a wide range of matters.
His home in Geula and his heart were open to everyone in need.

In conformity with the traditions of Ger, women were not admitted to his presence nor did he accept *pidyonot*.

His discourses were of rare brevity, seldom lasting more than a few moments. The brevity did not diminish their depth, and there was original thought in every one. Like his forefathers, he continued in the ways of Ger, by putting emphasis on learning, mainly Talmud and Codes. "There is no Hasidut without Torah," he told his *hasidim*. "Time" was the most valuable commodity in Ger. He demanded that his followers study Torah every available moment, and he expected them to follow his personal example of being in the *Bet Hamidrash* as early as 4 A.M. He would often make a surprise visit in the small hours to ensure that this was the case.

In 1926, he instituted a *Hafsakah*, an intermission, between *Shaharit* and *Musaf* on Shabbat morning and on Friday night before the evening service to enable his followers to devote time to study. In Ger, honor was given to the scholars and students of the Torah. Miracles were never the trademark of Ger, but almost everybody who had any connections with the rebbe had plenty to tell of miracles. He became a rebbe's rebbe; hasidic leaders from all over the world sought his counsel and submitted to his leadership. A rabbi once asked him: "What do you think of the present situation?" and he replied: "I recite Psalms." He took an active interest in the work of the Aguda, which he endearingly called the "Agudat Yisrael of my Fathers," and was one of the prominent leaders of the *Moetzet Gedole HaTorah*.

I visited the Rebbe one Friday evening in December 1971. Inside the spacious modern *Bet Hamidrash* in Rehov Malhe Yisrael in the Geula district of Jerusalem, there were nearly four hundred *hasidim*. Some were studying the Talmud; others were discussing the weekly portion of the Law or the *Sefat Emet* by R. Yehuda Arye Alter.

At about 10 P.M. four hours after the beginning of the Sabbath, the small side door suddenly opened and the Rebbe of Ger entered. Instantly, the atmosphere changed and a hushed silence enveloped the entire gathering. The *hasidim* rose to greet him and made a path for him through their midst. Briskly, he strode to

the center table, *hasidim* on both sides forming a cordon. He
looked at them, and they looked at him. No words were spoken.
To be near him was in itself an experience, and to catch his eye
was an honor. By a sign known only to the initiated, he indicated
those who were to join him at the table, a selection process called
Homot (the ceremony of the walls) by the followers of Ger. The
Rabbi and some forty selected followers took their seats. The
young *hasidim*, known in Poland as "the Cossacks of Ger," pushed
forward. The others leaned over each other and stood on tiptoe
to observe every gesture of their revered leader. After the singing
of one or two melodies, the Rabbi commented briefly on the
weekly portion of the Law. He spoke quickly and quietly, yet the
ideas were almost telepathically transmitted from hasid to hasid.
I could not hear his words, as I was at the far side of the *Bet
Hamidrash*, but a young hasid near him courteously and clearly
repeated the discourse as though he had heard every word.

Commenting on the verse[6] "And they told him all the words
of Joseph," the *Midrash* states that Joseph identified himself by
reminding his father that the last subject they had studied together
was the section on the heifer.[7] The heifer is killed in expiation of
an unsolved murder, symbolizing that the community is not responsible for a crime perpetrated in its midst. Similarly, the brothers of Yosef could not be blamed for selling him, for the act was
destined by Providence.

After the discourse, the *Gabbai*, Hanina Schiff, announced the
names and places of origin of the *hasidim* who were supplying
wine for the congregation that evening, thus: "Moshe Hayyim
David of Lodz, Aaron Shochet of Bene Berak, Moshe Keshenover,
Shmuel Yitzhak of Sokolow give wine." As they were named, the
hasidim arose, and the Rebbe wished them *Le-Hayyim* (to life).
After partaking of the wine and fruit (*peirot*) that had been brought
in, the Rebbe gave *Shirayim* to his *hasidim*, and Sabbath table melodies were sung. With the recitation of Grace after Meals, the *Tish*

---

6. Genesis 45:27.
7. Deuteronomy 21:6.

came to an end and the Rebbe disappeared as abruptly as he had entered.

He died in Hadassah Hospital, Jerusalem, after emergency internal surgery on 2 Adar 1977, and was buried on the Mount of Olives. The Ashkenazi Chief Rabbi, R. Shlomo Goren, said: "A spiritual light has been extinguished. He was a teacher of tens of thousands of *hasidim*. The Ark of the Lord, the father of Polish Hasidism, the glory of the people and the Torah."

R. Avraham Mordecai lost his only son in the Holocaust. At the conclusion of the *Shivah*, a delegation of prominent *hasidim* persuaded his brother R. Simha Bunem to become their leader. He was born in Ger on 23 Nisan 1898 and was named after R. Simha Bunem of Przysucha. He studied under the guidance of R. Mordecai Treisman and in the Yeshivah *Darke Noam* under R. Mendel of Pabianice. On 1 Elul 1915 in Warsaw, he married his cousin Yuta Henne (d. 1983), the daughter of R. Nehemia Alter (the third son of the *Sefat Emet*), who was *Dayan* in Lodz. The first twelve years of his marriage were blighted by misfortune. The couple waited twelve years for their first child, Hayyah Rada Yehudit, but she died at six months. After a further three years, they eventually had two children: a daughter, Rebecca Feiga (1930–1997), followed by a son, Yaacov Arye.

R. Simha Bunem, together with his father-in-law, visited the Holy Land in 1927 and remained there for a few years. In Elul 1934, he settled in the Mekor Baruch district of Jerusalem but returned to Poland in Nisan 1938. As a Palestinian citizen, he, together with his family, was able to leave Poland for the Holy Land in 1940. Though a renowned scholar, he was a cautious man who over the years developed sound financial acumen and amassed a personal fortune from real estate, both in Poland and in Israel. For twenty-nine years, he gave his allegiance to his brother, R. Yisrael, and kept out of the limelight when his brother became Rebbe. When his brother died intestate, he acceded to the request of the *hasidim* to become the fifth Rebbe of Ger. Despite his reputed wealth, he remained in his original small apartment and was renowned for his modesty. In his later days, he proved to be an energetic octogenarian.

At the sixth *Kenesiyah Gedolah*, the Rebbe, R. Simha Bunem, instituted the daily study of a page of the Talmud *Yerushalmi* side by side with the Babylonian Talmud. He thus opened a new vista on the study for many to whom the *Yerushalmi* was literally a closed book. He pioneered the settlement of young religious couples outside the main Orthodox centers of Jerusalem and Bene Berak, encouraging them to settle in Arad, Ashdod, and Hazor, where there were opportunities for apartments at lower rentals. In order to reduce the strain of the tremendous expense of weddings and celebrations of *Simhot*, he imposed an upper limit of the number of guests who could be invited to a festive meal. He stipulated that the maximum number of guests should be one hundred fifty, all others to be given light refreshments after the wedding ceremony. Nor should one spend more than two hundred twenty thousand Israeli pounds on an apartment. He furthermore urged his students to go to bed not later than 10 P.M.

He was opposed to giving back the Territories and he was the chief architect of the amendment to the anti-abortion law, which did away with the clause enabling women to have abortions for medical or psychological reasons. He was also a driving force behind the Religious Party's successful effort to ground EL AL flights on Sabbaths and Holy Days. He tried his utmost to stop the Mormons from establishing a college in Jerusalem. Nothing escaped his watchful eye, and even the cost of *etrogim* for Sukkot was subject to detailed regulations.

In 1986, his health began to deteriorate, and he ceased holding *Tishen*, the festive Sabbath meals. He died on the 7th of Tammuz 1992. He was survived by his daughter and his son, R. Yaakov Arye. He was succeeded, however, not by his living son, unprecedented in Ger, but by his half-brother, R. Pinhas Menahem. It now appears that the Rebbe actually nominated his son as his successor, but as this missive was not discovered during the seven days of mourning, and as the son was in any case reluctant to take on the burden, R. Pinhas Menahem became Rebbe.

R. Pinhas Menahem was born on 21 Tammuz (3 July) 1926, the son of R. Avraham Mordecai, then sixty years old, by his second wife, Feiga Mintza. His *bar mitzvah* took place two months before the outbreak of World War II. He came to the Holy Land with his father in 1940 and studied in the Ponevezh, *Hayye Olom*, and the *Sefat Emet* Yeshivot in Jerusalem. He was especially close to his father, who gave extraordinary attention to his upbringing and education. He was also guided by R. Simha Bunem Leizersohn (a brother-in-law of R. Shalom Zalman Aurbach). On 10 Tammuz 1946, he married Zipporah Alter, the daughter of R. Avraham Mottel Alter and the granddaughter of his uncle R. Bezalel Alter. In 1957 he became the principal of the *Sefat Emet* Yeshivah. He was a proven leader of men and was never content to rest on his laurels. His capacity for hard work was legendary.

He was one of the leaders of the rabbinical council and of the *Hinuch Atzmai*, and took an active part in the Aguda, frequently writing for its paper, *HaModia*. He was a master of the spoken word and his prose had the hallmark·of perfection. He had a genius for building bridges between the Torah factions that did not always see eye to eye with one another. He violently condemned the assassination of Prime Minister Yitzhak Rabin and before his death was working hard to create a united religious front for the 1996 election. The signing of the Oslo Accord affected him deeply. In common with most of the other hasidic rebbes, he strongly disapproved of the Israeli–PLO accord. "Just as a *Sefer Torah* becomes invalid if one letter is missing," stated the Rebbe, "so it is wrong to deprive the Holy Land of any of its territories."

His third son, the twenty-seven-year-old R. Yehuda Arye Leib, who married the daughter of R. Menashe Klein, Rabbi of Ungvar, New York, a member of the Ger *Bet Din* in Jerusalem, was injured by a car as he emerged from the ritual bath of the Ruzhin Yeshivah in the Romema district of Jerusalem, and he died from his injuries on 15 Tishri 1987.

In his last public letter, dated 15 Adar, just before the Fast of *Esther* 1996, the Rebbe wrote: "Once the forces of destruction are released, no difference is made between the righteous and the wicked. . . .[8] All Jews are responsible for each other. Let us uproot from our midst any animosity we may harbour against our

---

8. *Baba Kamma* 60a.

fellow Jews. Let us augment our feelings of kindness and good will. Let us enhance Torah study."

When he heard of the bomb in Dizengoff Square on the eve of Purim 1996 he cried out: "I cannot bear this any longer." On Purim, the theme of his discourse was King Saul, who went to battle fully aware that he would not survive. On returning home, he quoted to his wife the verse "And Moses went up to God." [9] He then bade her "Shalom." The Rebbe died in his sleep on 15 Adar 1996, and much of Jerusalem was brought to a standstill by the huge crowd of over one hundred thousand that accompanied the funeral procession, despite lashing rainstorms. In accordance with his wishes, he was buried next to his father in the courtyard of the yeshivah. Special permission had to be obtained from the minister of health, Dr. Ephraim Sneh. He left a letter requesting that his nephew R. Yaakov Arye should succeed him. His surviving sons are: R. Yaakov Meir, R. Shaul, R. Yitzhak David, and R. Daniel Hayyim.

In political terms, the most prominent hasidic Agudist leader has been R. Yitzhak Meir Levin, the son of R. Tzvi Hanoch Hakohen, formerly rabbi of Bendin, and Feige, the daughter of R. Yehuda Arye Leib Alter, the *Sefat Emet*. He was born in Ger on 19 Tevet 1894 and married his cousin Matil, the daughter of R. Avraham Mordecai Alter.

For a half-century he fought fearlessly in his native Poland to strengthen Torah Judaism. He was in charge of the Aguda, which then had more than two hundred thousand followers, six hundred *Bet Yaakov* schools, and many yeshivot. He was a prolific writer in the religious newspapers *Der Yid, Dos Yiddische Tugblatt, Diglenu, HaDerech*, and *Kol Yisrael*. In 1924 he represented the Aguda on the Warsaw Community Council, and eleven years later he visited the Holy Land at the head of an Aguda delegation. When the Nazis established the infamous *Judenrat*, he was a member of it for a short time. In 1940, he accompanied his father-in-law to the Holy Land. "Every day," said R. Avraham Mordecai, "Yitzhak Meir studies the tractate of the Agudat

9. Exodus 19:3.

Yisrael." One of the signatories to the Declaration of Independence, he became a member of the first Knesset in 1949, and then served in the Israeli Provisional Government (1948–1952) as minister for social welfare. He resigned during the controversy over national service for women.

On 22 January 1948, he informed the United Nations Working Committee at Lake Success that the *Agudat Yisrael* was united with all Jewry on the political future of Palestine. "The Land of Israel and the People of Israel form one complete entity, forever inseparable." At the Fourth *Kenesiyah*, held in Jerusalem in 1954, he was elected president of the World Actions Committee and chairman of the World Executive of the Aguda. "Let us be frank for a moment," he told the Knesset, in 1996, "Can country, language, or army be sufficient in themselves to safeguard our future in the spiritual sense? Surely, all these have no meaning and no value unless there is a real soul in the center of our activity." Even his opponents admired his courage and forthrightness. "The words of R. Levin came from an aching heart," said Prime Minister Levy Eshkol in 1967, "and showed a deep concern for the historic continuation of the Jewish People." He died in 1971.

Torah Thoughts

"In the Land of Moab, Moses resolved to expound the Law" (Deuteronomy 1:5). Rashi, commenting on this verse, writes that Moses explained the Torah to them in seventy languages of the world. Why was it necessary to expound Torah in seventy languages? Moses prophetically predicted that the children of Israel were destined to endure a long and bitter exile during which they would dwell among the alien nations of the world. He felt that disseminating the Torah in a multiplicity of languages would help combat hatred and prejudice and would enable the Jew to survive in dark periods of history (*Hiddushe Ha-Rim*).

On a visit to Warsaw, Sir Moses Montefiore met the Rebbe of Ger. The Baronet was concerned that Polish Jewry did not study secular subjects and were not even familiar with the vernacular.

If Mordecai, the hero of the Book of Esther, had not known his native tongue, argued the Baronet, he would not have been able to frustrate the plot of the king's servants (Esther 2:21–22). The Rebbe replied that, on the contrary, this very story gives a clear indication that Jews did not know the language of the country. The plotters would never have spoken in the presence of Mordecai, had they suspected him to understand their native language.

"No one could see anyone else or move about for three days" (Exodus 10:23). The actual Plague of Darkness was that the Jews did not "see one another." They were selfish, callous, and indifferent and were not concerned or affected by other people's troubles (*Hiddushe Ha-Rim*).

"And Moses stood in the gate of the camp and said: Who is on the Lord's side, let him come unto me" (Exodus 32:26). However, only three thousand people were guilty of worshiping the golden calf. Why, then, did the Almighty wish to destroy the entire nation? Wherein lay their fault? Their guilt lay in the fact that they did not protest and did not stop the few from perpetrating the heinous crime. Their crime was their indifference (*idem*).

"God said to the snake 'On dust you shall feed as long as you live'" (Genesis 3:14). Surely, there is no shortage of dust. The snake was assured of sustenance for the rest of its life. The real punishment was that the snake would never need to pray to the Almighty for food. This, in itself (*idem*).

"Juda is a lion's whelp; you stand over your prey like a lion, my son. He crouches and lies down, a mighty lion, who dare rouse him?" (Genesis 49:9). The greatest quality of Juda was that he was not dogmatic. He readily admitted his error, saying that "she [Tamar] is more righteous than me" (Genesis 38:26). Hence, he merited to be the ancestor of King David (*idem*).

"And Moses feared and said: 'Surely this thing is known' " (Exodus 2:14). Moses was perplexed and wondered why Israel had to endure such cruel servitude. When, however, he was confronted by informers and wicked men, he realized that they were not yet worthy of redemption (*idem*).

"And they went and came to Moses and to Aaron" (Numbers 13:26). In the words of Rashi, "Just as their coming was evil, so was their going." An evil thought is not considered an evil deed:

only when it is translated into action is it counted a sin. Consequently, although they went on with their evil plan, it was not counted against them, and they could still be considered "worthy." Once, however, they came to Moses with their unfavorable report, it was considered a sin (*Imre Emet*).

"Do not bury me in Egypt" (Genesis 47:30). Our Sages tell us that Jacob was motivated by a number of reasons in his wish not to be buried in Egypt. The soil of Egypt would ultimately become infested by lice that would swarm beneath his body. He was also afraid that the Egyptians would make him an object of worship. The Israelites, during their sojourn in Egypt lived in Goshen, and were not afflicted by the Plague of Lice. This made Jacob fearful that the Egyptians would regard the immunity of Goshen as due to him and would consequently regard him as an idol to be worshiped (*idem*).

Jacob, on his journey from Beer Sheva, took the stones of the place and put them under his head (Genesis 28:11). Subsequently, we read (Verse 18) that he took the "stone" that he used for his pillow. Rashi informs us that the stones began to quarrel with one another. One said: "Upon me let the righteous man rest his head," and each stone said, "Upon me let him rest his head," whereupon the Holy One, Blessed be He, straight away made them into one stone (*Hullin* 91b). Once there is unity, there is no room for jealousy (*idem*).

It is difficult to be a Jew and seven times harder to be a hasid. Jacob asked why the shepherds were waiting and did not roll the stone off the well (Genesis 29:8). Was it not a huge stone, and was it not enough reason for them to wait? It indicates that a Jew should not be afraid and not be intimidated, no matter however difficult the task is (*Bet Israel*).

R. Joshua, the son of Perahia, said: "Provide thyself a teacher, and buy thee a companion" (*Avot* 1:6). Why does the *Mishnah* use the term *buy*? If someone purchases a valuable article, he cherishes it, and if it is broken, he mends it. Similarly, if you find a fault in your companion, try your utmost to amend it (*Lev Simha*).

"You will order" (Exodus 27:20). The Hebrew word *order* can also connote "to be bound" or "to be tied," only by being closely attached to Moses can you survive (*idem*).

"And Abraham rose early in the morning" (Genesis 22:9). Despite the fact that he was about to sacrifice his only beloved son, his sleep was not disturbed, unlike Balaam (Numbers 22:9), who could not sleep at night (*idem*).

"All Jews are responsible for one another. Let us uproot from our midst any animosity we may harbor against our fellow Jews. Let us augment our feelings of kindness and goodwill. Let us endeavor to fulfill the verse 'When you go out to war against your enemies, you shall guard yourself from every evil thing; that He see no unseemly thing and He will turn away from you' (Deuteronomy 23:10). Let us cry out to the Rock of Israel, Blessed be He, Who liberates us from our enemies" (Letter of the Rebbe, 12 Adar 5756).

"The Zionist Movement, led by the Left, the Histadrut, that are founded on impure sources, far from Torah and *mitzvot*, led many of our Jewish brothers astray through false propaganda, bribery, lies, and demagoguey. They have corrupted the youth with a ruinous educational system, empty of any holy content, and all this in the name of the Land of Israel, as it were. And now they have got entangled in a situation of no peace and no security. There is unceasing bloodshed in all parts of *Eretz Yisrael*. They have joined hands, literally, with the enemies of Israel, whose hands are covered with innocent blood in *Eretz Yisrael* and abroad—people who are wicked even in the eyes of most non-Jews—a step that is incomprehensible to every thinking person. We have no one to rely on, but our Father in Heaven who promised our fathers to give us this land if we observe the Holy Torah" (letter from R. Pinhas Menahem Alter, Shevat 5755).

"And Moses brought forth the people out of the camp" (Exodus 19:17). It is the task of the spiritual leader to take the people out of the "camp," to remove all impurities and sensuality from the children of Israel (R. Yaakov Arye Alter).

Juda's plea to Joseph on behalf of his brother Benjamin (Genesis 44: 18–34) was full of pathos and beauty. Juda made eight references to their father. As he referred to the patriarch Jacob's anguish, he saw Joseph's unquenchable longing for his father revealed in his facial expression. Juda realized that by repeated mention of the aged Jacob, he would succeed in softening Joseph's heart (*idem*).

"And Isaac went to meditate in the field" (Genesis 24:63). The Targum and Rashi understand the word *meditate* to mean prayer and declare that Isaac instituted the Afternoon Prayer. Hence, the Talmud states that a man should always care about the Afternoon Prayer. For even Elijah's plea was favorably accepted only after he offered the Afternoon Prayer (*Berachot* 6b). Abraham, who originated the Morning Prayer, interceded on behalf of Sodom and Gemorrah but succeeded in rescuing only his nephew Lot. Whereas the moment Isaac offered the Afternoon Prayer, his prayers were immediately answered, and Eliezer's mission succeeded. As it says in the Torah: "And he lifted up his eyes and behold, there were camels coming" (Verse 64; *idem*).

2

Belz
The Sabra Rebbe

Though the flame of Jewish life was cruelly extinguished in Belz, Galicia, during World War Two, today, in the State of Israel, the fire of Belz is burning brightly, and the Belz dynasty remains a shining star in the hasidic constellation.

"The sun also ariseth and the sun goeth down," says Ecclesiastes.[1] This biblical verse comes to mind when one enters the new *Kirya* of Belz off Sorotskin Street in Jerusalem, where the Israeli-born R. Yissachar Dov Rokeah, popularly known as "Rab Berele" or "the Belzer Rov," maintains the traditions of Belz.

Berele, a charismatic and contentious figure who has continued to demand attention ever since the day he became Rebbe, was born in Tel Aviv on 8 Shevat 1948. In 1922, his father, R. Mordecai (1903–1950), the son of R. Yissachar Dov from his second marriage, had married Bathsheva, the daughter of R. Moshe

---

1. 1:5.

Aaron, the rabbi of Kobrin. He became rabbi of Bilgoraj in 1927. His brother R. Aaron advised him not to accept the rabbinate of Lvov. He had two daughters: Alta Bat Ziyon, who died in 1931; and Rebecca Miriam, who perished in the Holocaust, as did his wife.

He and his brother escaped the Nazi Holocaust. R. Modecai was indefatigable in his efforts to arouse the *Yishuv* to the plight of the Jews in Europe. "The Germans are more concerned with destroying Jewry than with vanquishing the Allies," he reiterated to gatherings, large and small. On 6 Nisan 1947, in Petah Tikvah, he married Miriam, the daughter of R. Tzvi Hayyim Glick, the son of R. Yaakov Yitzhak of Huszt.

In 1948, he visited England, Belgium, Italy, and France on behalf of Belz institutions. Despite his efforts, he did not escape dissension, and many *hasidim* felt that his activities were not in the spirit of his saintly brother.

R. Mordecai died on 25 Heshvan 1950 at the age of forty-seven and was buried in Tiberias. His son was then barely two years old, and the lack of a father's affection was, during the next eight years, compensated to some extent by his uncle R. Aaron. When R. Aaron died, the *hasidim* regarded Berele as the *Yenuka* ("the child"), a designation given to R. Yisrael (1873–1921), the son of R. Asher the Second of Karlin, who was four years old when his father died. A precocious child, a little spoiled and a little stubborn, he was adored by all. Berele's education was supervised by R. Avraham Yehoshua Feder and R. Shalom Brander. His mother did not wish him to become rebbe; she regarded this as too heavy a burden, and she tried her utmost to dissuade him from accepting the position. Legal arguments ensued before she finally submitted to the pressure of the *hasidim*, but she always remained perplexed and appalled by this decision.

On 16 Adar 1965, the youthful rebbe was married in Bene Berak to Sarah, the daughter of R. Moshe Yehoshua Hager, the son of R. Hayyim Meir of Vizhnitz. Just as the wedding at Ustilug in the early nineteenth century between R. Shmuel, the son of R. Dan of Radziwillov, and the daughter of R. Yosef of Hrubieszov fired the imagination of the *hasidim* so the Belz/Vizhnitz wedding was the most publicized and picturesque Jewish wedding of the year. On Monday evening (the wedding took place on Wednesday) the Rabbi of Vizhnitz, R. Hayyim Meir, made a traditional "beggar's banquet" to which all the poor of Bene Berak and the surrounding areas were invited and each guest received five Israeli shekels. Thousands of *hasidim* from all over the world were participants or spectators. The entire quarter was illuminated by colored lights and over three thousand people attended the banquet. Over five thousand *halot* (loaves) were consumed. The young couple had met briefly for the first time at their betrothal, ten months before the wedding. They saw each other for the second time when the bridegroom lowered the veil over the face of his bride, before she was led to the bridal canopy that had been set up in the courtyard, in front of the fort-like towers of the Vizhnitz Yeshivah.

Following the wedding, Berele and his wife, a graduate of the *Bet Yaakov* Seminary, lived in Bene Berak, and the young husband continued his studies under the guidance of his father-in-law. After his ordination by R. Dov Berish Weidenfeld and R. Yosef Grunwald, R. Berele was encouraged by R. Hayyim Meir Hager of Vizhnitz, R. Yisrael Alter of Ger, and R. Yehuda Yekutiel Halberstam of Klausenburg to take over the leadership of Belz.

In 1966, on Shabbat *Nahamu* (the Sabbath of Comfort, when the prophetic portion of Isaiah begins with the word: "Comfort ye, comfort ye, my People"), R. Berele became the Rabbi of Belz, and from then on he made his home in Jerusalem. He had stepped into the shoes of a living legend. Unlike his late uncle, the Rebbe is highly organized and the services are held at the appointed statutory times. Twelve years after the wedding, a son, Aaron Mordecai, was born to him on 7 Heshvan 1976, and R. Berele was the *mohel*.

On 25 Sivan R. Berele and his son visited the ancestral cemetery at Belz to "invite their ancestors to the wedding." On 16 Av 1993, in Kiryat Belz, Jerusalem, R. Aaron Mordecai married the eighteen-year-old Sarah Leah, a student of *Bet Malkah* and the daughter of R. Shimon Lemberger, the rabbi of Makov, the son-in-law of R. Elhanan Halpern of London, and now living in Kiryat

Ata. The father of R. Shimon was R. Nathan Nata, a hasid of Belz. They now have two sons and a daughter.

R. Berele, a man of great complexity, has formidable energy and a fertile imagination. His success did not come without effort and ceaseless work. He is singleminded and has infinite capacity for taking pains. Unlike the *hasidim* of Satmar, Belz has comparatively few wealthy followers, and it is almost miraculous how the Rebbe—with limited financial resources—is able to achieve so much and create such vast Torah institutions. He is imbued with a sense of infallibility. He is by nature proud and touchy and clings tenaciously to his own ideas. At the same time, he is a caring and warm person, a mentor to the young. There is undeniably a competitive element in his nature, and he prefers to make all decisions alone. Courageous and audacious, he is capable of taking the initiative and his views are pungently expressed. He has tremendous drive, enjoys power, and loves getting things done. He can be astonishingly open but is often inscrutable and a strict disciplinarian.

He is not, as his opponents allege, a cold and ruthless person who uses the most loyal individual and then discards him when he is no longer of use. His course has never been in doubt, and he does not flinch from saying what he thinks. He has been accused of being inflexible and uncompromising and of never seeing the other person's point of view if it does not coincide with his own.

When he formed his own *Bet Din* and a new board to supervise *kashrut*, he alienated not only the *Eda Haredit* of Jerusalem but also the *hasidim* of Satmar. A number of ugly skirmishes between Satmar and Belz took place. Satmar students even vandalized the Belz *Shtiebl* in Ross Street, New York. When the Rebbe visited New York in March 1981, he was given police protection.

After Ger, Belz undoubtedly has the largest hasidic following. On New Year and the Day of Atonement as many as four thousand *hasidim* worship in the Belz *Bet Hamidrash*. The foundation stone of the new *Kirya* of Belz was laid in 1977. The masterplan envisages a huge synagogue with five thousand seats (for which the foundation stone was laid on 10 Sivan 1984), the Rebbe's house, a number of banqueting suites to cater for large and small functions, facilities for *kollelim* and yeshivot, Talmud Torah schools, and schools for girls, playgrounds, shopping centers, and apartments for five hundred families. The *Kirya* already houses four hundred families and is a beehive of activity. The Rebbe himself officiates on Friday nights and at *Musaf* on Sabbath. The Service on New Year's Day rarely finishes before 5 P.M. He delivers discourses before the blowing of the *shofar* and before *Kol Nidre*. He reads the Law during the High Holy Days and acts as a *Baal Tekeya*.

The Rabbi himself acts in the dual capacity of *sandak* and *mohel*. He is a member of the *Degel HaTorah* Council of Sages, which is controlled by R. Eliezer Menahem Shach of Bene Berak. In 1981, he established his own *Bet Din* and his own *shechita*, also a *machon l'bedikat shaatnez,* for modern developments have brought new problems that necessitate greater vigilance in determining whether a garment contains both wool and linen. The language of instruction in his educational institutions is Yiddish, but one hour per day is devoted to Ivrit. The girls, however, are allocated more time for secular studies, and the Rebbe fully utilizes municipal and governmental funds to support his institutions.

During the 1996 elections, he urged his followers to vote for the Aguda but did not direct them to vote for the prime minister. The Rebbe has always taken an independent line and is considered one of the most dove-ish haredi spiritual leaders. In the past the Rebbe has supported the peace process and the Oslo Accords. His views are in keeping with the traditional Haredi injunction not to provoke the Gentiles. He recently issued a blistering condemnation of Prime Minister Binyamin Netanyahu and his government. In 1996, he told his followers that the government had shown considerable ineptitude, as a result of its inexperience.[2]

Warning against a tendency toward greater militancy on the part of the Haredi public, he said that the command to live by the sword was a blessing that had been granted to the descendants

2. Genesis 8:22.

of Esau and not to the sons of Israel. He warned of the danger in
which Israel found itself as a result of government action and the
fact that the State had become isolated.

The Belz Yeshivah began in Katamon in 1952 with eight students under the guidance of R. Yehoshua Deutsch. Soon after, a
site of five thousand three hundred square meters was acquired in
Rehov Agrippas, Jerusalem. A five-story yeshivah was erected,
many of its students originating from the United States and different parts of Europe. When laying the foundation stone on 2
Elul 1954, the Rebbe said: "I lay this foundation stone to enable
Jewish children to acquire Torah and the fear of Heaven and it is
my wish that they should be able to eat, drink, and sleep here,
and have all their needs taken care of."

The Rebbe insisted that no less than three students should share
a room, that the language of instruction should exclusively be
Yiddish, and that no donations should be accepted from
nonobservant donors. He was anxious that time be devoted to the
study of *Keddushat Levi*, by R. Levi Yitzhak of Berdichev, and
Maaseh Rokeah, by R. Eleazar Rokeah of Amsterdam. The yeshivah maintains a high standard of scholarship and produces principals of yeshivot, *dayanim*, and lecturers. In Tel Aviv his uncle also
established a Talmud Torah *Mahzike HaDat*, a *Yeshivah Ketanah*,
and a small *kollel*. The activities of the Belz *hasidim* in Bene Berak
started in 1954 with the establishment of a small *shtiebl*.

R. Berele has expanded and enlarged all these centers of learning for boys and girls: from kindergartens for the very young, to
yeshivot and *kollelim* for young married men in Jerusalem, Bene
Berak, Rishon Le-Zion, Haifa, Ashdod, Arad, Bet Shemesh, Kiryat
Gat, and Hazor. A network of schools for girls, *Benot
Yerushalayim* and *Bet Malkah*, flourishes wherever *hasidim* of Belz
live. The small Talmud Torah, established in Jerusalem in 1953
and relocated by the Rebbe to Zichron Moshe, now has a roll of
more than one thousand children.

The Rebbe, moreover, has established a mini-welfare state with
splendid facilities. There is *Ahavat Hesed*, a charitable committee
to help the needy; *Mifal Halbashah*, providing garments for deserving brides and bridegrooms; *Agudat Ezra U'Marpeh*, supplying

medical facilities and visiting nurses for the sick, paramedics, and sophisticated equipment for blood donations; *Oneg Simha*, offering help with the arrangements of *Bar Mitzvah* and wedding celebrations; *Vayizra Yitzhak*, finding accommodations for the elderly; *Zos Asis*, in charge of providing refreshments for *Shalom Zachor*, circumcision, and *Pidyan HaBen* celebrations; *Gemah Terufah*, helping to pay for medication; *Mifal Kamha D'Psicha*, for the allocation of food for Passover; *Mishmeret HaKodesh*, providing facilities for the correction of *Sifre Torah* by qualified scribes; a *Hevra Kedusha*, offering meals during the week of *Shivah* (seven days of mourning); *Gemah HaKlali*, which helps young couples acquire apartments at a reasonable cost; and *Maaseh Rokeah*, an institute for the publication of the works of the rebbes of Belz.

A special body, called *Naaseh V'Nishmah*, with branches in Tel Aviv, Haifa, Netanya, Bat Yam, and Pardes Hannah, organizes facilities for studies and outreach for *Baale Teshuvah*, especially for Russian immigrants. There are *Shtieblech* of Belz in London, Manchester, Antwerp, Vienna, Zurich, Montreal, Borough Park, Monsey, and Williamsburg.

The founder of the dynasty of Belz, a town now in Belarus, was R. Shalom ben Eliezer Rokeah (1783–1855), a militant opponent of *Haskalah*. The high incidence of apostasy among the *Maskilim* convinced R. Shalom that *Haskalah* represented a danger to Judaism. He refused to temporize with the Reformers, categorizing as rank heresy the slightest deviation from the traditional path.

In defense of traditional Judaism, his son and successor, R. Yehoshua (1825–1894), formed the *Mahzike Hadat* (Upholders of the Law) in 1878. The Rebbe was the unofficial spokesman of Galician Jewry and the appointments of rabbis, ritual slaughterers, and communal functionaries required the imprimatur of Belz. He was one of the first hasidic rebbes to engage in politics, and the *Mahzike Hadat* was the first attempt by Orthodox Jewry to unite for political action in order to protect their traditional way of life. The second son and successor of R. Yehoshua was R. Yissachar Dov (1854–1927), the third rebbe of Belz, who extended the power of the dynasty, so that Belz became for Galicia what Ger was to Poland. "The entire world," *hasidim* used to say jokingly, "journeys to Belz."

Large numbers of *hasidim* of Belz were also found in Czechoslovakia, Hungary, and Romania. To the poet Jiri Langer (1894–1943) Belz was the "Jewish Rome." The symbolism in the writings of Franz Kafka (1883–1924) owes much to the inspiration and influence of Belz, as do the writings of Jiri Langer. With the blessing of the Rebbe, Sarah Schenierer started a school for twenty-five girls in a tiny room in the Jewish quarter of Cracow. This was the beginning of the *Bet Yaakov* movement, whose alumni were to become the anti-assimilationists and upholders of Jewish traditions.

On 22 Heshvan 1927, R. Aaron Rokeah, who was born on 17 Tevet 1880 and was named after R. Aaron of Brzezany, succeeded his father. His mother, Bat Rehumah, died when he was four years old, and he was brought up by his stepmother, Hayyah Devorah, the daughter of R. Avraham Shmuel of Chernobyl. In 1896, he married his cousin Malkah, the daughter of R. Shmuel, the rabbi of Sokal. Like his ancestors he was a man of many interests and a man of action, and his influence was far-reaching. When Hitler became the chancelor of Germany on 30 January 1933, R. Aaron declared: "Hitler is the very personification of the devil. He is worse than Amalek or Haman."

For four perilous years, 1940–1944, the Rabbi lived precariously in Nazi Europe. When it was ascertained that Belz would come under German jurisdiction, the Rebbe, in a situation of *Pekuah Nefesh*, left Belz on the last train to Sokal on the night of *Simhat Torah*. When the Russians organized a mass evacuation to Siberia, the Rabbi left for Przemysl, where he spent a whole year. By Hanukah 1943 he was in the ghettos of Bochnia and Cracow, arriving in Budapest on 18 Adar 1943. He withstood unspeakable hardships. His son R. Moshe was burned alive. "It is kind of the Creator," the Rabbi exclaimed in sorrow, "that I, too, was allowed to contribute a sacrifice." He changed his name first to Aaron Singer and then to Aaron Twersky, in order to confuse the Nazis who pursued him relentlessly.

A concerted effort to rescue him was set in motion by his followers, especially in the Holy Land. Chief Rabbi Herzog, R. Moshe Shapira, R. Yitzhak Meir Levin, R. Moshe Blau, Berish Urtner, and his *hasidim*, Elimelech Rumpler and R. Hayyim Nata Katz of London, all interceded on his behalf with the Palestine high commissioner, and the necessary certificates were issued. Traveling through Slovakia, Romania, Bulgaria, Greece, Turkey, Syria, and Lebanon, he arrived in the Holy Land on 9 Shevat 1944. After a brief stay in Haifa, he settled in Tel Aviv. He refused to make his permanent home in Jerusalem. "The sancitity of Jerusalem is so great that I am not able to live there. Besides, I would like to dwell in a town which is entirely inhabited by Jews." He made his home at 63 Rehov Ahad HaAm, where he lived for thirteen and a half years.

The Rebbe lived quietly and did not intervene in public affairs, but on the rare occasions that he did, he was regarded as authoritative. The Rebbe broke the tradition of Belz neutrality when he urged his followers, at the election of the first Knesset in 1949, to support List 2, the United Religious Front, which was made up of the Mizrachi, Hapoel HaMizrachi, the Aguda, and the Poale Agudat Yisroel. "Everyone is obliged to participate in the coming elections," declared the Rebbe.

In the Holocaust, the Rebbe lost his wife, who was killed in Prezemysl, his three sons (R. Moshe, R. Yisrael, and R. Yehuda Zundel), four daughters (Rebecca Miriam, Mirel, Eidel, and Sarah Brachah), his sons-in-law (R. Shmuel Frankel, R. Eliyahu Hayyim Kahan, R. Yisrael Rosenfeld, and R. Moshe Eliakum Briah Zak), daughters-in-law, brothers, and twenty-six grandchildren. Two of his children, Avraham Yehoshua Heschel and Eliezer Menahem, died very young.

After obtaining *Hetter Mea Rabbanim* (dispensation by one hundred rabbis), on 9 Tammuz 1947 he remarried Esther Hurwitz Hager, the daughter of R. Yitzhak Hager. This marriage ended in divorce. He subsequently married, on 9 Adar 1949, Hannah, the daughter of R. Yehiel Hayyim Labin of Makova, a descendant of R. Shimon of Yaroslav and Yitzhak Eizig of Zydaczov. She was the widow of R. Yosef Meir Pollack of Beregzasz, who perished in the Holocaust. She had two young children, Avraham Alter and Beilah Hayyah, whom the Rabbi undertook to look after and whose weddings he arranged. It is noteworthy that the Rebbe could not bear to mention the losses that he had sustained in the Holocaust, but only on the eve of the Day of Atonement did he enumerate the many relatives he had lost.

During the Sinai Campaign (28 October to 5 November 1956), he spent one day in fasting and ceaseless prayer for Israel's victory. Alone in his room, he pleaded for the "tiny Israeli army fighting against seven armies." When he finally emerged, he declared: "My sons, we have won with the help of the Almighty." He readily accepted grants from government sources: "We are paying taxes, and it is only right that we should get something in return."

I was privileged to see the Rebbe in 1957. The month was June and the Sabbath was due to end just before 7 P.M. Tel Aviv's innumerable cafes, restaurants, cinemas, and bars were already open and were thronged with pleasure-seekers, but a different atmosphere pervaded the Rebbe's home. Although "three stars" (indicating that the Sabbath had ended) had appeared in the sky, the Rebbe of Belz was preparing for his first Sabbath morning meal. In its disregard for the conventional prayer times, Belz followed Kotsk. "The evil man has enveloped the earth in darkness," the Rebbe said of Hitler, "there is neither day nor night. He has deprived me of all sense of time" The biblical verse "Day and Night shall not cease"[2] was taken by the Rebbe to mean that time had been suspended with the advent of Nazism, which was evil incarnate.

It was a hot evening and the *Bet Hamidrash* was crowded. The windows were shut and the Rebbe was dressed in heavy garments, with a *streimel* and a very heavy Turkish *tallit*. He looked emaciated, all soul and very little body. He delivered a terse discourse in a low voice, audible only to those who sat next to him. But even those who could not hear were impressed and awed by his mere presence. He left the table for the traditional *Hafsakah* (in-

---

2. Genesis 8:22.

terval), which lasted more than an hour, and he returned about 9
P.M. Four large candles were kindled by a follower who had already recited *Havdalah,* the prayer that signals the conclusion of
the Sabbath. The Rebbe and his followers partook of a single fish
dish that the *hasidim* call *der lichtiger fish* ("the luminous fish"),
for the lights had been lit. Then there was another interval. It was
about 2 A.M. on Sunday morning when the Rebbe finally recited
Havdalah, having extended the Sabbath for seven hours or so.

The very last discourse of his life was based on the verse in
the *Shema* "That your days may be multiplied, and the days of
your children, upon the land which the Lord swore unto your
fathers to give them, as the days of the Heavens above the earth."[3]
The Rabbi stressed the importance of education and told his followers that they must strive to make a bridge between heaven and
earth.

The Rebbe ate little and kept irregular hours, three attendants
caring for him in eight-hour shifts. His asceticism may have been
rooted in a childhood incident. *Hasidim* relate that when he was
a small boy, his grandfather, R. Yehoshua, found him eating with
great relish and sternly rebuked him: "Have you come down to
earth merely for this?"

R. Aaron died on 21 Av 1957 at the age of seventy-nine in the
Shaare Zeddek hospital in Jerusalem. Following the ruling of R.
Dov Berish Weidenfeld, he was interred on *Har HaMenuhot* in
Jerusalem and not near his brother R. Mordecai in Tiberias. The
prediction of *Sar Shalom* (the first rebbe of Belz) that "Belz would
be a source of Torah and fear of God until the advent of the
Messiah" is being fulfilled.

Torah Thoughts

"I am old and do not know when I will die" (Genesis 27:2). "A
man," says the Talmud (*Berachot* 5a) "should always incite the good
impulse to fight against the evil impulse. If his soul does it, well

3. Deuteronomy 11:21.

and good. If not, let him study the Torah. If he subdues it, well
and good, if not, let him recite the *Shema*. And, ultimately, let
him remind himself of the day of death." Isaac had no need to
remind himself of his day of death. He was throughout his life in
complete control of his evil impulses (R. Shalom of Belz).

"These are the names of the sons of Israel who went with Jacob
to Egypt" (Exodus 1:1). The Hebrew text literally means "who
are coming" and not "who came." This indicates that the Israelites never regarded themselves as natives and did not become assimilated with the Egyptians (*idem*).

Commenting on the great mutiny of Korach and his compan-
ions against Moses, the Rebbe of Belz stated: "Korach opened his
mouth against Moses, saying, 'You take too much on yourselves,
seeing that all the congregation is holy' (Numbers 16:3). The rebels
were therefore punished, in that the earth, too, opened 'her mouth'
and swallowed them" (Verse 32).

"They went down alive in Sheol with all their belongings"
(Numbers 16:33). Why were Korach and his associates punished
by going down *alive* in Sheol? This was to give them another opportunity to repent (R. Joshua of Belz).

"The enemy said, I will pursue, I will overtake, I will divide
the spoil" (Exodus 15:9). Our Sages tell us that our fathers were
redeemed from Egypt in the merit of three things: they did not
change their names, their language, or their dress. The consonants
of the Hebrew word for "spoil" (*Shalol*) indicate the three qualities: *Shem*, *Lashon*, and *Levush* (*idem*).

"These are the generations of Noah. Noah was in his generation a man of righteousness" (Genesis 6:9). Some rabbis held this
to be a disparagement. He was righteous only by comparison with
his own generation. Had Noah lived in the time of Abraham, he
would have been accounted as of no importance (*Sanhedrin* 108a).
If the Torah describes Noah as "a man of righteousness, wholehearted and one who walked with God," why do some rabbis
belittle him? The rabbis never underestimated him. On the contrary, they felt that Noah was so humble that had he lived in the
time of Abraham, he would have regarded himself as completely
unworthy (*idem*).

"He is my God, and I will glorify Him" (Exodus 15:2). Rashi states that God did reveal Himself, and the children of Israel pointed to Him—as if it were with their finger—exclaiming: "This is my God!" They visibly felt the Divine presence. True faith is manifested when God remains invisible and does not manifest Himself physically. "This is my father's God and I will exalt him." Though He was invisible, they still did not lose their faith (*idem*).

On the sixth day of the month (Sivan) were the Ten Commandments given to Israel. However, in R. Josi's view, the event took place on the seventh day of Sivan (*Sabbath* 86b). The exact dates of the festivals of Passover and Tabernacles are given in the Torah, but the date of the festival of *Shavot*, the Season of the Giving of the Torah, is subject to controversy. The reason for not recording this momentous event in the Torah can be explained that the acceptance of the Torah does not depend on time (R. Issachar Dov of Belz).

"Of the first of your dough, you shall give to the Lord, a portion for a gift throughout your generations" (Numbers 15:21). The Hebrew word for "dough" not only means "coarse meal" but also "bed" or "cradle." (Proverbs 7:16 and Psalms 132:3), meaning that form the moment you get up, you should devote your energies to the service of·the Almighty (R. Berele of Belz).

"But he called the past to mind, Moses his servant. Where is he who saved them from the sea, the Shepherd of his flock? Where was he who put the holy Spirit among them? Whose glorious arm led the way by Moses' right hand who divided the waters before them to win himself everlasting renown" (Isaiah 63:11–12). Why does the Prophet Isaiah recall the physical deliverance and not the spiritual awakening of the Giving of the Torah? The reason for this is that in times of sorrow and stress, when troubles become overwhelming, it is not possible to cultivate spirituality. Deliverance from distress takes priority over all else. (ibid.).

3

Vizhnitz
A Center of Yiddishkeit

In the flourishing township of Bene Berak is the large, autonomous hasidic settlement *Kiryat Vizhnitz*, named after the townlet
of Vizhnitsa (Vijnita, in Romanian). It is the home of the rabbis
of Vizhnitz, a dynasty that has produced eight generations of
hasidic leaders in the last two centuries.

The foundation stone of the *Kirya* was laid on the site of an
abandoned orange grove near Zichron Meir on 2 Sivan 1950. The
Shikkun grew rapidly, and problems were resolved with dispatch
and ingenuity. By 1973, it housed over one thousand families and
now has a population of over six thousand. The street names tell
the story of the dynasties of Kosov and Vizhnitz: Rehov Ahavat
Shalom, Rehov Torat Hayyim, Rehov Imre Baruch, Rehov Zemah
Zaddik, Rehov Demesek Eliezer, Rehov Admor M'Vizhnitz.

Predictably, the chief building is the magnificent Yeshivah *Bet
Yisrael V'Damesek Eliezer.* Erected with the help of the philanthropist Meir Shalom Rosenberg and modeled after the far-famed yeshivah destroyed by the Nazis in the Bukovina, it has an enroll-

ment of three hundred students. The curriculum requires students
to study for two hours prior to the morning service, both Talmud and *Shulhan Aruch Orah Hayyim* with all its commentaries.
The yeshivah also houses the library of the late R. Meir Meiri,
the author of *Humash Torah Meiri*. The head of the yeshivah is
R. Menahem Ernster, who was born in 1924 in Klausenburg and
studied in the Vizhnitz and Satmar Yeshivot. In 1948, he married
Shevah Brachah, the daughter of R. Hayyim Meir.

After completing their studies at the yeshivah, the students
progress to the six different *kollelim*, where they study *Yoreh Deah*,
Parts One and Two, leading to rabbinical ordination. They are
guided by R. Shmuel Wozner, the Rabbi of Zichron Meir, and
R. Yaakov Meir Stern. The students receive monthly stipends in
addition to allowances for each child, and exceptionally gifted
students receive extra money. The stipends are augmented by help
from parents or by the salaries that the young wives earn working as teachers or secretaries. Graduates of the *kollel* have been
appointed to rabbinic posts in all parts of the world.

The *Kirya* is virtually self-sufficient, particularly in regard to
its educational facilities. Young children attend kindergarten or
one of the three nursery schools, after which, until the age of
fourteen, boys attend the Talmud Torah *Imre Hayyim*, which has
an attendance of over two thousand children in thirty-three classes.
There are fifty dormitory places for children who do not reside
within the *Kirya*. After the age of fourteen, the boys attend the
Yeshivah Ketanah (Junior Yeshivah), run by *Yad Haruzim*, headed
by R. Yaakov David Vizhnitzer, where they are encouraged to
study *mishnayot* by heart, some of them knowing as many as one
thousand.

The girls are enrolled in *Bet Yaakov* schools, many of them
going on to the Teachers' Seminary at Zichron Meir, which is
under the umbrella of the *Hinuch Atzmai*. Nor is adult education
neglected. There are regular *shiurim* after the morning service and
at the end of the working day.

The *Kirya* has its own *shehita* and its own *Bet Din*, whose
members are: R. Meshullam Zusya Luria, R. Moshe Shaul Klein,
and R. Arye Tobias. It is well looked after by social and welfare

organizations: *Bet Avot Vizhnitz* houses over one hundred elderly people; the *Gemilat Hesed* fund grants interest-free loans to the needy; *Ezrat Nashim* provides financial aid for indigent students; and there are over twenty-two different committees providing necessities for its members, such as *tefillin*, furniture, and medical supplies. The *Bikkur Holim* (the society for visiting the sick) takes care of the ailing, and a permanent building fund, *Binyan Ade Ad*, enables people to acquire apartments relatively cheaply. In the central banquet hall, residents, and even nonresidents, celebrate their festivities, while a hotel, *Malon Vizhnitz*, caters for the many visitors to the *Kirya* and has a banquet hall that can accommodate three hundred people.

"Where there is no food, there is no Torah," says the *Mishnah*.[1] It was soon realized that one of the first responsibilities of the *Kirya* was to provide the *hasidim* with the means to earn a living. In response to this imperative, the settlement has its own diamond factory, bakery, printing press, butcher's shop, greengrocery, and a special bakery where unleavened bread for Passover is produced by hand. Its twelve ritual baths open at 3 A.M. every morning and are visited by more than one thousand people every day. The *Kirya* has its own generator, the maintenance of which does not require a Jew to work on the Sabbath.

The *Kirya* is particularly proud of its high birthrate and is colloquially known as the "university for child-bearing." The average family has six or seven children, and ten or twelve is not unusual. Marriages are arranged by *shadhanim* (professional matchmakers), and couples are matched according to cultural backgrounds and compatibility of families. The *hasidim* point out that those who are quick to "fall in love" can just as quickly fall out of love. Arranged marriages are essential in settings where the sexes are segregated from infancy. Boys and girls play separately, young men and young women pray separately, and there is no casual mingling at festivities. As a result, juvenile delinquency, promiscuity, broken marriages, and divorces are virtually unknown in the *Kirya*.

---

1. *Avot* 3:2.

The Rebbe plays a prominent part in the community. Friday night is the highlight of the week's activities, when the Rabbi officiates at the Reader's desk, and at the end of the service over one thousand worshipers wait to greet him but do not shake his hand. He enters the *Bet Hamidrash* with the words: *Gut Shabbos, Gut Shabbos, Heiliger Shabbos, Teiyrer Shabbos, Shreit Yiddlech, Gut Shabbos* ("Good Sabbath, Holy Sabbath, Dear Sabbath. Jews, welcome the Sabbath"). Every Sabbath he conducts three public meals in a building adjacent to the synagogue. The Friday night *Tish* rarely terminates before 2 A.M. His discourses are interwoven with *gematrias* (a method of biblical exegesis based on the interpreting of words according to the numerical value of the letters in the Hebrew alphabet), and *notarikon* (the abbreviation of Hebrew words or phrases). He does not enjoy challenge from those around him and tends to surround himself with men who are always sure to give agreement and support.

The rebbes of Vizhnitz believe that joy is one of the basic tenets of Judaism. A man should rejoice in his day-to-day life as well as when he seeks communion with his Creator. How should a man rejoice? By means of concentration and fervor. It is a touching experience to hear the Rebbe sing *Nishmat* ("the breath of every living being," part of the morning service for the Sabbath) or *Hallel* (hymns of praise recited on the New Moon and festivals), to the tunes of his grandfather, such melodies as *Kol Mekadesh* ("All who sanctify the Sabbath") or *Bene Hechale* ("Members of the Palace"), composed by the kabbalist R. Yitzhak Luria.

Every day, petitioners come to the Rebbe, and each is greeted with the utmost tact and lovingkindness. There is nothing stereotypical about these interviews; some last a few minutes, others for hours. Each visitor is important, and children are treated with particular tenderness, being addressed in endearing diminutives: Yisroel becomes Yisraelniu; Mendel, Mendele; and Nahum, Nahumniu.

The Rebbe today is R. Moshe Yehoshua, the son of R. Hayyim Meir. He was born in Grosswardein on 13 Sivan 1916. He studied under his uncle, R. Eliezer of Vizhnitz. In 1937, as a young man, he became Rabbi of Vilkovitch and later of Grosswardein.

On 2 Nisan 1942, he married Leah Esther (1921–1993), the daughter of R. Menahem Mendel Panet of Des, a descendant of Zanz.

In 1943, he settled in the Holy Land and lived in Tel Aviv. His father joined him in 1947 and helped him set up *Kiryat Vizhnitz* in Bene Berak. R. Moshe Yehoshua is the head of *Mo'etzet Gedole HaTorah* and is very active in the Aguda. He recently protested against the rulings of the Israeli Supreme Court on *Halachah*: "They, the Judges of the High Court, do not understand the meaning of the Sabbath, and they permit *Hillul Shabbat*." He has also attacked the Reform movement, which, in his opinion, is turning Jews into *Goyim*.[2] The Rebbe urges his supporters to study not only one page each day of the Babylonian and Palestinian Talmuds, but also sections of the *Hovot HaLevavot* ("Duties of the Heart") by Bahya ben Yosef ibn Pakuda (1050–1120). He says that this work will help to instill trust in God, love of God, and asceticism, which are no less important than the Commandments. He places great emphasis on cleanliness and personal hygiene. Some years ago he expelled a number of dissident families from the *Kirya*. Nor do cordial relations exist between him and his brother R. Mordecai, the Rebbe of Vizhnitz in Monsey.

R. Moshe Yehoshua has two sons and four daughters. The daughters are married to the Rebbe of Sqvira, the Rebbe of Belz, R. Avraham Teitelbaum of Monroe, and R. Menahem Mendel Ernster, who is now the head of the yeshivah in the *Kirya*. His younger son, R. Menahem Mendel, born in 5 Kislev 1958, married, in 1976, the daughter of R. Avraham David Horowitz. Formerly of Strassbourg, later a member of the *Edah Haredit*, he is now the Rabbi of the *Kirya* and is the designated successor. He has one son and three daughters.

Vizhnitz, like Ger and Belz, is constantly expanding. In addition to *Kiryat Vizhnitz* in Bene Berak, there are institutions in Jerusalem in Har Nof, where the center has a *Bet Hamidrash*, a Talmud Torah *Imre Hayyim*, a yeshivah, and a *shikkun*. There is a Vizhnitz branch in Rehovot, established in 1980, where several hundred couples now reside. In the last three years, educational

---

2. *Jewish Tribune*, London (28 January 1996):7.

establishments have been founded in Ashdod. "Our mission is to establish Torah institutions everywhere" sums up the Rebbe's ambition.

The Rebbe's elder son, R. Yisrael, was born on Israel's Independence Day and was ordained by R. Pinhas Epstein and R. David Jungreis. He married Miriam, the daughter of R. Zusya Twersky, the Rebbe of Chernobyl of Bene Berak. He is erudite and a great servant of the Lord. As the elder son, he was in complete charge of the financial and religious management of the *Kirya* for six years. However, in 1983, after a series of squabbles and altercations, he was summarily dismissed from his post, all contact was broken off, and he was virtually excommunicated. His scholarly and articulate younger brother, R. Menahem Mendel, became his father's favorite and heir presumptive.

When R. Yisrael's mother died in 1993, the event, rather than bringing him closer to the family, proved a further cause for estrangement. He attended the funeral but sat *shivah* separately. All the hasidic rebbes and prominent personalities who visited the Rebbe during the *shivah* subsequently called upon R. Yisrael. When his two sons and four daughters were married into illustrious hasidic families, Vizhnitz-Monsey, Sqvira, Sziget-Satmar, Teitelbaum-Nir Batur, and Panet-Des, the most prominent hasidic rebbes participated in the festivities, while his father and younger brother were conspicuous by their absence.

R. Yisrael lives isolated in a small apartment in Rehov Sefat Emet, Bene Berak. He did not establish a rival fellowship, but he prays in a nearby *shtiebl*. A number of *hasidim* of Vizhnitz, who prefer anonymity, support him financially, and when he visits London from time to time, he is very much welcomed by R. Elhanan Halpern. He attended the *shtiebl* of Ger in Lampard Grove, Stamford Hill, on the Sabbath and not the Vizhnitz *Bet Hamidrash* in Upper Clapton. In vain have the Rebbe of Ger and R. Kohn of *Toldot Aaron* tried to make peace between father and son and create family harmony, but their efforts were repulsed. R. Yisrael's brothers-in-law, particularly, R. Berele of Belz, often visit him, but he is completely ignored by his younger brother. All doors to Vizhnitz are closed to him, and in his isolation, his moral and personal courage shines brightly, for he never utters a word of criticism against his father and remains unwavering in his devotion. This has earned him widespread respect from those who are impressed by his steadfastness and courage.

An insatiable longing for his father intensified as the years roll on. Unexpectedly and unannounced, he visited him when his father was vacationing in Switzerland in the summer of 1996, but his hopes of a reconciliation were dashed. "I cannot start a new war," his father said to him, meaning that he cannot fight against the establishment that now looks to the younger son as the successor. The cause of this disagreement, unparalleled in the history of Hasidism, is difficult to ascertain. It is impossible to speculate on the motives behind this. The French statesman Leon Gambetta, during the German occupation of Alsace/Lorraine, said: "Let us think of it always, but speak of it never." These words could be applied here.

Similarly, the followers of Vizhnitz never even mention him, and his name is omitted from the 350-page telephone directory published by the *Kirya*. It is said that R. Yisrael lacked discerning worldliness, drive, and determination. As a young man in a hurry, not a professional administrator, he was reluctant during his tenure of office to seek advice and thereby incur fatherly reproof and correction. He was overgenerous in granting loans to needy *hasidim*, which repeatedly resulted in large debts that then had to be paid off by his father. There were, naturally, rows and recriminations, as he constantly ignored warnings for the need to balance the budget of the *Kirya*. His temperament did not make him an ideal subordinate and led to constant disagreements. It must have been a traumatic decision to remove R. Yisrael from his post. The paradox remains, and we are no closer to understanding why he was removed from the bosom of a family whose motto is "lovingkindness and compassion."

The Kosov-Vizhnitz dynasty was founded by the kabbalist R. Yaakov Kopul (d. 1787) of Kolomyja in Galicia, who was a devoted follower of the Besht. R. Kopul's son, R. Menahem Mendel (1769–1826), settled in Kosov in Eastern Galicia, near the Hungarian border. In 1790, he married Sheine Rachel, the daughter of R. Shmuel of Kosov. He lived by three principles: love of God, love of Israel, and love of the Torah. He, like the Besht, maintained that his threefold ideal could be achieved through music, and his melodies echoed through Hungary, Romania, and Czechoslovakia.

His traditions were continued by his son R. Hayyim (1795–1854). R. Hayyim's youngest son, R. Menahem Mendel (1830–29 Tishri 1885), settled in Vizhnitz, which then was part of Austria, and married Miriam, the daughter of R. Yisrael Friedman, founder of the Ruzhin-Sadagora dynasty. Modeling himself after his father-in-law, R. Menahem Mendel, who was head of the *Kollel* of Vizhnitz and Marmaros, built himself a palatial residence with a large *Bet Hamidrash*, surrounded by gardens and orchards. He employed a man whose sole duty it was to distribute money anonymously to charitable causes. Such vast sums were involved that his brother-in-law, R. Nahum of Stefanesti, remarked: "If the Rabbi of Vizhnitz had kept for himself all the money he has given away to charity, he would have been richer than Rothschild." R. Menahem Mendel's son, R. Baruch (1845–20 Kislev 1893), also made his home in Vizhnitz, where he published his father's writings. He died at the age of forty-eight, leaving twelve children.´

The most outstanding of R. Baruch's progeny was R. Yisrael (1860–1936), known among the *hasidim* as the *Ohev Yisrael* ("lover of Israel"). At the age of fifteen he married Hinda, the daughter of R. Meir Horowitz of Dzikov. He succeeded his father as Rebbe of Vizhnitz when he was thirty-three. He was particularly interested in education, setting up a Talmud Torah and a yeshivah, *Bet Yisroel*. With the outbreak of World War One, he found refuge in Grosswardein (Nagyvarad, in Hungarian) in Transylvania. At first, the mitnaggedic community gave him an unfriendly, if not hostile, reception, but gradually he won their affection.

After the war he did not return to Vizhnitz, for he yearned to settle in the Land of Israel, and his son R. Eliezer became rabbi in Vizhnitz in his place. He was involved in a bitter dispute with R. Hayyim Tzvi Teitelbaum over the presidency of the *kollel*, a fund for the needy in the Holy Land. Since they were unable to settle their differences, they were made jointly responsible for the fund. A staunch supporter of the Aguda, R. Yisrael often urged his followers to vote for the Aguda candidates at elections.

Fourteen years after his death, he was reburied in Bene Berak on 13 Adar (Fast of Esther) 1950. His son welcomed the coffin with the Vizhnitz melody of "Shalom Aleichem" (Welcome, Ye Ministering Angels). Three of R. Yisrael's five sons settled in the Holy Land. R. Hayyim Meir Hager, the founder of *Kiryat Vizhnitz*, was born in Vizhnitz on 15 Kislev 1888 and was ordained by R. Meir Arik, R. Shalom Mordecai Schwadron of Brzezany, and R. Binyamin Arye Weisz of Czernowitz. In 1908, he married his cousin Margalit, the daughter of R. Zeev Twersky of Rahmastrivka, a descendant of the rebbes of Chernobyl. The Rebbe divided his time between Vizhnitz and Vilcovitz, his first rabbinic post. In 1935, he visited the Holy Land accompanied by his brothers R. Baruch and R. Eliezer. In 1940, the Yeshivah of Vizhnitz was closed and in the same year the Russians occupied the Bukovina. His home was always open to all who were homeless and destitute. Although it was dangerous, he visited the communities in Marmaros and conducted clandestine services.

In 1940, Grosswardein was taken over by then Fascist Hungary. Jews of military age (twenty to forty-eight) who had become classified as "unreliable," and thus deemed unfit to bear arms, were drafted into the *Munkaszologalat* (Hungarian Labor Service System). By 1942, one hundred thousand men served in these units, with over fifty thousand of them outside Hungary's borders, mostly in the Ukraine. After the German occupation of Hungary in March 1944, the Final Solution program was launched. On 1 May, Adolf Eichmann's representative, Theodor Dannecker, arrived to supervise the concentration of the Jews into a ghetto near the town center. By 6 May, more than ten thousand Jews had been placed in the ghetto. The first transport to Auschwitz began on 24 May, and nearly every day until 3 June some three thousand Jews were sent there, until the ghetto was virtually empty. The Rabbi escaped with only his *tallit* and *tefillin*. For a time, he chopped wood in a labor camp. Miraculously, the Rabbi's family survived the Holocaust.

Eventually, after an arduous journey, he made his way back to Grosswardein, which became a center for returning Hungarian and Romanian Jews. Many Jewish children, who had survived in Budapest, were brought there, as food shortages were a lesser problem. At the end of the war, in Elul 1945, only eight thousand Jews had resettled there, perhaps two thousand of whom were former residents who had survived the war. The Rebbe tried to rebuild the shattered community.

R. Hayyim's brother R. Eliezer (1891–1946) found refuge in the Holy Land in 1944. He was his father's favorite son. "I have five books of Moses," said his father of his five sons. "When the doors of Paradise are closed to me, I will state that I am Eliezer's father, and all the gates will be opened." In 1907, R. Eliezer married Havah (d. 1954), the daughter of R. Yitzhak Meir Heschel of Kopicienice. He spent World War One in Vienna and, in 1922, became the Rabbi of Vizhnitz, where he established the Yeshivah *Bet Yisrael Damesek Eliezer*.

On his arrival in the Holy Land, he set up a *Bet Hamidrash* and a yeshivah in Tel Aviv, but became very ill only two years later. Although in pain, he would not permit the doctors to hush the *hasidim* who were singing and dancing in the nearby synagogue. "They do not disturb me," said the Rabbi to the doctor, "on the contrary, their songs and dances give me new strength." He died on 2 Elul 1946 and was buried on the Mount of Olives. He left no children.

R. Hayyim Meir had little success in postwar Grosswardein and decided to emigrate. After one year in Antwerp, he settled in Rehov Lilienblum in Tel Aviv in 1947. He had so many followers that a hall had to be rented to accommodate them all on the High Holidays. After three years, he was ready to found his own settlement. "Because only by building and establishing new centers of Torah here, can we effectively strengthen the faith." Acquiring thirty-three *dunams* in Bene Berak, he established the first hasidic *shikkun* to be set up since the establishment of the State of Israel.

R. Hayyim Meir died at the age of eighty-four on 9 Nisan (22 March) 1972. Fifty thousand people from all over Israel attended his funeral. At the yeshivah, *Hakafot* (circuits) were made around the coffin. He was succeeded by his son R. Moshe Yehoshua.

R. Naftali Hayyim Adler, born in Jerusalem on 11 Heshvan 1913, was the son of R. Mordecai Yehuda, a descendant of the dynasties of Lelov and Przysucha. Orphaned while very young, he was brought up by his stepfather, R. Baruch Hager of Seret. After studying in the yeshivot of Hungary, he was ordained by R. Pinhas Zimetbaum, rabbi of Grosswardein, and R. Yitzhak Yaakov Weisz. In 1938, he married Hinda, the daughter of R. Hayyim Meir Hager of Vizhnitz. Miraculously escaping the Holocaust, he came to the Holy Land in 1944 and, for a time in 1952, was the rabbi of the Vizhnitz *hasidim* in Tel Aviv. In 1953, he taught at the Yeshivah *Yachel Yisrael* in Haifa.

He subsequently established a *Bet Hamidrash Ohel Naftali*, and *kollelim* for young married men and *Baale Batim* in Netanya, with branches in Haifa, Tel Aviv, Jerusalem, and Bene Berak. He published *Nezah Shebemalchut*, a *Haggadah* for Passover, as well as festival prayer books, according to Vizhnitz liturgy. His son R. Mordecai was killed on the way to the synagogue on 15 Av 1990, and R. Naftali Hayyim Adler's wife died in 1993.

He died on 9 Adar 1995 and was succeeded by his son R. Yisrael Eliezer Adler of Rehovot. Born in Haifa on 25 Tevet 1956, he studied in the Yeshivah *Bet Avraham* in Jerusalem.

Ramat Vizhnitz

On the heights of Mount Carmel, overlooking the blue waters of the Mediterranean and the Bay of Haifa, where the road twists and turns before it reaches the wooded plateau, stands *Ramat Vizhnitz*, a hasidic center established by R. Baruch Hager.

R. Baruch, the fourth son of R. Yisrael, the *Ohev Yisrael*, was born in Vizhnitz on 2 Heshvan 1895. His father called him the "wise one." He was ordained by R. Meir Arik of Buczacz and R. Abraham Steinberg of Brody. He married Henia, the daughter of R. Yissahar Dov Rokeah of Belz, a union that ended in divorce. His second wife, Tzyril, was the daughter of R. Eliezer Nisan

Horowitz of Safed, a descendant of Dzikov. Her first husband, R. Mordecai Yehuda Adler, left her with one son, Naftali Hayyim.

From 1923 on, R. Baruch occupied a rabbinic position in the Bukovina, and in 1934, he became rabbi in Seret-Vizhnitz where he established a yeshivah, *Bet Yisrael Tamchin D'Oreita.* Like his father and brothers, he was active in the Aguda and advocated the establishment of agricultural centers for the training of religious *Halutzim.* A courteous and considerate man, he listened thoughtfully to the opinions of others, presenting his own views with a gentle persuasiveness that often carried the day.

During World War Two, he was transported·to Transnistria, where he spent two and a half years in hiding and suffered great hardships. He arrived in Israel in Sivan 1947. While his brother was planning to establish a *shikkun* in Bene Berak, R. Baruch founded his settlement in Haifa. On 3 Tammuz 1954, the cornerstone was laid. Many religious Jews were attracted to *Hadar HaCarmel* and its illustrious yeshivah, *Yachel Yisrael.* The *shikkun's* large synagogue, *Mekor Baruch*, seats some six hundred men and four hundred women. There is a kindergarten, a Talmud Torah, an elementary school (recognized by the Ministry of Education), a school for girls, a home for elderly people, a *kollel* for married students, a Torah library, dormitories, and modern kitchen facilities. There is also a *Mishnayot* Society where *kaddish* is recited on behalf of the bereaved for the eleven months of mourning and *mishnayot* are studied on the days of *yahrzeits.*

The *Shikkun Seret-Vizhnitz* places special emphasis on helping Russian immigrants become acclimatized to the new Torah-culture, offering Jewish education and a network of youth clubs. In order to mitigate spiraling food prices, Vizhnitz maintains a nonprofit supermarket for large families at specially discounted rates. The *shikkun* also provides emergency first aid, sees to the visiting of the sick, helps to meet medical expenses, and refers people in need of special medical care to the appropriate doctors. It also offers grants and loans, and new clothing to young couples about to get married. It has a mother-and-child rest home, administered by professional and experienced staff, to enable mothers to regain their strength after childbirth, prior to returning to their homes.

The Rebbe was pleased with the progress of the settlement: "Red Haifa is getting whiter and whiter," meaning, of course, that the Labour-controlled teeming city was becoming more observant.

The Rebbe died on 2 Heshvan 1964 at the age of sixty-eight and was buried in Bene Berak. He was survived by three sons and one daughter. Two of the sons of his second marriage, R. Eliezer and R. Moshe, divided their father's patrimony. R. Eliezer, who was born on 11 Tishri 1925, studied in Seret and married Hayyah, the daughter of R. Oizer Braun, a descendant of the *Yismah Moshe*.

The second son, R. Moshe, who was born in 1926 and married Perel, the daughter of R. Hayyim Menahem David Horowitz of Dzikov, became the head of the yeshivah. "My aim is to maintain and expand the glorious path of my ancestors," stated the Rebbe. A publishing house has been added to the settlement, and it has printed a commentary on the Sabbath Table Melodies of Kosov and Vizhnitz. In January 1973, a new building, *Zeev Hesed V'Eliezer David Halevi*, was consecrated. It provides additional facilities for the students of the yeshivah, and a center for research into the history of Vizhnitz.

Torah Thoughts

"The rich man must not give more, nor the poor man less" (Exodus 30:15). The wealthy shall not "increase" implies that they should not become proud, nor should the poor "decrease," meaning that they should not feel inferior for contributing just half a shekel. Observing the Torah and *mitzvot* will enrich the poor (R. Menahem Mendel of Vizhnitz).

"And Joseph fell on his neck and wept" (Genesis 46:29). Jacob, however, neither fell on Joseph's neck nor did he kiss him. The reason given by Rashi is that Jacob was reciting the *Shema*. If it was the time for the recitation of the *Shema*, why did Joseph not recite it? If, on the other hand, it was not the time, why did Jacob recite it? When Jacob beheld Joseph, whom he had already given up for dead, he was so overwhelmed with joy that he felt that he had to channel it to the service of the Almighty. So he recited the *Shema*. Another reason for Jacob reciting the *Shema* is that when he entered Egypt, the land of idolatry, he felt that he had to affirm his loyalty to the Almighty (*idem*).

"Therefore shall a man leave his father and his mother, and become attached to his wife and they shall become one flesh" (Genesis 2:24). The Hebrew word for "to leave" can also mean "to help." Marriage does not remove a man's filial obligations (*idem*).

The High Holy Days are a period of repentance. Repentance should take the form of joy and not of sadness or melancholy. For joy is one of the pillars of Hasidism, as our Sages tell us: "The Divine Presence rests upon a man 'neither through gloom nor through frivolity, but only through joy'" (*Sabbath* 30b). Hence, Joseph said to his brothers: "And now be not grieved" (Genesis 45:5). "Even when you feel sorry and are full of remorse, there is no room for sadness" (*idem*).

"Behold, I set before you this day a blessing and a curse" (Deuteronomy 11:26). It refers not only to the blessings and curses that were pronounced on Mount Gerizim and on Mount Ebal on entering the Holy Land, but to everyday life, for free will is axiomatic in Judaism. In the words of our Sages "everything is determined by Heaven, except the Fear of Heaven" (R. Joshua Hager).

"And Moses was grown up and went out unto his brethren" (Exodus 2:11). The Hebrew *vayigdal* means "becoming great." He became "great" because he went out to his brethren, because of his association with his fellow Jews. This was the secret of his greatness (R. Hayyim Meir).

"Abraham sat in the tent door in the heat of the day" (Genesis 18:1). Abraham was watching the road for passers-by to offer them hospitality. The numerical value of the Hebrew word for "heat" is the same as for the word *hayyim* ("life"). We should aim that every day should be full of "life," full of Torah and good deeds, so as to make life worthwhile (R. Yehoshua of Vishnitz).

"Our educational trend is holy. Among those who receive education in our establishments, you will not find those who tear up and burn *mezuzot*. Our education is based on sound foundations, and not on the secular way of life. It is inconceivable that after we have gone through the Holocaust, it is possible here in Israel that Jews should be persecuted only because they are attached to their faith" (*Ibid*). "Take heed unto yourselves, lest ye forget the Covenant and make you a graven image . . . which the Lord your God has forbidden" (Deuteronomy 4:23). The worst crime is to perpetrate a transgression and regard it as if it were a *mitzvah*. It is bad enough "to make a graven image" but worse still that you assume and pretend that "God commanded you" (R. Baruch of Seret).

4

Kiryat Zanz
A Rebbe's Dream

Twenty minutes' walk from Netanya, a cosmopolitan Mediterranean resort, stands *Kiryat Zanz*, the home of four hundred families and one of the largest hasidic settlements in Israel outside Bene Berak and Jerusalem. It was founded by R. Yekutiel Yehuda Halberstam of Klausenburg. The foundation stone was laid on 4 March 1956, and the settlement was built according to Jewish law. Its most impressive building is the Great Synagogue, the centerpiece of which is a three-hundred-year-old Italian Ark, constructed of beautiful red-veined wood. It has seats for over one thousand worshipers and is used mainly on the High Holy Days and other special occasions.

Directly opposite the Great Synagogue is the small *Bet Hamidrash*, which is in constant use for prayer and study. In the evening after work, the men of the *Kirya* gather together to study the Talmud and the Codes. The Rabbi set a standard of scholarship for his followers, quoting the talmudic dictum "an ignorant man cannot be truly pious." [1] "To me," he once declared, "a hasid is not one who just comes to my weekly discourse or sits at my table, but one who learns eighteen hours a day and studies eighteen pages of the Talmud or recites eighteen chapters of the Psalms."

Diverse Torah institutions cater to every age. The primary school, with its attractive layout and modern equipment, includes a kindergarten and a gymnasium. There is a Talmud Torah, *Darke Avot*; a yeshivah, *Ketanah*; and a boarding school, *Bet Hannah*, where girls receive elementary education. The dormitory is open to girls outside the *Kirya*, and free education is provided. The language of instruction is Yiddish (not Hebrew), although Hebrew is, of course, a key subject.

The pride of the community is the main yeshivah, which also reflects the Rabbi's high standard of scholarship. A student who masters only three hundred pages of the Talmud qualifies for the title of *Zurvah Mirabbonam* (a young student of rabbinics). A student who commits to memory five hundred pages of the Talmud, with its commentaries, is given the title of *Haver* (Associate), while the mastery of one thousand pages entitles one to the coveted degree of *Morenu* (Our Teacher). The highest degree, that of *More Morenu* (Revered Teacher) is reserved for those who have mastered the entire Talmud. Talmudic scholars who visit the yeshivah regularly never fail to be impressed by the sight of teenage students reciting many pages of the Talmud from memory. The yeshivah has a comfortable and contemporary dormitory in the *Kirya*.

Advanced students, all of them married, continue their studies in a *kollel*, a number of whose graduates hold rabbinic and educational posts in Israel· and other countries. Every student receives a free apartment and a monthly stipend, which is supplemented by parents and the young working wives of the students.

The Rabbi's efforts were not confined exclusively to his *hasidim*. He was particularly concerned with the status of Israel's Yemenite and North African Jews and became incensed when he

---

1. *Avot* 3:21.

heard of discrimination or intolerance toward the Sephardim: "How can we have anything but admiration for a community that has produced the Golden Age of Spain, and such luminaries as Yitzhak Alfasi, Moses Maimonides, Yosef Caro, Hayyim Ibn Atar, Shalom Sharabi, and Avraham Azulai?" For oriental Jews the Rabbi established *Yeshivat Maharshad*, named in memory of his father-in-law, R. Shmuel David Unger. The Rebbe held the Sephardim in high esteem, calling them *Heilige Shevatim* (holy tribes). The *Kirya* also maintains an orphanage for Sephardi children and a synagogue, where they can follow their own traditional liturgy and where the style of worship is oriental. "Let us show that all Jews, whatever their origin, can live together in harmony," declared the Rebbe.

The *Bet Avot* (home of the fathers) provides pleasant, self-contained apartments for its elderly residents, many of whom are retired Americans. Also in the *Kirya* are a diamond factory, a shopping center, a post office, a bank, and *mikvaot*. Only religious Jews are admitted as residents. Television is not allowed, but radios are tolerated. Its hotel, *Galei Zanz*, has its own handsome synagogue. Bathing facilities for men and women are provided on the beach on different days.

The most interesting aspect of the *Kirya* is probably the *Laniado Hospital*, the first religious hospital to be built for many years. At the time the hospital was founded, there were no medical facilities for the residents of the large metropolitan region that stretches from Hadera in the north to Kfar Saba in the south. The growth rate of the city of Netanya, the fifth largest town in Israel, has long been one of the highest in the country. The recent wave of mass immigration from the Soviet Union has accelerated this growth, as forty thousand new immigrants have chosen Netanya as their home, and the population is due to reach an estimated quarter-million by the end of the millennium.

The hospital began its existence in June 1975 with a four-room outpatients' clinic, and at the end of 1976 it became a full-fledged hospital. In 1978, a leading firm of architects was commissioned to draw up a long-term masterplan for a medical center on a ten-acre site adjacent to the original building. Step-by-step, new departments and new wings were opened, and the hospital became known as the *Zanz Medical Center*. There are at present 169 beds in the various departments, with an additional one hundred thirty-two beds in the *Bet Avraham* and *S. Daniel Avraham* Geriatric Centers. With the completion of the new medical building, the hospital will have over four hundred beds in service. The hospital also has an extensive range of ambulatory care services.

It has departments of internal medicine, cardiology and intensive coronary care, and obstetrics (with an annual delivery rate of more than two thousand five hundred babies); a male fertility laboratory; a pediatric department; and surgery and urology units, where three thousand operations are performed each year. It also has a department of ophthalmology, featuring laser implant surgery, where more than ten thousand patients are treated every year. It has recently purchased the most up-to-date, state-of-the-art equipment to perform cataract operations using the Fhaco-Emulsification Technique, known as "Diplomax." To meet the needs of cancer patients, the hospital has opened its own oncology department. Residents of the *Kirya*, instead of having to make weekly trips to Tel Aviv or Petah Tikvah for chemotherapy, can be treated at home by doctors who have special expertise in chemotherapy treatment.

The hospital also provides visits by teams of physicians, nurses, physiotherapists, and social workers, which serve housebound patients. It has a mammography section, where examinations to help in breast cancer prevention and its early detection are provided under the guidance of Israel's Cancer Society. Residents can also receive treatment in the Hemodialysis Unit, which is equipped with fourteen dialysis machines. The nuclear medical unit is able to perform noninvasive functional imaging tests of the bones, thyroid, kidney, lung, gallbladder, liver, and heart.

The hospital is run according to the *Halachah* and without compromise of the highest standard of medical practice. There is a Tache Outpatient Clinic that looks after forty-five thousand patients annually. An additional asset to the hospital is the extensive medical library, with its recently installed computerized data retrieval system, enabling doctors to have immediate access to the latest information and techniques.

Many of the nurses are graduates of the hospital's own teaching faculty, the Tessler School of Nursing, where the students are trained to uphold the sanctity of life in a loving and caring manner. Special programs are arranged to train Soviet and Ethiopian immigrants to become registered nurses. Like most countries, Israel suffers from an acute shortage of qualified nurses, since Orthodox girls are reluctant to become nurses because of the lack of a suitable religious environment. In the nursing school at the hospital, Hebrew and religious studies are combined with the nursing curriculum.

In 1993, some twenty thousand patients were treated in "Emergency" and thirty-five thousand in 1995. No person is ever turned away, regardless of their religious affiliation or ability to pay. The Laniado Hospital is widely admired as a model of tolerance and good medical practice. It attracts trained medical staff from around the world and is under the supervision of the Israeli Ministry of Health, with an international board of directors drawn from Europe, Canada, the United States, and Israel. The late Rabbi often stated that of all the communities and religious institutions he founded, the Laniado Hospital was the holiest of the holy.

The hospital has fully lived up to its guiding principle "that every effort shall be made to alleviate the physical sufferings of all patients and uplift their mental outlook in order to provide them with the best overall therapeutic treatment." The late Rabbi felt that all hospital workers should have a warm Jewish heart. They should love the patient, and their aim should be to cure the person, not merely the disease.

Life in the *Kirya* revolves around the person and personality of the Rabbi. He supervises all the religious and spiritual activities. Fruit and vegetables are not sold until a tithe has been taken, and strict rules are observed during the seventh year (*Shemitah*). Every Friday the entire *Kirya* is examined to ensure that the *eruv* (the symbolic boundary within which people may carry things on the Sabbath) is intact. There is no vehicular traffic in the *Kirya* on the Sabbath. It has a *Hevra Kadisha* (burial society) and its own plot at the Netanya cemetery. In the Zanz tradition they follow the view of Rabbenu Tam (1100–1171), the French Tosaphist, in terminating the Sabbath one hour later than is the norm.

The founder of the *Kirya* was R. Yekutiel Yehuda Halberstam, the Rabbi of Klausenburg, who was born in Rudnik on 4 Shevat 1904. When his father, R. Tzvi Hirsch, died at the age of forty-four in 1918, the fourteen-year-old Yekutiel Yehuda delivered a three-hour eulogy. He studied under R. David Tzvi Zehman of Dukla and was ordained by R. Yehiel Meir Halstock of Ostrowiec, R. Meir Arik, and R. Shmuel Engel. One of the projects he completed as a young man was a comprehensive study of the halachic opinions involving sunset (in Hebrew, *Bain Hashmashot*) that determine when one day ends and the next begins. This would have been a major contribution for a mature scholar, and the fact that its author was still an unbearded youth created a profound impression on the entire community.

R. Hayyim Tzvi Teitelbaum of Sziget (1882–1926) sought out the young scholar as his son-in-law. The young man married R. Teitelbaum's daughter Hannah in 1921; thus, the houses of Halberstam and Teitelbaum were once again united. After living with his father-in-law for five years, he accepted the position of rabbi of the hasidic community *Yereim* of Klausenburg (also known as Cluj-Napoca or Kolozsvar), which had a well-developed network of educational and charitable institutions.

He was firm and uncompromising. With extraordinary talent and capacity for work, he earned a reputation as a dynamic rabbi, laboring hard and inspiring others to do likewise. He was an exacting and, at the same time, a stimulating teacher. Unlike R. Moshe Shmuel Glasner (1856–1925), a leader of the Mizrachi movement in Hungary, and his son R. Akiva Glasner (d. 1944), who both sought a more liberal approach, the Rabbi was firm and uncompromising, especially when it came to challenging the large Neolog (Conservative) community under the Zionist leaders Drs. Jozsef Fischer and Rezso (Rudolf) Kasztner, his father-in-law.

The Rabbi's twenty years in Klausenburg were fruitful and fulfilling. During this period, he gained renown as a rabbinic leader. This was, however, to come to an abrupt and tragic end with the German "New Order," which brought destruction to the Jews of southeastern Europe. Two-thirds of Romanian Jews perished during the war. The ghettoization of the Jews of Klausenburg, numbering 16,763 souls, began on 1 May 1944 and was completed within one week. The ghetto was liquidated through the deportation of the community to Auschwitz in six transports between 25 May and 9 June 1944.

The Rabbi saw his community scattered and deported by the Nazi murderers. He himself was interned in a number of labor camps in Hungary and transferred to the ghetto of Nagy Banya. For a time he was forced to work in the ruins of the Warsaw Ghetto, where conditions were cruel and the work virtually beyond human strength, starting at 4 A.M. and finishing late at night. In 1944, he was taken to the hell that was Auschwitz, Dachau, and Mildorf. He describes his experiences: "I, myself, was about to be murdered on several occasions, by those evil ones, let their memories be blotted out. More than once, I found myself spread out on the ground, murmuring the prayer: 'In Your hand I return my spirit . . . when suddenly I heard a command that I rise and return to the camp. Such things occurred with virtually everyone who had been there. They had been in mortal danger, but rescued at the very last moment." [2]

During the Nazi domination, the Rabbi's wife and eleven of his children perished. Such a tragedy would have broken a lesser man and caused him to lose faith, but the Rebbe emerged with a fiery determination to rebuild a hasidic community that had been completely demoralized. In 1947, it had a Jewish population of close to six thousand five hundred, consisting of survivors and those who had moved there from other parts of Romania.

The postwar years were almost as traumatizing as the war years had been. Immediately after the liberation, he went from camp to camp, nourishing the broken shards of humanity with the teachings of their Fathers.[3] He helped the Rebbe of Stolin, R. Yohanan

2. *Humash Shiur*, Toldot 5743, quoted by S. Greenwald, "The Late Zanz/Klausenburger Rav," in *Torah Lives* (New York: *Mesorah Publications*, 1995), p. 10.

3. Meyer Birnbaum and Yonason Rosenblum, *Lieutenant Birnbaum* (New York: *Mesorah Publications*, 1993), p. 49.

Perlow; R. Yitzhak Meir and R. Avraham Ziemba, nephews of R. Menahem Ziemba; and many orphans who had become estranged from the Jewish way of life. His once-flowing beard had been shaved off in the concentration camps, and with little more than stubble on his chin, he dedicated himself to the rehabilitation of those broken remnants of Jewry. He established kosher kitchens, yeshivot, religious schools for girls, *Batei Midrashim* (study centers) for adult study, and printing presses to reprint religious books.

Desperately, he attempted to sort through the pathetic human wreckage: children without parents, parents without children, husbands without wives, and wives without husbands. He listened, talked, counseled, comforted, publicized the plight of those unfortunates, and exerted all possible influence for their rehabilitation. Working at the Feldafing, Landsberg, and Foehrenwald Camps, containing four to six thousand DPs (Displaced Persons), he soon gained a wide reputation as a "wonder rabbi." He tried to help those who were still ailing souls, suffering from the psychological effects of their past experiences, and worried about their uncertain future.

General Dwight D. Eisenhower, who was then commander-in-chief of the European Theater of Operations (later to become the president of the United States), visited the camps and was especially interested in meeting this "wonder rabbi." It was the Day of Atonement and the arrival of the general did not disturb the Rabbi's devotions. Afterwards, he told the general: "I was praying before the General of Generals, King of Kings, the Holy One, Blessed be He. The earthly general had to wait." Eisenhower was impressed by this man, for here was no cowering refugee but a leader of men, working to rebuild a community. He asked if there was anything he could do to help. "Yes," replied the Rabbi. "The Festival of Tabernacles is coming soon, and it is impossible to procure the 'Four Species' here in the camp." To some people this might have seemed like a trivial request, but the Rabbi stressed its importance and religious significance for the spiritual rehabilitation of these forlorn survivors. The general, to his credit, acceded to his request and even sent a special airplane to Italy to procure an ample supply of the "Four Species" in time for the festival.

In order to mobilize the conscience of Jewry, the Rabbi traveled to the United States and spoke widely in different communities. He returned to Germany after a few months, but it did not take him long to realize the futility of remaining in Europe, the valley of the shadow of death. In 1947, he settled first in Manhattan's Upper West Side, then in the Williamsburg section of Brooklyn, and finally in the Crown Heights section of Borough Park, as well as establishing a community in Union City, New Jersey. He founded *hadarim* for boys, and girls' schools. In 1952, he founded the very first *kollel* in the United States. He also established a yeshivah, *She'erit HaPeletah* ("surviving remnants"),[4] which over the years expanded rapidly. He eventually transformed the *Bet Moses* Hospital into a large and vibrant yeshivah. In order to accommodate the growing Zanz community, the Marcy Theater was acquired in 1954 and converted into a beautiful and spacious synagogue. Branches of the Zanz Yeshivah were soon established in Montreal and Mexico City.

Shortly after his arrival in New York, the Rabbi married Hayyah Nehamah, the daughter of R. Shmuel David Halevi Unger (1886–1944), formerly rabbi of Nitra. R. Halberstam had five daughters and two sons. At first, he followed his father's-in-law political ideology and associated himself with the Aguda. When, in October 1951, the Zionist leader and then president of the World Jewish Congress Dr. .Nahum Goldman invited a number of Jewish organizations to establish the Conference of Jewish Material Claims against Germany and to secure funds for the relief, rehabilitation, and resettlement of Jewish victims of Nazism, the Rabbi was one of the few Orthodox leaders to urge Orthodox Jewry to participate in the negotiations. Under the treaty between the German Federal Republic and Israel, concluded in 1952, the State of Israel received large payments, and many Orthodox institutions and individual victims of Nazi persecution benefited from this agreement.

---

4. 1 Chronicles 4:43.

Even while the Rabbi was establishing his roots in the United States, his heart was in Israel. He constantly spoke of the miracle of its rebirth and counseled many of his followers to settle there. He quoted his great-uncle, R. Yehezkel Halberstam of Sieniawa, who visited the Holy Land in 1869 and later remarked: "If a man loves the Land of Israel, it becomes his friend, the best friend a man can ever have." The Rabbi constantly spoke of the close links between Zanz and the Holy Land.

His ancestor, the founder of the dynasty of Zanz (Nowy Sacz), R. Hayyim Halberstam (1793–1876), had attained a reputation as leader of the entire hasidic community of Galicia and was a renowned and outstanding rabbinic scholar. His responsa reflect the social and religious life of Galician Jewry in the mid-nineteenth century, and through his erudite writings, he refuted the allegations of both *Mitnaggedim* and *Maskilim* that Hasidism was synonymous with ignorance. He himself longed all his life to settle in the Holy Land but was unable to do so. Six years before he died, he had raised enough money to build a synagogue in Safed. His son-in-law R. Moshe Unger of Dombrova settled in Safed and was soon joined by another son-in-law, R. Naftali Hayyim Horowitz, the son of R. Meir of Dzikov.

R. Yekutiel Yehuda first visited Israel in 1955 and for seven years searched for a site that would be suitable for his *hasidim*. Jerusalem was the obvious choice, almost too obvious. "Jerusalem is already steeped in holiness," the rabbi explained. "I want to add to the holiness of the rest of the Land of Israel." For a similar reason, he rejected Safed and Bene Berak, which had been suggested by the Israeli government.

During his visit, the Rabbi met David Ben Gurion, who had, in December 1953, resigned as prime minister and was living in Sede Boker in the Negev. Expressing his love for this southern region, Ben Gurion urged him to settle in the Negev. But the rabbi was not convinced. "The Torah states,"[5] he said, "that Avraham

---

5. Genesis 12:9.

journeyed, constantly going towards the south," that is, the Negev, as southern Judah was called. Avraham did not begin in the Negev but eventually reached there. Similarly, the Rabbi felt that he, too, should not initially settle there.

The Rabbi's travels finally led him to Netanya, where he met its founder mayor, Oved Ben Ami. At the mayor's suggestion he acquired three hundred *dunams* of land that would become the setting for his community. The site, which had originally belonged to a group of Belgian Jews, had many advantages: the climate was idyllic, the panorama pleasing, and it was close enough to a major growing city to provide employment for its inhabitants.

There was little question what this settlement would be called. The Rabbi identified closely with his great-grandfather, the founder of the Zanz dynasty, and the community would be the resurrection of the town made famous by him. The new settlement would henceforth be known as *Kiryat Zanz*. The date for its dedication was chosen with equal care. R. Elimelech of Lejask, "the Rebbe Reb Melech," was one of the pioneers of Hasidism in Poland and was another great individual whom the Rabbi considered his spiritual ancestor. The dedication, therefore, took place on R. Elimelech's *Yahrzeit*, the anniversary of his passing from this world. The foundation stone was thus laid on Sunday, 4 March 1956 (21 Adar), and was attended by many *hasidim* from all over Israel and the United States.

Four years later, in 1960, the Rabbi arrived in Israel with a Scroll of the Law and a nucleus of fifty American immigrants who proceeded to make their home in the *Kirya*. From one quarter, however, the Rabbi had to contend with opposition. His cousin and uncle by marriage R. Yoel Teitelbaum, the Rebbe of Satmar, viewed this move as being tainted with secular Zionism. The Rebbe responded with this censure:

> How absurd to suggest that I am following in the footsteps of the secular Zionists. On the contrary, I am following the paths of the disciples of Rabbi Israel Baal Shem Tov and of Elijah, the Gaon of Vilna, and of the great medieval sages like Nahmanides who either visited Israel or settled in the Holy Land. I am not

afraid of the secularist government which is transitory and can very suddenly pass away. One must not detract from the sanctity of the Land of Israel, which does not depend on the government in power or on the conduct of the inhabitants. Even in the time of Avraham our father, when the Canaanites lived in the land, the Land of Israel was still selected and sanctified over all other countries in the world. We might reasonably draw the analogy of a Scroll of the Law which had fallen into the hands of a heretic. It does not lose its sanctity, but on the contrary, it is our sacred duty to retrieve it, and maintain its sanctity. The Land of Israel will likewise always be holy, even though it may be temporarily contaminated by non-religious elements.[6]

Religious Jews, especially those in the Western world, were urged by the Rabbi to settle in Israel because "an influx of Orthodox Jews would transform the State into a veritable wall of fire which would render it indestructible. The achievements of Torah-true Jews, imbued with a spirit of self-sacrifice, would amaze the entire world."

The Rabbi remained in the forefront of negotiations with architects, building contractors, and engineers, and was involved in every detail of the development. Plans were based on an optimistic projection of growth, and the key buildings were designed to cater for an expanding community.

The high point of the week in the *Kirya* in the Rabbi's lifetime was the Sabbath, which to a large extent was dominated by the Rabbi's *Tish* on the Friday night. One Friday night in 1960, quite late in the evening, at about 11 P.M., I paid him a visit. The Rebbe entered the *Bet Hamidrash*, chanting the traditional greetings to the Sabbath angels: "Shalom Aleichem—Peace be with You, Ministering Angels, Angels of the Most High, coming from the King who ruleth over kings, the Holy One, Blessed be He."

At the table he was flanked by his two sons, R. Tzvi Elimelech and R. Shmuel David, as well as by his two sons-in-law, R. Shlomo

---

6. H. Rabinowicz, "Hasidism and the State of Israel" (*Associated University Press*, 1982), pp. 148–149.

Goldman and R. Dov Berish Weiss. After the recitation of the *Kiddush*, the sanctification over the wine, he broke one of the twelve loaves, representing the twelve tribes of Israel, which were arrayed before him. The traditional courses were interspersed with Sabbath melodies, handed down from the hasidic masters. The Rebbe only tasted each dish, while the remainder was passed around as *Shirayim*, for the *hasidim* believe that the Rebbe sanctifies everything he touches. Imprisoned sparks, they believe, are released and restored to their original source. The *hasidim* ate and sang, but most of all they watched and listened, for every gesture of the Rebbe was significant.

The climax was reached around midnight when the Rebbe began a lengthy, unrehearsed discourse on the weekly Torah portion. The entire vast spectrum of talmudic, rabbinic, hasidic, and kabbalistic literature was at his fingertips, and he quoted freely and extensively. Many of his followers were major talmudic scholars. He frequently paused for their comments or corroboration.

Another Sabbath highlight was *Shalosh Seudot*, the third Sabbath meal. The lights were out, and in the gathering dusk the Rebbe spoke in illuminating phrases, and his *hasidim* sang mystical melodies. The meal ended before midnight.

The Rebbe led an ascetic life, rising every morning at 5 A.M. and spending the early hours immersed in study. Like many other hasidic masters, he commenced the morning service quite late. A special rota of students provided him with a quorum (*minyan*). The afternoon service seldom started before 7 P.M., and the evening service took place at midnight. The Rebbe himself acted as *Baal Keriya* (the Reader of the Law) on Sabbaths and Festivals, and the service on Sabbath morning rarely terminated before 2 P.M.

On Monday mornings the Rebbe lectured to the more advanced married students, and at various other times, he delivered discourses on talmudic and halachic topics. Every Tuesday from 11 A.M. to 2 P.M., he was "at home" to his followers. Scores of people from the *Kirya* and from all over Israel, as well as from abroad, came to him with petitions. These related to the entire spectrum of human problems—recovery from sickness, longing for a child, the need to finding a suitable mate for one's child, and the difficulty of earning a living. The hasid wrote his name and that of his mother on a petition (*Qvittel*), but not that of his father—a custom traced by the *Zohar* to King David, who prayed "Save the son of Thy handmaiden." A *pidyon* (redemption money) accompanied the petition. The amount varied according to the finances of the petitioner, and it was usual to give a sum that corresponded to the numerical value of the Hebrew word *Hai* ("life"), that is, eighteen.

The Rebbe followed the traditions of R. Hayyim Halberstam, who published very little during his lifetime, although many of his expositions have appeared in the monthly periodicals of the *Kirya*. He delivered a major two-hour discourse once each month on the Sabbath on which the Blessing for the New Moon is recited (*Shabbat Mevorchim*). He also preached on key occasions during the year, such as on the Sabbath before Passover (*Shabbat Hagadol*) and on the Sabbath before the Day of Atonement (*Shabbat Teshuva*). On New Year and the Day of Atonement, he joined his community in the large communal synagogue for worship. He delivered a discourse lasting one and a half hours before the blowing of the *shofar* (ram's horn) on the New Year and before the opening prayer on the eve of the Day of Atonement.

To the Rabbi, Israel was a spiritual Eden, a foretaste of the Golden Age to Come, though he faced daily disillusionment, for it grieved him to witness any un-Godly act in the Holy Land. His life in Israel was not devoid of problems, technical as well as spiritual. Once, when the construction of the *Kirya* was in full swing, a severe shortage of cement blocks developed. In response to this urgent need, a factory had to be set up. Religious and national issues were not quite so easy to resolve. At one point, in 1963, such an issue almost brought about his departure from Israel, and only the personal intervention of the then president, Zalman Shazar, dissuaded him from taking this drastic step.

He had many ideas for encouraging fellow Jews to observe the Commandments. One example of such concern took place when he sent out young scribes to examine *mezuzot* (the parchment that is enclosed in a metal, wooden, or plastic case and attached to doorposts) and *tefillin*. "It is not enough to just observe the Commandments," he said, "they must also be observed correctly. It is vital that the phylacteries one wears should be without defect." The Rabbi was confident that the spiritual influence of his *Kirya* would have far-reaching effects and that eventually people would not say, "*Kiryat Zanz* near Netanya," but "Netanya near *Kiryat Zanz.*"

Following the example of R. Meir Shapiro, who in 1923 instituted the *Daf Yomi*, the daily study of a page of the Talmud, the Rebbe, in 1968, founded the *Shas Kollel*, involving the study of seventy pages of the Talmud each month, envisaging that, within four years, the entire Talmud would be completed. A *Siyum* actually took place in the *Binyane HaUma* in Jerusalem. Another innovative proposal was *Mifal HaShas*, the study of thirty pages of the Talmud each month, to be followed by a written test.

Encouraged by the success of the *Kirya*, he established a *Shikkun Zanz* in the northwest of Jerusalem at Tel Arza in 1964. It has many housing units, and a large number of families are living there. It has a synagogue, a *kollel*, a Talmud Torah *Darke Avot*, a yeshivah for the young, a kindergarten (*Bet Hannah*), and a *Bet Hamidrash*, in which, perhaps surprisingly, the services are conducted in a non-hasidic ritual, *Nusah Ashkenaz*, rather than the liturgy of R. Yitzhak Luria, adopted by the *hasidim* in the eighteenth century. R. Shmuel Raphael Reich and R. Yehuda Belz were among the prominent founders of the *shikkun*.

Among the Zanz institutions in Bene Berak (Rehov Yehuda Halevi and in Kiryat Herzog), there are two *Bate Midrashim*; a Talmud Torah, *Darke Avot*; a yeshivah, *Divre Hayyim*; and a home for older people. Two *Bate Midrashim* and a kollel, *Avreichim*, flourish in Petah Tikvah. There are also Zanz hasidic communities in Tiberias (*Kiryat Shmuel*) and in Safed.

Owing to ill health, the Rabbi had to spend his last years in New York where, in 1968, he underwent cardiac surgery, but he kept up his links with the *Kirya*. He died on 9 Tammuz 1994 and was interred in the Zanz hasidic section of the Netanya cemetery. His two sons divided his patrimony. R. Tzvi Elimelech, born in New York in Heshvan 1953, married, in 1970, the daughter of R. Shmuel Unsdorfer of Montreal, Canada, now the rabbi of the Zanz community in Petah Tikvah. R. Tzvi Elimelech succeeded his father as Rebbe in Israel. His other son, R. Shmuel David, born in New York in 1957, married the daughter of R. Aaron Wider, Rabbi of the Linzer Community of Brooklyn, and assumed the position of Rebbe of Zanz in the United States. The two brothers are, however, accepted as joint rebbes by the Zanz *hasidim* who live outside Israel and the United States. It was a heartwarming experience for the *hasidim* to witness the two brothers conduct a joint *Tish* in the *Kirya*. The late Rabbi's sons-in-law, too, are active in Torah institutions in Israel and the United States.

The Rebbe, in his "Last Will and Testament," forbade any eulogies to be delivered at his funeral. It was his wish that only his name and the name of his father be inscribed on his tombstone, with no laudatory epithets. He urged his followers that peace and harmony should reign among them, and this his two sons are faithfully maintaining.

Torah Thoughts

A man should repent his transgressions in his youth and not wait until he reaches old age. Hence, R. Hanina ben Hahinai said: "He who keeps awake at night, such a man commits a mortal sin" (*Avot* 3:5). "By night" implies that he waits until the evening of his life before repenting (R. Hayyim Halberstam).

Why was the Temple built on Mount Moriah and not on Mount Sinai, where the Torah was given? The *Akedat Yitzhak*, the binding of Isaac, when Isaac was ready and willing to give his life to the Almighty, took place on Mount Moriah. A human being's spirit of self-sacrifice is superior to any other quality, and for this reason Mount Moriah took precedence over Mount Sinai (*idem*).

When R. Hayyim was once asked: "What does the Rebbe do prior to prayer?" he replied: "Before prayer, I pray that I shall be able to pray." As the *Mishnah* says (*Berachot* 30b): "The pious men of old used to wait an hour before praying, in order that they may concentrate their thoughts upon their Father in Heaven."

"These are the generations of Noah. Noah was a righteous man" (Genesis 6:9). The behavior of a father can be detected in the appearance of his children.

R. Hayyim Halberstam of Zanz asked one of his followers what he would do if he found a big purse of golden coins. The man replied, "I would naturally return it to the owner straight away." To this, the Rabbi answered: "You are nothing but a fool." He put the same question to another hasid, who replied that he would not hesitate to keep the money. "You," the Rabbi said, "are a wicked person." When this question was posed to a third hasid, his reply was: "How can I foretell how I would act in such an eventuality?" Him, the Rabbi called a wise man.

The Rebbe of Zanz believed in taking care of one's physical needs. He once said to a hasid: "Have my wardens looked after you? Did they give you enough food and drink?" "Rebbe," replied the hasid, "surely I did not come here to eat and drink. I came here for spiritual nourishment." "True," said the Rebbe. "Your soul did not come to this world just for physical nourishment. But if you fail to feed it, it will soon leave your body."

"He has not perceived iniquity in Jacob, neither has he seen perversity in Israel" (Numbers 23:21). When a Jew commits a sin, he is distressed and full of remorse. Is it possible for a Jew to transgress and be joyful? (*idem*).

"God departed when He had finished speaking to Abraham, and Abraham returned to his place" (Genesis 18:33). Despite Abraham's failure to save Sodom and Gemorrah from total destruction, Abraham did not lose his faith in the Almighty. He was fully aware that "God of faith, devoid of iniquity, righteous and fair is He" (Deuteronomy 32:24). "He returned to his place," which implies that he continued to serve the Almighty as hitherto (R. Ezekiel of Sianawa).

"God of the Hebrews has met with us" (Exodus 5:3). The children of Israel called Hebrews *Ivrim*, which means "passers-by." This can be taken to mean that we are not permanent residents in this world, but merely transients en route to the World-to-Come (*idem*).

"He may impose forty strokes but no more" (Deuteronomy 25:3). The Talmud amplifies this, saying, forty save one, that is, thirty-nine (*Makkot* 22b). Punishing him with thirty-nine lashes and not with the maximum of forty is to impress upon wrong-doer that he still has to repent and should not assume that he has received his full punishment (*idem*).

"And all the blessings should come upon you and overtake you" (Deuteronomy 28:2). Surely the word *overtake* is superfluous? But the Hebrew word *overtake* can also denote appreciation. It is not enough to receive a blessing from God, it is just as important to appreciate it (the Rebbe of Zanz).

5

Habad
The Global Lamplighters

Notable among the hasidic settlements is Kfar Habad, situated in central Israel, in the Lod Valley, on the main road from Bet Dagon to Sarafand, an hour's drive west of Jerusalem and near Ben Gurion Airport. It was founded in 1949 by the sixth Rebbe of Lubavitch, R. Yosef Yitzhak Schneersohn (1880–1950) of New York.

The first Habad settlement in Israel is situated on the ruins of a former Arab village, Safariya, on a three hundred-*dunam* site. The site was allocated by the Jewish National Fund, which cleared the land, built the roads, and trained the newcomers in agricultural methods. The settlement began with seventy-four families in 1949, who were soon joined by another fifteen from Morocco and then by Russian immigrants. Conditions were extremely primitive, but with the Rebbe's continual encouragement, the pioneers persisted. Now some three thousand people live there, most of them engaged in farming, and it is the largest independent agricultural settlement in Israel.

In Kfar Habad, the Talmud Torah (established in 1954) is under the supervision of the religious department of the Ministry of Education, with dormitories for out-of-town students. Its timetable is equally divided between talmudic and secular studies. In the kindergarten, with two hundred and fifty children, boys and girls are taught separately after the age of three. The pride of the settlement is *Yeshivat Tomche Temimim*, whose students come from all over the world. They are aged between seventeen and twenty-five, a number of students knowing whole tractates of the Talmud by heart. I met a student, Israel Barenbaum, who had come from Kiev in 1978 and now knows the whole talmudical tractate of *Kiddushin* by heart. As part of their education, students are encouraged to spend at least one year in the Rebbe's yeshivah in New York. Graduates of the yeshivah become rabbis, teachers, slaughterers, and scribes, or work as administrators within the Lubavitch education system. Some of the students of the yeshivah have come from *Yeshivah Ketanah*, which is under the guidance of R. Eliyahu Kook. Special departments in the yeshivah cater to students from Morocco and Yemen, or to those who wish to qualify for the rabbinical diploma or, alternatively, become ritual slaughterers.

Every morning before the service and every evening after dinner, there are lectures on Habad, for Habad is the acronym of the Hebrew words: *Hochmah* (wisdom), *Binah* (understanding), and *Daat* (knowledge), three kindred faculties. *Hochmah* is the initial idea, *Binah* is the development of the idea, and *Daat* is its logical conclusion. It is an intellectual Hasidism. Habad believes that the mind has dominion over the heart, and faith must be allied to understanding.

Attached to the yeshivah is a *kollel* (also established in 1954) for advanced students of rabbinics. They serve one year in the Israeli Army. "An excellent thing is the study of the Torah combined with some worldly occupation," says the *Mishnah*,[1] and the yeshivah at Kfar Habad offers vocational training, which makes it a rarity among yeshivot, both mitnaggedic and hasidic, where the ideal is the study of Torah for its own sake.

---

1. *Avot* 2:12.

With the help of the JOINT (American Jewish Joint Distribution Committee) and ORT (Organization for Rehabilitation through Training), Kfar Habad has set up a printing press. Much of the machinery was provided by the Jewish Master Printers and the Jewish Aid Committee in London. Equipped with a modern plant and machinery, they produce not only prayer books but innumerable Lubavitch publications. There is also an agricultural school, and a carpentry school, established in 1954, provides training in woodworking and carpentry. Since 1964, there have been locksmith and tool workshops and facilities for training in electronics, motor mechanics, and agro-mechanic techniques. R. Yehoshua's talmudic dictum "Give half to God, and keep half for yourself"[2] is taken literally in Kfar Habad. Students devote fifty-eight hours each week to intensive study of the Bible, Talmud, Codes, Hasidism, and secular subjects; the rest of the time is allotted to vocational training.

Girls attend the *Bet Rivkah* schools, set up in 1959, which provide an elementary education in religious and secular studies to the age of fourteen. A Teacher Training Seminary provides a two-year course leading to the State Teacher Certificate. The comprehensive curriculum provides the students with a broad education in accordance with the requirements of the Ministry of Education. The late Rabbi is quoted as saying, "The *Bet Rivkah* schools must become spiritual centers not only for Kfar Habad, not only for Israel, but for the whole world,"[3] and indeed, graduates of the seminary become teachers in Habad schools in Israel, the United States, France, and Italy. There are also schools for girls, where sewing and wigmaking are the specialities.

The Vocational Departments, too, provide the students with extensive religious training as well as the general education required by the Ministry of Education. The synagogue, *Bet Menahem*, erected in 1965, was furnished by the students of the school of

---

2. *Pesahim* 68b.

3. *Challenge* (London, Lubavitch Foundation of Great Britain, 1973), p. 147.

carpentry. Three synagogues serve the community, and a special house of worship exists for the Moroccan members, so that they may follow their own liturgy. An important addition to the village opened in 1969: a Youth Center, *Bet Shazar* (house of Shazar), known also as the House of the President, in honor of the first president of Israel, Zalman Shazar, who was named after the first rabbi of Habad. This building is extensively used as a venue for Youth Conventions, Winter Review weekends, and a variety of other occasions important to the village and its neighboring settlement.

In February 1992, the community erected a brick replica of the Rebbe's residence, the imposing Brooklyn World Lubavitch Headquarters at 770 Eastern Parkway, New York. It houses a library of over seven thousand volumes, as well as a number of lecture halls for the use of the members of the *kollelim*. It serves as a vast distribution center of Habad literature. No television is allowed in the settlement, and at the approach of Passover, schoolchildren from all over the area come to watch the making of the hand-baked *shemura matzot* in the special bakery.

On 21 Iyar 1955, a tragedy occurred. Five students and a teacher were reciting the evening service when they were attacked and murdered by Arab Fedayan terrorists. The victims were buried with their prayer books. The Rabbi exhorted the inhabitants not to panic. A School of Printing and Graphic Arts, called *Yad HaHamisha* (Memorial of the Five), was set up in their memory. To strengthen the village, Georgian families were encouraged to settle there, and thus a part of the former Soviet Union was transplanted to the village.

Many young people visit the village on the Sabbath, on festivals, on High Holy Days, and on other occasions, such as *Yud tet Kislev* (commemorating the release of the founder of the movement, R. Shneur Zalman of Liady, from a Tsarist prison in 1798); *Yud Shevat* (the tenth anniversary of the death of R. J. Y. Schneersohn); and *Yud Bet Tammuz* (commemorating the release from prison of Rebbe J. Y. Schneersohn), when Habad *hasidim* celebrate in characteristic fashion. At regular *ferbrengen* (get-togethers), they study the *Tanya* and *Likkute Torah*, a series of mystical commentaries by R. Shneur Zalman of Liady, as well as the discourses of the late Rebbe.

Yeshivah students are exempted by Law from military service, but during the Sinai Campaign of 1956, a number of Habad students waived their right and joined the Army. After the war, members of the settlement set up a program headed by the late Mrs. Shifra Golombovicz, the director of the Habad War Orphans Program. A resident of the village, herself a war widow (her husband, David, fell at the Suez Canal), she ensured that the orphans received personal and educational care.

No apartment building in the *Kirya* has more than two floors, as the Rebbe was anxious to retain its village aspect. It was his wish that it should always retain the nature of a *dorf* ("village"). Periodically, large groups of boys, IDF war orphans, gather in the village to celebrate their joined *Bar Mitzvot. U'Faratzta* ("And thou shalt spread abroad, to the west, to the east, to the north and to the south")[4] is the theme of a lively melody popular with Lubavitch *hasidim*, and this was the motto of the late Rebbe of Lubavitch. From his headquarters at 770 Eastern Parkway in Brooklyn, he directed his spiritual empire and expanded the already far-reaching manifold activities of the movement. In 1969, a settlement for women was established in *Kfar Habad Bet* by the children of the original settlers.

In 1979, *Nahlat Har Habad* near *Kiryat Malachi* was founded. With an industrial school, a diamond polishing factory, and a textile factory, it has now become the home of many families, including many recent immigrants from Georgia. Over three hundred thousand boys and girls in Israel's cities and villages attend weekly classes under *Zivot HaShem* (God's Children's Army), which the Rebbe founded in 1950 for boys under *Bar Mitzvah* and girls under *Bat Mitzvah* age.

Shikkun Habad, established in 1961, in the northwest of Jerusalem, has modern apartments, a Talmud Torah, a kindergarten (*Gan Hannah*), and a girls' school, *Bet Hannah*, named after the Rebbe's mother. Another Habad *Shikkun* is rapidly rising in Lod.

---

4. Genesis 28:14.

Among other Lubavitch educational establishments in Israel is *Yeshivat Torat Emet* (established in 1922) in Rehov Mea Shearim, now the main center for Habad learning in the Holy City.

Unlike other hasidic institutions, which were created primarily to cater for their own followers, Lubavitch aims to embrace the wider community. Its objective is to create new *hasidim*. In all, thousands of pupils are educated under its auspices. Nor are adults ignored. The movement stresses that however estranged a Jew may be from Torah-true Judaism, he can be made conscious of his heritage, provided that the right approach is used. The *Zeire Agudat Habad* (Young Habad), for example, is charged with many activist missions that are designed to bring Judaism to Jews by blowing the *shofar* at the New Year for patients in hospitals. For many years, it has carried out *Operation Tefillin*. Thousands of visitors to the Western Wall are urged to put on phylacteries and recite the appropriate benedictions. "The Commandment of *Tefillin*," said the Rabbi, "unites mind and heart, intellect and emotion."

There are today one hundred and eighty Habad Houses throughout Israel. Habad personnel visit over one thousand settlements, from Mount Hermon in the north to Elat in the south. There is an active center in Hebron, adjacent to the Cave of the Patriarchs, containing lecture halls, dining rooms, and a ritual bath. In Shiloh, the first cultural city of the Israelites, where the Tabernacle was erected, after the conquest of the Holy Land under Joshua, there is a Habad *Bet Hamidrash* for the *Hesder* yeshivah, named *Bet Menahem*, and in Efrat, there is the *Kirya Shoshanah* in memory of the mother of R. Yosef Yitzhak Hakohen Gutnik, the Australian philanthropist. It includes a *kollel*, a section for *Baale Teshuvah*, and a program for training rabbis for *Shelihut*.

Today, some 1,300 Habad-Lubavitch institutions span more than thirty-five countries on six continents, from Tasmania in the Southern Hemisphere to Zaire in Equatorial Africa. In the United States alone there are more than two hundred and twenty centers. After the Soviet Union crumbled, Lubavitch emerged from underground and established some sixty institutions of Jewish learning in the Commonwealth of Independent States. A new

$500,000 marble synagogue on the sixth floor of the four-star Furama Hotel was opened recently in Hong Kong. There is a worldwide budget of over $100 million.

The seventh Rebbe, who has been described as "the most phenomenal Jewish personality" of our times, was born on 11 Nisan 1902 in Nikolayev and came from a line of hasidic rebbes in Byelorussia. His father, R. Levi Yitzhak, was a noted kabbalist and a grandson of the third Rebbe, R. Menahem Mendel of Lubavitch. Menaham Mendel and his brothers Yisrael Arye Leib and Dov Ber were taught by an outstanding teacher, R. Shneur Zalman Wilenkin, who had a small Talmud Torah in his own home. He was known for his wonderful skills as an educator as well as for his gentle, unassuming personality. Even as a child, Menahem Mendel stood out from the crowd because of his extraordinary intellectual qualities and his maturity. In Warsaw, on December 1929 (14 Kislev), at the age of twenty-seven, he married his cousin once removed Hayya Mushka (1901–1922 Shevat 1988), who was the second daughter of R. Yosef Yitzhak Schneersohn of Lubavitch.

R. Menahem Mendel lived for a time in Berlin. There, during 1929, his wife attended courses at the Deutsche Institut fuer Auslaender, which was under the auspices of Humboldt University of Berlin, and she is mentioned in their *Mitteilungen* (Bulletin) of 23 March 1929 as having attended Course No. 57/45. At that time, they lived at the Oranienburger Strasse, No. 33, with a family called Bruhn.

R. Menahem Mendel himself was a registered *Gasthoerer*, that is, a student who is restricted to attending occasional lectures of Humboldt University, either because he has other commitments or because he is not fully qualified to attend on a regular basis.[5] His status is given as Russian/Ukrainean, Jewish, and sometimes as Student at Rabbinical Seminary, living at different addresses. His age is given variously as thirty-two, thirty-four, and thirty-

---

5. Letters to the author by Dr. W. Schutze, head of the Archives of Humboldt University, Berlin, 23 August 1995, 5 December 1995, and 19 December 1995.

five. There is validation of his registration for the following se-
mesters (running April to August, and October to March): Summer 1928, Winter 1928/1929, Summer 1929, Winter 1929/1930,
and Summer 1930. It would appear that during 1929, when his
father-in-law spent ten months in the United States, R. Menahem
Mendel took his place in Riga.

Another piece of information received from Humboldt University concerns one Mark Gourary, a Jew (probably the Rebbe's
brother), who enrolled there as *Gasthoerer* in mathematics for the
summer semester 1932, giving his age as twenty-four and as living
in Kantstrasse 133, Berlin-Charlottenburg. It is difficult to recon-
cile this piece of information with the others and with the Rebbe's
reputed departure for Paris.

At the advent of the Nazis in Germany, the couple moved to
Paris. It is difficult to ascertain from the French University records
that the Rebbe attended the Sorbonne and studied or graduated
in electrical engineering or mathematics there, as is maintained by
the innumerable biographers of his life.

After the Nazi victory in France, when three-fifths of the territory of metropolitan France was occupied by the Germans, he
lived for a time in unoccupied France, first in Vichy, then in Nice,
and finally he fled from Marseilles to the United States. On 23
June 1941, he arrived in New York, where his father-in-law had
established himself the previous year. He settled in Crown
Heights, New York, where he became the chairman of the *Merkaz
L'Inyone Hinuh* (the Central Organization of Jewish Education of
the Lubavitch Movement). In 1947, he flew to Paris and brought
over his mother, Hannah, who had survived the Holocaust. His
younger brother, R. Dov Ber, and his wife's younger sister and
her husband, Menahem Orenstein, were murdered by the Nazis
in Treblinka.

After the death of his father-in-law on 10 Shevat 1950, he reluctantly became the seventh Rebbe of Lubavitch. He excelled as
an administrator, no less than as a scholar. He extended the activities to North Africa, and Habad teachings were brought to
Casablanca, Marrakesh, Serfou, and Meknes. His followers were
expected to demonstrate to their fellow Jews the *mitzvot* of don-

ning *tefillin*, kindling the Sabbath lights, pronouncing the benedictions of *etrog* and *lulav*, sounding the *shofar*, and eating *shemura*
matzot. He organized a Peace Corps to bring Judaism to Jews in
many out-of-the-way places. With fleets of vehicles, known as
Mitzvah Tanks, the Rebbe's adherents propagate Judaism.

His unique analytical style of thought has resulted in a monumental contribution to Jewish scholarship. Many volumes of the
Rabbi's talks and writings have been published. Central among
them are one hundred volumes of *Likkute Sihot* (collected Talks
of the Rabbi) and *Iggrot Kodesh*, twenty-six volumes of a chrono-
logical collection of the Rebbe's correspondence and letters total-
ing more than eight thousand. His correspondence covered subjects ranging from mysticism to Talmud, hasidic philosophy to
science and world events. He was forthright in his views and criticized the various scientific theories concerning the age of the
world. He denied evolution and maintained that the world is only
5,757 years old. The discovery of fossils was to him by no means
conclusive evidence of the great antiquity of the earth.[6] He was
against the concept of family planning, which he regarded as a
destructive process, and regarded population explosion as God's
will.

In the "Who is a Jew?" controversy of 1970, he opposed easy
conversions and exercised, from afar, a strong right-wing influence
on Israeli politics. Intensifying his attacks on the state of religion
in Israel, he accused the ministers of the National Religious Party
of displaying insufficient zeal, and he was dissatisfied with the separation of religion and state as being inappropriate, he felt, for a
people destined to be a "kingdom of priests and a holy nation."
He believed that the Torah encompasses the universe: every new
invention, every theory, piece of knowledge, thought, and action—
everything that happens must be interpreted from the point of
view of the Torah.

---

6. Edward Hoffman, *Despite All Odds: The Story of Lubavitch* (New
York: Simon & Schuster, 1991), p. 126.

The Rabbi opposed mass meetings and public protests against the former Soviet authorities on behalf of Russian Jewry. His own approach was based on *stadlanut* ("persuasion") at diplomatic level. He called upon the Orthodox ministers of the Israel government to show "the same courage in protecting the honor of the Torah as the soldiers on the Suez Canal in protecting Israel's frontiers." He persuaded the aged Chief Rabbi Unterman to stand for re-election in 1973 and attacked Chief Rabbi Goren's ruling on the Langer case, even telling him to resign.

Though nonpolitical, in the election campaign for the 1988 Knesset, he backed the Aguda, which increased its representation from two to five members. An ardent supporter of a Greater Israel that would incorporate the West Bank, the biblical Samaria, and Judea, he opposed the 1979 Camp David Peace Treaty with the late President Anwar Sadat of Egypt. "For all we gave away," he stated, "we received nothing in return."[7] He further intervened in favor of Israel's ill-fated "Peace in Galilee" Drive into Lebanon in 1982. In 1990, his supporters frustrated a Labour Party attempt to form a government.

He was also against the Peace Accord of Rabin and Peres with the Arabs and maintained that any sacrifice of territory would weaken Israel's defense position, and any shrinking of Israel's vital borders would be dangerous. He consistently opposed any kind of land for peace on the grounds of *Pekuah Nefesh* (the positive biblical command enjoining the duty to maintain personal safety and the avoidance of danger to life). Unilateral concessions, he maintained, do not encourage the other side to make concessions but rather to redouble their demands.[8]

When asked by the author why he never visited Israel, the answer given was that he would never be allowed to leave the promised land once he had set foot in it. "I have never left New York," he told the British politician Baroness Alma Berk in 1972, "since the death of my father-in-law."

He discouraged university education. Lubavitch is an outreach

---

7. Ibid., p. 165.
8. *Jewish Chronicle* (16 April 1982), p. 20.

movement, reaching out to the alienated, the assimilated young Jews on campuses, families in isolated communities, and anyone in need of help. No section of the community is excluded: young or old, men or women, scholars or laymen. In the field of education there are now thousands of Habad students scattered in some hundreds of schools around the world, from Hong Kong to Tel Aviv, from Budapest to Chicago. Habad eagerly embraces modern communications and has a bank of twenty fax machines that are used to distribute, in a dozen different languages, the late Rebbe's discourses throughout the world.

In the course of forty-five years, the Lubavitch publishing house, *Kehot Publication Society*, has become one of the largest Jewish publishing houses in the world. It has issued 1,250 titles: books, journals, pamphlets, cassettes, and educational material, designed for all ages, in many languages. The *Tanya* has been published over three thousand times all over the world.

Despite the deterioration of the Crown Heights area, the high crime rate, and several tragic incidents (a black child was killed in 1991 by a car escorting the Rebbe, followed by a black riot in which an Australian Habad hasid was killed), the Rebbe urged his followers to remain there and to preserve it as a thriving Jewish community. In his prime, nearly five thousand people were received by him in private audience each year, and hundreds of letters passed through the hands of his secretariat. On the eve of *Shemini Atzeret*, in October 1977, he suffered a heart attack. He was distressed when Barry Gourary, the son of his brother-in-law R. Shemarya, removed four hundred valuable books from his library in 1985. It is known that the nephew sold an illuminated Passover *Haggadah* of 1757 for $69,000. This resulted in vexatious litigation in American courts of law, lasting twenty-three court days, between 1986 to 1987. Elie Wiesel and R. Dr. Louis Jacobs were expert witnesses. The judge, Charles P. Sifton, ruled in favor of the Rebbe.[9]

---

9. David Margolick, "Suit on Books Gives Look at Hasidim," *New York Times* (18 December 1985), quoted in Jerome R. Mintz, *Hasidic People* (Cambridge: Harvard University Press, 1992), p. 403.

In 1992, the Rebbe suffered repeated seizures, and the right side of his body became paralyzed. He also suffered a second cardiac arrest. He died on 3 Tammuz (12 June) 1994 and was buried at the old Montefiore cemetery in the New York Borough of Queens. Many people now visit his grave and leave messages. A house has been acquired adjacent to the cemetery, where petitions are constantly received by fax, with the request that they be put in the Rebbe's sepulcher. In his "Last Will and Testament" he did not name a spiritual successor, and R. Yehuda Krinsky was named sole executor. His entire personal worldly assets consisted of a mere fifty thousand dollars, which he left to the Lubavitch Foundation. During his forty-year stewardship, the Rebbe transformed the movement from a practically moribund branch of Hasidism into a powerful and expanding international movement. It is unlikely that a successor will be named in the foreseeable future, and the movement continues to be run from its New York headquarters by R. Yehuda Krinsky, R. Leibel Groner, and R. Benjamin Klein.

The messianic promotion of the Rabbi was imprecise. He never, at any stage, claimed that he was the Messiah, but the views that he had expressed on messianism in the last few years struck a cord with many of his followers around the world. They are still stubbornly convinced that the Rebbe was the long-awaited Messiah who, as the twelfth-century Jewish philosopher Maimonides predicted, would usher in a period "without sickness, war, jealousy or death." The Moshichistim, as they are known inside the movement, still believe in the Rebbe as the Messiah. This messianic fervor has grown in the past few years when Habad started to use modern technology, bumper stickers, bleepers, and Madison Avenue–style advertising, to convince Jews that the arrival of the Messiah was imminent. There are bound to be internal divisions in such a mass movement, which has no shepherd. It seems that his *hasidim* are following in the footsteps of the *hasidim* of R. Nahman of Braclav, who have remained leaderless for nearly two hundred years.

Lubavitch has a long association with the Holy Land. The founder of the movement, R. Shneur Zalman (1745–1812), believed that the rebuilding of the Land would commence before the Coming of the Messiah, and the rebuilding of Jerusalem would take place before the ingathering of the exiles. He himself was tempted to follow in the footsteps of R. Menahem Mendel of Vitebsk and settle in the Holy Land. According to hasidic legend, R. Dov Ber, the Maggid of Mezhirech, appeared to him in a dream, urging him not to leave his followers in Europe without a leader.

Having denied himself the privilege of living in the Holy Land, he did his utmost to support those who settled there. He constantly and consistently urged his followers to support the *Yishuv.* He urged them to contribute at least once a week to this deserving cause. He made this point in no fewer than forty letters, and five sections in the fourth part of the *Tanya* deal with this subject.

Not content with writing letters, he traveled extensively, personally soliciting contributions. On two occasions, he was imprisoned by the Russian authorities for sending large sums of money to the Holy Land, then under the jurisdiction of Turkey, Russia's enemy. His son, R. Dov Ber of Lubavitch (1773–1827), took a similar attitude and warned those responsible for the funds not to divert the money to any other cause. He recommended placing collection boxes in every house. He quoted the views of the rabbinic authorities that a man who owned land in Hebron is saved from the tribulations of the grave.

He encouraged his son-in-law R. Yaakov Slonim to settle there, and R. Dov Ber himself acquired a small plot in Hebron. *Kollel* Habad appealed to Sir Moses Montefiore for help. In 1833, the traveler Menahem Mendel of Kamienice noted that the Habad *Kollel* in Hebron consisted of worthy people who were charitable and hospitable.[10]

It is not certain whether the present Habad synagogue in the Old City of Jerusalem stands on the site of the original synagogue, which was established in 1848. The community consisted of fifty families, and the synagogue was financed by Sir Albert (Abdulla)

---

10. Shalom Dov Ber Levin, *Toldot Habad B'Eretz HaKodesh* (Brooklyn: Ozar Hahasidut, 1988), pp. 79–83.

Sassoon (1818–1896), the first baronet of Kensington Gore. This synagogue was the first to be renovated after the Six-Day War.

R. Shalom Dov Ber (1860–1920), the fifth rebbe of Lubavitch, was antagonistic to Zionism and criticized Herzl for visiting the Temple Mount. In 1911, his relative R. Shneur Zalman (son of R. Levi Yitzhak) settled in Hadera and married the daughter of the wealthy philanthropist Yosef Hindin. During World War I, his son-in-law Levi Yitzhak joined *Nili* (from the Hebrew initials for the "Glory of Israel" will not die),[11] the pro-British and anti-Turkish underground movement, headed by Aaron Aaronsohn. In 1912, *Yeshivat Torat Emet* was established in Hebron. Seven disciples were sent by the Rabbi to study there, but the outbreak of war in 1914 forced them to return to Russia.

R. Yosef Yitzhak Schneersohn (1880–1950) visited the Holy Land for seventeen days in Av 1929, meeting the religious leaders R. Yosef Hayyim Sonnenfeld, R. Avraham Yitzhak Halevi Kook, R. Yaakov Meir, and the Chief Justice of the High Court, Mr. Gad Frumkin. "During the twelve days that I have been in Jerusalem," said the Rabbi, "I have gained a lot and achieved a lot. I have visited every place. I leave Jerusalem, taking with me the tremendous impression it has made on me. May God grant that the Messiah should be revealed soon." It was his wish that a hasidic settlement be established in the Holy Land, and many years later this wish was fulfilled.

Contrary to popular belief and despite the glare of publicity and elaborate public relations, the Lubavitch *hasidim* in Israel today are not so numerous. Ger and Belz have a greater following, but the fervor, dedication, and intense loyalty of its adherents more than compensate for the lack of numbers.

Torah Thoughts

"And the Lord God called to the man asked him: 'Were are you?' (Genesis 3:9) R. Shneur Zalman of Liady was asked by a Russian

---

11. I Samuel 15:29.

officer: "Surely, God, being omnipresent, knew where Adam was? Why did he ask him 'Where are you?'" And the reply was: "This question is not limited to Adam, but applies to us all. God's call comes to every human being, asking, 'Where are you? What are you doing with your life?' "

"These are the things which the Lord has ordained to be done" (Exodus 35:1). Why does the verse state, "These are the things," in the plural, when the Israelites were only given the single command to keep the Sabbath? The expression "to do" (*la'assot*) implies positive action, whereas the commandment here was actually to refrain from doing, that is, not work on the Sabbath. However, "these are the things" includes all the thirty-nine categories of work forbidden on the Sabbath. During the week, a person's service by way of the thirty-nine categories is intended to refine and purify the sparks of holiness within creation. On the Sabbath, however, the sparks refined during the week are elevated. This is the purpose of fulfilling all the *mitzvot*: to refine and elevate material existence. For this reason, the word *things* is in the plural, for all the *mitzvot* are included in the Sabbath. The expression "to do" is used to imply positive action, because the Hebrew word *la'assot* also means "to rectify," that is, to refine and elevate all weekday activity (the Rabbi of Lubavitch).

"These are the accounts of the *Mishkon*, the *Mishkon*, the dwelling of the testimony" (Exodus 38:21). The repetition of the word *Mishkon* in the verse alludes to two sanctuaries: a spiritual sanctuary above, and a physical sanctuary below. However, the word *testimony* refers explicitly to the second *Mishkon*, the physical sanctuary, for testimony is necessary only when the existence of something is concealed, not when it is revealed. Since Godliness is not revealed within physical existence, it was necessary to testify that the Divine Presence dwelled within the Sanctuary.

Lag B'Omer commemorates the passing away of R. Shimon bar Yochai. He left instructions for each and every Jew in his generation and in all succeeding generations celebrate this date with "great joy," for on this day R. Shimon bar Yochai and the Holy One, Blessed be He, were united in the loftiest fashion. This concept applies to all Jews, as it is stated: "The Jews should rejoice in their

Maker," and "God rejoices in His works (i.e., Jews)." Lag B'Omer gives special strength to this concept of the joy experienced by Jews in their unity with God. Although we cannot compare ourselves to R. Shimon bar Yochai, we can nevertheless be successful in this service. To illustrate with a parable: a small child cannot see far. But when a "giant" lifts the child onto his shoulders, the child can see a great distance. In our case, the service of R. Shimon bar Yochai gives strength to all succeeding generations, comparable to the "giant" who, with his strength, raises the small child to the heights. When we utilize this strength properly, amidst joy, we will surely be extremely successful (*idem*).

We can learn a lesson from soccer. The *Talmud Yerushalmi* (*Avodah Zorah* 3:1) tells us that an eagle carried Alexander the Great into the heavens. From there, the world looked to him like a ball. Similarly, the *Zohar* (3:10) comments "the entire world revolves in a circle like a ball." In soccer, the intent of the game is to propel the ball through a gate. Hence, the ball, that is, the world, has been given to every Jew with a similar intent. The *Mishnah* comments: "Each individual is obligated to say 'For my sake the world was created.'" The world is given to each individual with the purpose that he bring it through the "gates of the king," despite the many obstacles and difficulties that must be overcome. In soccer, the opposing team tries to prevent the scoring of a goal by the players. At the same time, they try to put the ball through the opposing players' goal, "the opening of *Gehinom*." So it is in our lives: the obstacles and challenges we encounter must arouse in us the attribute of victory, a quality that activates the essence of the soul. In soccer, the presence of the opposing team causes a player to run and to jump—not to be content with slow, step by step, progression. Also, the game is won through the efforts of the feet, symbolic of deed and action, rather than the head. Certainly, the game must be played with thought. Nevertheless, the most important aspect is deed and action. Similarly, in our service there are parallels to these concepts.

These remarks are not intended to take a person away from his studies and cause him to go out and play ball. That would be ridiculous. However, since there are children who, as of yet, do not fully appreciate the preciousness of Torah and want to play ball, they should be able to do so "for the sake of Heaven." By "educating a child according to his way," that is, taking something like soccer, which he enjoys, and showing him how it can be done "for the sake of Heaven," we ensure that "even when he grows older he will not depart from it" (*idem*).

6

Jerusalem and a Unique Community

Today, the Holy City is a thriving center of Hasidism, the home of more than thirty hasidic rabbis and innumerable hasidic yeshivot, but until after the Second World War few hasidic leaders lived there. It was facetiously asserted that Jerusalem did not need a hasidic rebbe, for it had the *Kotel*, the Western Wall, "the greatest rebbe." Why give a *Qvittel* to the rebbe, when there is a *Kotel*, and it does not even take *pidyonot*?

The early hasidic pioneers of the eighteenth and nineteenth centuries lived in either Safed or Tiberias. R. Nahman of Braclav did not even visit Jerusalem, the explanation for this seeming neglect of the Holy City being in the realm of hasidic eschatology.

R. Avraham Shlomo Biderman, the rebbe of Lelov in Jerusalem today, was born in Cracow in 1929 and married Hayyah, the daughter of R. Zundel Hager of Kosov. They have two sons and five daughters. In the lifetime of his father, he was the rabbi of the *hasidim* of Lelov in Jerusalem and Bene Berak.

Over one hundred and fifty children study in his Talmud To-rah, *Tiferet Moshe*, named after his father. He has *kollelim*, *Or Avraham* and *Zemah David*, as well as a soup kitchen, *Berach Moshe*, where on average two hundred poor people are provided with meals daily, from early morning until late in the evening. Every year, the Rebbe spends the Sabbath before the fifth of Elul, the *Yahrzeit* of his ancestor R. David, in Meron, at the graveside of R. Shimon bar Yochai.

His father, R. Moshe Mordecai, was born in Jerusalem in 1903 and lived for two decades in Tel Aviv, until in 1964 he finally made his home in Bene Berak. A descendant of the "Holy Jew," he followed the Przysucha custom of praying late in the day. The Morning Service rarely finished before the evening, and on the Sabbath, he combined the midday meal with *Shalosh Seudot*. I vis-ited him in December 1972 when the Sabbath was over, yet the rabbi had just completed the Morning Service. Nine students were waiting for him to make up a *minyan* (quorum). On Passover he would live in a special apartment.

On 13 Heshvan (the traditional anniversary of the death of the Matriarch Rachel), he visited her grave at Bethlehem and then the graves of the Patriarchs at Hebron. "When one is in trouble, one goes first to the mother and then to the father," explained the Rebbe. He spent most of his day preparing himself for prayer, praying that he should be able to pray.

The founder of the Lelov dynasty was R. Moshe (1777–1851). When he reached the age of thirteen, his father, R. David (1745–1813), a disciple of R. Elimelech of Lejask and of R. Yaakov Yitzhak, the "Seer of Lublin," exhorted him to make his home in the Holy Land. "I have not been worthy to do so," said his fa-ther, "but you should go there and hasten the Redemption." When his first wife died, he married Rebecca Rachel, the daughter of the "Holy Jew." His father-in-law encouraged him to undertake the journey. R. Moshe needed little urging: "When, with the help of the Almighty, I shall arrive safely in the Holy Land, I will go directly to the Western Wall in Jerusalem where I will lift up my voice like a trumpet and I will hasten the advent of the Messiah."

The path to the Holy Land was far from smooth; problems, both personal and financial, had to be overcome. His wife strongly opposed her husband's journey. She was reluctant for him to leave his ever-growing following and could not be won over. Other voices were also raised in opposition. "The Polish Jews are foolish," said R. Yisrael Friedman of Ruzhin, "to let such a *Zaddik* leave their midst." R. Moshe was not to be dissuaded, and his faithful disciple R. Shlomo of Radomsk helped raise funds.

R. Moshe left Poland in 1850, accompanied by his two sons and ten followers but not by his wife. The voyage took two months, and on the eve of *Rosh Hodesh* Heshvan, he arrived in Acre. He stayed for a short time in Safed and Tiberias, but Jerusalem drew him like a magnet. When he arrived in the Holy City, he was exhausted and in rapidly failing health. He could not even walk to the Western Wall, and his sons had to carry him there. Arabs attacked the little group and R Moshe did not reach his destination. He died in his seventy-fourth year on 13 Tevet 1851, seventy-four days after arriving in the Holy Land. His last wish fulfilled, he was buried near the grave of the Prophet Zechariah in Jerusalem.

His descendants left their impact on the *Yishuv*. For thirty-two years his son R. Eleazer Menahem Mendel (1827–1883) lived a life of hardship and penury in Jerusalem, but his sufferings did not lessen his ardor. Every day, regardless of the weather and the constant risk of attack by marauding Arabs, he made his way to the Western Wall to spend three hours reciting the Afternoon and Evening Prayers. Four times each year, he made pilgrimage to Hebron. He was buried on the Mount of Olives on 16 Adar 1883.

His son R. David Tzvi Shlomo (1844–1918) was educated in the home of R. Aaron of Karlin. Like Sir Moses Montefiore before him, he encouraged Jews to settle outside the Holy City. He was instrumental in obtaining large sums of money for the building of fifty homes in *Bate Warsaw* in Jerusalem. He was also responsible for the finances of the *kollel*. His kindliness was proverbial. During the First World War, a Turkish officer provided him with food, which was then in short supply. The Rabbi promptly distributed it among the needy. "I am old. I have lived. I must strengthen those whose life is just beginning."

The traditions of the family were maintained by his second son, R. Shimon Nathan Nata (1870–1930). A native of Safed, he studied in the yeshivot of Eastern Europe for fifteen years and returned to the Holy Land in 1926. The torch of Lelov was carried on by his son R. Moshe Mordecai.

Rab Arale's *Hasidim*—A Unique Community

R. Avraham Yitzhak Kohn, the charismatic leader of the *Toldot Aaron* or *Shomre Emunim hasidim* ("Guardians of the Faithful Community"), popularly known as R. Arale's *hasidim*, died in December (27 Kislev) 1996.

This group, one of the youngest sects of Hasidism, consisting of 350 *hasidim* and their families, in all about 2,000 souls, is barely half a century old, and its adherents reside mainly in the Mea Shearim area. They are distinguished by their dress. The men wear Jerusalem garb: on the Sabbath they wear black *streimels*, on weekdays, grey-striped kaftans; boys do not cut their earlocks; women wear black headscarves, black stockings, and grey or black dresses with long sleeves; girls dress modestly, and they wear opaque stockings.

The community is governed by *takkanot* (regulations) that meticulously control members from the cradle to the grave. Once a month they must attend a general meeting. It is forbidden to speak during prayers. A prayer shawl must be worn by married men during the Friday night service. A prayer belt must be worn by the officiant, and he may not wear woolen garments because of the possibility of *shaatnez*. Services must be attended punctually, and no study is allowed during the repetition of prayers, but the prayer book must be followed closely at all times.

Women must shave their heads and cover them with a scarf and not a wig. A man and his wife may not walk together; the husband must walk in front of her. A man must take a ritual bath every morning. If he fails to do so, then he is not allowed to be called up to the reading of the Torah. Members are expected to make financial contributions to maintain communal facilities, and whoever is called up to the reading of the Law is required to make a donation. Psalms must be recited every day.

A member who infringes any of the rules is liable to sanctions and even expulsion. It is the duty of every member to keep an eye on his neighbor, and children must not make friends outside the sect.[1] R. Arale's followers are not allowed to shave their beards or cut off their sidelocks. Nonconforming strangers are allowed a little leeway, but if they habitually attend the synagogue, they are exhorted to adopt the community's lifestyle and become permanent members. Whoever marries within the community must conform to the *takkanot*.

Radios are permitted, but television is strictly banned. The Torah admonition "be fruitful and multiply and replenish the earth" is taken literally, and they have large families—fourteen children is not unusual. The inability to have children is seen as a great misfortune, and those who are unable to conceive make pilgrimages to holy places. The boys marry at eighteen, and the girls are often much younger. The bride's head is shaved on the day following the wedding. Child delinquency is unknown, and divorce is very rare. They are renowned for their warm hospitality.

The annual budget of the community in 1996 was over $2 million. The community categorically refuses any subsidy from the government or even from the *Vaad HaYeshivot*. Nor do they appear to approve of the Agudist *Hinuch Atzmai*. No special provisions have so far been made for the girls, who attend the old *Yishuv* institutions of the *Benot Yerushalayim*.

Zionism is rejected as secular and nonreligious. They do not associate with the Aguda but adhere to the ideology of the Satmar *hasidim* of Williamsburg. They do not participate in municipal or Knesset elections, and their official language is Yiddish. Their association with the *Neture Karta*, however, has become very tenuous.

---

1. Daniel Meijers, *Ascetic Hasidim in Jerusalem* (Leiden: E. J. Brill, 1992), pp. 62–65.

"All my bones shall say, Lord, who is like unto Thee."[2] By praying aloud and pronouncing each word carefully, they maintain, one can drive out "strange" thoughts. Nearly one thousand boys up to the age of fourteen or fifteen are educated at the Talmud Torah, many of them coming from families who cannot afford to pay the required fees. They begin the study of the *Mishnah* at eight, and one year later, they start Talmud study. Only one hour per day is devoted to arithmetic. Boys who do well are rewarded with a trip to the grave of R. Shimon bar Yochai in Meron. Girls, on the other hand, are taught reading, writing, geography, and arithmetic.

The Yeshivah *LeZeirim*, for post-Talmud Torah scholars, is attended by more than two hundred students guided by a specialist staff of dedicated teachers. Discipline is strictly maintained, and any repeated misdemeanor or latecoming is punished by expulsion. In the *Yeshivah Gedolah*, students, who study there to the age of eighteen or nineteen or until marriage, apply themselves with intense enthusiasm and are led by teachers who are outstanding in their scholarship and piety. This yeshivah was one of the first to provide students with food and dormitory facilities.

Hevra VeShinantam enables young students to revise at night what they have studied, and once each year they are tested on their knowledge and are rewarded with prizes. A number of boys, even before their *Bar Mitzvah*, are able to recite from memory many pages of the Talmud. The *Hevra Tselosa D'Aharon* trains children to be devout in prayer. They are taught to respond *Amen* ("So be it") and *Yehe Sheme Rabba* ("May His great Name be blessed for ever and ever, and for all eternity") with devotion, in conformity with the talmudic saying[3] that "he who answers '*Amen*' and '*Yehe Sheme Rabba*' may avert even a decree of seventy years," and the name *Shomre Emunim* is taken to mean "those who observe the saying of 'Amen.'" It is obligatory to recite "Amen" when hearing blessings, and the person who says "Amen" is regarded as if he had recited the blessing himself.

2. Psalms 35:10.
3. *Sabbath* 119b.

A large *kollel* network exists for young men for the continued study of the Torah. The *kollelim* consist of four departments: a *kollel* for young scholars; *Orhot Hayyim* for continuing study; a *Teacher's kollel*; and a *Kollel Dayanim*. There is also a *Hevra Mishnayot*, where *mishnayot* are studied and memorial prayers offered for the souls of the departed every day for eleven months after a death and on the person's *Yahrzeit*. There are, furthermore, a number of *hevrot* that provide welfare benefits and interest-free loans for those in need.

The founder of this dynasty, R. Aaron Roth or Rab Arele (1894–1946), was born in Ungvar, Hungary. His father, R. Shmuel Yaakov, was a pious greengrocer who traced his descent from R. Shabbatai ben Meir HaKohen, known as the *Shach* (1621–1662), and to R. Yeshayahu Horowitz, known as the *Shelah*. As a young boy, R. Aaron studied in the yeshivot of Galicia and of Waitzen in Central Hungary, under the direction of R. Yeshayahu Silberstein and R. Moshe Forhand, respectively. In 1916, he married, at the age of twenty-two, Sima, the daughter of Yitzhak Katz who was the head of the Yeshurun Synagogue in Budapest. During World War I, he became acquainted with many of the rabbis who found refuge in Budapest, among them R. Engel of Radomysl, R. Yissahar Dov Rokeah of Belz, and R. Tzvi Elimelech Shapira of Blazova.

R. Aaron rejected easy answers and tried to solve problems in depth. His enthusiasm was infectious. He was a perfectionist, and the frequent inability of others to live up to his high standards of study and prayer greatly frustrated him. He was the author of many books and pamphlets, full of scholarship and wry observations. Although frail and ailing, the moment he started to pray he was transformed. Prayer was more than "service of the heart," it was an act of ecstasy, or spiritual elevation. Wherever he went, he attracted kindred spirits who idolized him. His rebbe called him "the good Jew" and urged him to become a rebbe.

When R. Tzvi Elimelech Shapira died in 1925, R. Aaron went to the Holy Land. He stayed for four and a half years and formed a small hasidic group. On the advice of his doctors, he returned to Satmar, where this self-styled rebbe aroused much antagonism.

He found more peace in Beregszaz (Beregovo). In 1940, having obtained a certificate to enter the Holy Land, he returned there, on almost the last boat from Romania. Even the usually belligerent R. Hayyim Elazar Shapira of Munkacs spoke in laudatory terms about R. Arele, saying: "A man of such qualities and attributes would have been a novelty even in the time of R. Yisrael Baal Shem Tov."

R. Aaron suffered even fools gladly. On one occasion, when a shoemaker abused and ridiçuled him, R. Aaron listened without a word. Before the Day of Atonement he went to the shoemaker: "I have come to apologize to you," he said. He begged his followers to lead disciplined lives. "Sleep for five hours. You do not need more," he wrote to his *hasidim*. "After prayers, study for half an hour and recite a few Psalms. Eat enough to satisfy yourself, but from time to time, stop in the middle of a meal and do not eat anymore, for this is also counted as fasting. Each week, you should fast for one day until noon, and the best day for this is Friday. During the month of Elul, and during the winter days, fast three times each week until noon."

His morning weekday services took more than two hours, and on the Sabbath he commenced the service at 9 A.M. and did not conclude until past one o'clock in the afternoon. He perspired so much that he had to change his clothes three times. His emphasis was on simple faith and ecstatic prayers. He maintained that a man must dig deeply into the recesses of his heart in order to recognize God, at Whose word the world came into being. He died on 6 Nisan 1947 and was buried on the Mount of Olives.

In his "Last Will and Testament," he urged his family not to become involved in politics. "Do not be among those *hasidim* who slander each other. Do not associate with such people. The aim of R. Yisrael Baal Shem Tov was to establish harmony and unity." He urged his son R. Avraham Hayyim and his son-in-law R. Avraham Yitzhak to stay on good terms and "be submissive to one another." He did not specify a successor but stated "the leadership would be indicated to them by Heaven."

After the death of R. Arele, R. Avraham Yitzhak became rebbe, and his brother-in-law became the principal of the yeshivah, a dual leadership that did not endure for long. When they fell out with one another, the overwhelming majority followed the son-in-law, and only a small minority adhered to the son. The followers of the son-in-law maintained that a vote by the community decided the "succession." R. Aaron Rokeah of Belz and R. Friedman of Husyatin, on the other hand, urged R. Avraham Hayyim to succeed his father. On the advice of the Rebbe of Belz, the son was to be known as the Rebbe of *Shomre Emunim*, and the son-in-law as *Toldot Aaron*.

R. Avraham Yitzhak Kohn was born in Safed on 6 Tevet 1914. His father, R. Aaron David, was a descendant of R. Elimelech of Lejask and of R. Dov Ber the Maggid of Mezhirech. His mother, Sheindel Brachah, the daughter of R. Moshe Deutsch of Sziget, was a descendant of R. Shmuel Heller, the rabbi of Safed, who amassed one of the greatest private libraries in the Old *Yishuv*.

When he was a child, his family left for Europe owing to the lack of adequate higher educational facilities in Israel at that time. They lived in Hungary where he studied at the yeshivot in Carole under R. Yoel Teitelbaum and also under R. Yisrael Freind and his son R. Moshe Arye Freind of Honiad, who later became a member of the *Bet Din* of the *Eda Haredit*. He was ordained by R. Yoel Teitelbaum, R. Yehuda Rosner, R. Yaakov Shalom Klein, and R. Yosef of Papa. He displayed unusual talents and was very diligent in his Torah studies and his devotion in prayer. In 1940, he married Yente, the daughter of R. Arale, in Honiad. His father-in-law stated: "I looked everywhere for a suitable son-in-law, and nowhere could I find a young man as God-fearing as Avraham Yitzhak." In 1957, he named his community *Toldot Aharon*.

The new Rebbe was an extremist, closely associated with the *Eda Haredit*. He was a sympathizer of the late R. Amram Blau, then the leader of the *Neture Karta*. The Rebbe never visited the *Kotel* himself but permitted his followers to visit it and also allowed some of his followers to settle in Bet Shemesh. It is not surprising that a number of his yeshivah students participated in violent demonstrations, sponsored by the *Haredi* militants.

The Rebbe used to act as the *mohel* and as the *sandek* at the same time. He wore a prayer shawl at *Kiddush* on Friday nights and followed the traditions of the rebbes of Komarno by omitting passages from the *Mishnah* in the *Tikkun Leil Shavuot* (the liturgy used on the eve of the Pentecost Festival). R. Yeshayahu Karlitz, known after his chief work as *Hazon Ish* (1878–1953), regularly testified that the Rebbe was well versed in the whole of the Talmud.

During a trip to the United States, he was received by R. Menahem Mendel Schneerson of Lubavitch, with whom he retained a close relationship, and he tearfully reprimanded anyone who spoke unflatteringly of Lubavitch. He was the author of *Asifat Michtavim, Derech Emuna, Tikvat Hageula,* and *Divre Emuna*—Yiddish discourses—and he also republished the works of his father-in-law, especially his work *Shomer Emunim,* which consisted of homilies concerning faith, reward and punishment, redemption, confidence, and Providence. Apart from Ger and Belz, no other rabbi in Jerusalem attracted so many followers on a Friday night, when more than three hundred people crowded into the large *Bet Hamidrash.* His prodigious labors bore fruit: he raised a generation of diligent and devoted disciples. He was also behind the founding of the *Bet Lepletot* Orphanage.

On 20 Heshvan 1995, the Rabbi fell on his way to the *Bet Hamidrash* and suffered a stroke, which deprived him of the power of speech. Despite intensive physiotherapy, there was no marked improvement. He appeared in the synagogue only when he acted as *sandek* (a person given the honor of holding the baby on his knees during the circumcision ceremony). He was kept alive by his doctors and the tender care of his family for nearly two years, but he never fully regained his speech.

During his illness, the community was administered by a committee and by his elder son, R. Shmuel Yaakov, the father of fourteen children. He is the son-in-law of R. Yeshayahu Schneebalg, rabbi of Bene Reim, and now *Dayan* of the *Bet Din* of *Mahzike Hadat.* The Rebbe instructed that the words of the liturgy, the *Unesaneh Tokef,* recited on the High Holy Days during the *Musaf Amida*: "On Rosh Hashanah will be inscribed and on Yom Kippur will be sealed how many will pass away from the earth and how many will be created," should be intoned at his funeral. He died on 27 Kislev 1997. The Rebbe was survived by six sons (R. Shmuel Yaakov, R. David, R. Aaron, R. Moshe, R. Yisrael Hayyim, and R. Yosef Yoel) and three daughters (Shifra Leah, Reizel, and Dina) who married, respectively, R. Shmuel Zalman Katz of Brooklyn, R. Tzvi Shlomo Biderman of Monsey, and R. Naftali Tzvi Rotenberg, who is the rabbi of *Toldot Aaron* in Bet Shemesh, a thriving community. One daughter, Sheindel Brachah, died in childbirth.

The Rebbe was buried on the Mount of Olives next to his father-in-law and was eulogized by five of his sons (his sixth son, R. Yosef Yoel, being on his return journey from Australia), and by R. Meir Brandsdorfer, a member of the *Eda Haredit Bet Din*, who also paid tribute to him at the tombstone consecration.

The Rebbe's elder son, R. Shmuel Yaakov, born in 1940, was educated in the Yeshivah of Vizhnitz in Tel Aviv and was a devout follower of the Rebbe of Vizhnitz; he is generally regarded as a moderate. In 1963, he married Sarah Hannah, the daughter of R. Isaiah Schneebalg of Bene Reim. They have eleven children. He is the head of the *Kollel* of Zydaczov.

A number of the late Rebbe's followers, however, sympathized with his younger son R. David (born in 1942), a follower of Satmar, who was closely attached to R. Yidele Horowitz of Dzikov (d. 1989), who lived in Jerusalem from 1947. R. David married the daughter of R. Tzvi Naftali Labin, the rabbi of Zydaczov, who at one time had a *shtiebl* in Clapton Common, London, but later settled in New York. They have sixteen children.

The late Rebbe was blessed with many grandchildren; only one son, R. Yosef Yoel, remains childless. Instead of voting on a single successor, it was decided through the good offices of the *Bet Din* of the *Eda Haredit* to appoint two of his sons as successors. R. David took over his father's main synagogue, *Toldot Aaron* in Shifte Yisrael, and R. Yaakov Shmuel the smaller *Ein Yaakov* Shul in Mea Shearim, and styled himself as the head of the community of *Toldot Avraham Yitzhak*. He already has a yeshivah of eighty students, a Talmud Torah for one hundred seventy children, a *Yeshivah Ketanah* and a *Yeshivah Gedolah*, and a *kollel*. In all, two hundred fifty families owe allegiance to him. He is, more-over, supported by R. Moshe Teitelbaum, the Rebbe of Satmar, and Rabbis Meir Brandsdorfer and Daniel Parish.

R. Arale's son R. Avraham Hayyim, now the rabbi of Beregszaz in Bene Berak, was born in Satmar in 1924. In 1945, he married Batyah Hayyah, the daughter of R. Mordecai Goldman of Zwehil. They have eleven children. Since his father died in 1947, he has lived in the Mea Shearim area, almost opposite his dynamic brother-in-law. Relations between them have been far from cor-dial. He is a friendly and unpretentious man, who welcomes all visitors with warmth and spontaneity. He has a very melodious voice and encourages his *hasidim* to dance. Hands, as well as feet, are caught up with the passion of the dance, which becomes a form of self-expression, even to the point of self-oblivion.

His scholarship is combined with considerable business acumen. At one time, he owned a thirty-*dunam* (about 7½ acres) site, ac-quired many years before, and for which he had grandiose plans. He dreamed of erecting a yeshivah, a Talmud Torah, a synagogue, a school for girls, a home for the elderly, a hotel, an industrial center, and apartments. So far, only a few apartments have been completed, and the Rabbi maintains a small *kollel, Huke Mate Aaron* in the old *Bet Hamidrash* of his late father in Mea Shearim.

While his brother-in-law was creating and expanding a cohe-sive community, he was preoccupied with unrealistic building plans and ambitious ideas for the future. Mea Shearim became too small for two rival establishments. In 1976, he moved to Bene Berak where he erected a magnificent building in Rehov Sefat emet, which houses a yeshivah, a *kollel*, a Talmud Torah with a roll of over two hundred children, and an institute for the publi-cation of his father's and his own works. He has, however, only a small following. Redemption tends to be the main motif of his discourses. He quotes the *Zohar*, which predicts that the Redemp-tion will come after domination by alien and irreligious elements. His comments are illuminating, and his opinions are expressed with precision and wit. He commutes regularly to Jerusalem, where his elder son, R. Aaron, is the spiritual guide of the *Shomre Emunim* in Jerusalem.

Torah Thoughts

The Talmud (*Taanit* 31a) says that "in the World-to-Come the Almighty will make a dance for the righteous, and He will sit in their midst in the Garden of Eden and everyone will point his finger towards Him." The Hebrew word for dance, *mahol*, can also be translated as "forgiveness." The Almighty will ask forgiveness of the righteous for the pains and poverty they suffered in this world (R. David of Lelov).

Ben Zoma says: "Who is wise? He who learns from all men, as it is said (*Avot* 4:1): 'From all my teachers I have obtained understanding' " (Psalms 119:99). A wise man is always willing to learn. I once heard the Rebbe of Lelov say, "A peasant asked his neighbor: 'Tell me, do you really love me?' and was answered in the affirmative. The peasant then continued: 'You do not love me at all, because if you truly loved me, you would know what is troubling me' " (*idem*).

"You should love your neighbor as yourself" (Leviticus 19:18). R. David of Lelov once said, "How can you say that I am a *Zaddik*? when I know full well that I love my children and grandchildren more than I love my fellow Jews."

Moses announced the approaching end of his leadership by saying: "Today I am 120 years old. I can no more go out or come in" (Deuteronomy 31:2). This surely cannot refer to his physical condition, for we read that when he died, his eyes were undimmed and his vigor unimpaired (Deuteronomy 34:7), implying that as he suffered none of the infirmities of age, it must refer to his spiritual qualities. He could no longer advance any higher on his spiritual rung (*idem*).

"Let them ask every man of his neighbor and every woman of her neighbor jewels of silver and jewels of gold" (Exodus 11:2). Borrowing from the Egyptians and becoming indebted to them would prevent them from ever returning to Egypt (R. Moses of Lelov).

"The Seder is now concluded. Just as we were privileged to arrange it, so may we merit to perform it." The Passover is different from all other festivals, for the Paschal lamb is an integral part of the ritual. We, therefore, conclude the Seder service by praying to the Almighty that the Temple may be restored, and we be able once again to offer the Paschal lamb (*idem*).

"Now the Holy One, Blessed be He, the Torah and Israel are one." The light of the Holy Name, Blessed be He, resides in the letters of the Torah, and when a man moves his lips in holiness and endeavors with all the power of his thought to comprehend the innermost light of the holy letters, he becomes a veritable receptacle of the Holy *Shechinah* (*Shomer Emunim*).

Now the fool who walks in darkness desires only a plain approach. He is satisfied with the literal meaning of his study and prayer. He does not believe that in every generation the Holy One, Blessed be He, affords illumination to the holy people of Israel when they longingly yearn for him. "For I the Lord change not" (*Malachai* 3:6). There is no change in His name, Blessed be He, for all the three sets of the Holy Torah are eternal. As it is written "and to cleave to him" (Deuteronomy 11:22). Scriptures speak of loving God and fearing Him. Shall we say that this only applies to former generations? Surely not. For the Torah is eternal and unchanging (*idem*).

"And the woman saw that the tree was good to eat, and pleasing to the eye" (Genesis 3:6). The eyes can be the source of all evil, as the Satan stressed "on the day that you shall eat it, your eyes will be opened" (Genesis 3:5). The only way to avoid cupidity is to shed tears of remorse (*idem*).

"Speak now into the ears of the people and let them ask every man of his neighbor" (Exodus 11:2). This, so the rabbis tell us, is in order that the promise to Abraham might be fulfilled, so that they, the nations, should not say that "they shall serve them and they shall afflict them" He permitted to be fulfilled, but the promise "and afterwards they shall go out with a great substance" He did not bring to fulfillment (*idem*).

"And Moses took with him the bones of Joseph" (Exodus 13:19). While the whole house of Israel was preoccupied in borrowing gold and silver from the Egyptians, Moses was busy collecting the bones of Joseph. For Joseph made his brethren promise that they would take his bones out of Egypt. Why did Moses not participate in despoiling the Egyptians? The items "taken from the Egyptians" were ultimately used for the erection and furnishing of the Tent of Meeting. As Moses did not contribute toward the building of the Tent of Meeting, he had no need to amass any wealth (*idem*).

Dishonor is preferable to honor. For honor begets pride, but modesty cultivates humility. The Talmud tells us (*Sabbath* 88b), "Those who are insulted and do not insult, hear themselves reviled without answering, act through love and rejoice in their suffering." Scripture says: "Let those that love you be like the sun when it emerges in all his strength" (Judges 5:31). A man who searches for honor is never satisfied. He is always under the impression that he does not receive the honor due to him. Consequently, he becomes angry and loses his temper, and this is regarded as idolatry (*idem*).

I have seen among the writings of the holy R. Shalom Dovber of Lubavitch, may his memory be for a blessing, that there are many categories of sleep. There is a sleep that is no more than a light nodding, when the sleeper is half-awake. There is the category of real sleep. There is the category of deep slumber. And, far worse, God forbid, there is the category of fainting, where it is necessary to massage the sleeper, to strike him, and to revive him with every kind of medicine in order to restore his soul. . . . And there is a category of still deeper unconsciousness that is known as a coma where, God forbid, only a tiny degree of life still remains in deep concealment so that even shouting at the sleeper and striking him fail to revive him. In this age we are in this deepest state of unconsciousness. To be sure, there are still to be found holy men in Israel who are still alert. And even the ordinary holy Israelite is in the category of: "I sleep, but my heart is awake" (Song of Songs 5:2). But there are some whom nothing can succeed in awakening, as, God forbid, in the last of the stages we have mentioned. Only if God has pity on him, to some extent, can such a one be restored to his former vigor, as the discerning will understand. So there are those whom neither suffering nor anything else can avail, God forbid. They have descended to the lowest degree. But efforts at revival can be effective for those who are in the category of a faint and, a fortiori, for those only in the category of sleep. And there are those who are only half asleep and who wake up as soon as they are called by name, even though they fall asleep again (R. Aaron Roth, in *Hitraggershut ha-Nefesh*).

The Rebbe called for more input in our prayers. Everyone requires salvation of one kind or another. And only through the power of prayer can one achieve it. The vitality that people in the Orthodox community invest in the observance of the Commandments has a profound effect even on the nonreligious Jews, and it influences the lifestyle of those of our brethren who are estranged from the Torah. Quoting the well-known anecdote concerning the Gaon of Vilna—that he became a Gaon "from five minutes," that is, every minute was precious to him—the Rebbe appealed to his followers not to squander the precious few minutes before and between prayers, but to put them to good use in the service of the Almighty (R. Shmuel Yaakov Kohn).

7

Servants of the Lord

The Zwehil Dynasty

The modest Yeshivah *Bet Mordecai*, founded in 1939 by R. Shlomo Goldman, the Rebbe of Zwehil, has been expanded beyond recognition by the present Rebbe, R. Avraham Moshe Goldman. The voice of Torah resounds there by day and by night from the hundreds of students, under the guidance of R. Michael Silber, the author of *Lev Yam* (treatises on several tractates of the Talmud). Students are examined regularly by prominent rabbis. The yeshivah recruits its students from a junior yeshivah and is under the supervision of R. Arye Gotlieb. The Talmud Torah, which will soon be moving into a new building, is maintained by trained teachers who give each child individual attention. Many children who live on the outskirts of Jerusalem travel there daily in a school bus.

Students of the *kollel* receive substantial sums of money every week, so that they and their families can live in comfort. There are charitable funds such as *Keren LaNesiim*, which provide financing to enable students to acquire apartments, and the *Vaad Simha*, which allocates funds to cover the cost of wedding festivities.

The Rebbe also established the *El HeHarim* Institute whose main object is editing and publishing manuscript writings of the rebbes of Zwehil and Zloczov, such as the seven-volume erudite discourses of the principal of the yeshivah, the works of R. Yitzhak of Radziwillov, and a book of *Zemirot* (Sabbath melodies).

The four-story building is now nearing completion in Rehov Shmuel HaNavi. The foundation stone was laid in Kislev 1990, and the first phase of the building was completed in 1994. This edifice will house a large synagogue, a yeshivah, a Talmud Torah, a kindergarten, kitchens, playrooms, and a dormitory. There is also a Zwehil *Bet Hamidrash* and a *kollel* in Rehov Eliezer Hamodia in Betar.

The present Rebbe, the seventh rebbe of Zwehil, is R. Avraham Moshe, whose life and works can be summed up in the mishnaic maxim: "Love peace, pursue peace. Love your fellow-creature and draw them near to the Torah." [1] He was born in 1920 and studied in the *Hayye Olam* Yeshivah in Jerusalem. He married the daughter of R. Moshe Sternbuch of Bene Berak and has six sons. One of his brothers, R. David, is rabbi in Bene Berak. The rebbe has never left Israel and never signs any political or religious proclamations.

One of his treasured possessions is a Scroll of the Law that had belonged to his ancestor R. Yehiel Michael of Zloczov (d. 25 Ellul 1786), a disciple of the Besht and the founder of the dynasty. R. Yehiel Michael had five sons whom he called "the five books of Moses." His fourth son, R. Moshe, who died on 10 Iyar 1831, made his home in Zwehil, which is now Novogrod Volinsky. On his tombstone were inscribed the words: "Moshe the servant of the Lord died."

He was succeeded by R. Yehiel Michael (1788–1712 Tishri 1851), whose son, R. Mordecai I, who died on the eve of *Sukkot* 1901, had twenty-one children, nineteen of whom died in his life-

---

1. *Avot* 1:12.

time. The two surviving sons became rebbes: the elder, R. Michael, in Korzec, and the younger, R. Shlomo, at the age of thirty-one, the fourth rebbe of Zwehil, where he lived for twenty-five years. He was unbending and uncompromising. When a number of residents sent their children to school on the Sabbath, he would not permit the fathers to be called up to the Law in the synagogue and even forbade the water carriers to supply them with water.

But, then, he lived through hard times, not just the Ukrainian pogroms perpetrated by Simon Petlura, Anton Denikin, and Machno, but also through the ordeals perpetrated by the Yevsektsiya (the Jewish Section of the Communist Party), whose aim it was to abolish Jewish traditions, customs, and beliefs. There was a mass closure of Jewish houses of prayer, accompanied by other repressive measures: the baking of *matzot* was greatly restricted and often entirely forbidden, and the teaching of Hebrew and religion to young people under eighteen was made a punishable offense.

In 1926, the Rebbe emigrated to the Holy Land. On arriving in Jaffa on the Fast of Gedaliah, he said: "I am now throwing overboard my mantle of rabbinics," and for three years he lived in the *Bet Yisrael* district of Jerusalem in complete anonymity. He made his home close to that of R. Yisrael Shochet, the *gabbai* of the *Tiferet Yisrael* synagogue, which is also known as the Synagogue of Nisan Bak. The Rebbe would often spend the entire night there, after studying all day at the *Hayye Olam* Yeshivah. He was generally known as "the Jew from Zwehil."

When his identity was eventually discovered, it made no difference to his way of life. He never employed a beadle but walked every day, and sometimes twice a day, to the *Kotel*, where he sat among the poor and the lonely. Nothing could deter him from his regular visits, and even in the time of disturbances, when conditions were dangerous, he maintained: "He who fears God has no reason to fear the Gentiles." Nor would he go a day without immersing himself in the ritual bath. He was an ascetic, fasting regularly. It was not unusual for him to fast on three consecutive days. He had only one meal a day, never eating before late afternoon. On the Sabbath, however, he had all three statutory meals.

He lived in a tiny, one-story house of three rooms that he himself erected without any technical aid. There were no locks or bolts
on the doors, which were always open wide. His followers constantly and persistently urged him to move to a more dignified
residence, one befitting his status, but he paid no heed to them.
On the eve of the Sabbath, he would recite the whole book of
Psalms and every day he studied eight pages of the Talmud with
Rashi's commentaries. He regularly observed the midnight prayer
(*Tikkun Hazot*), which he recited sitting on the ground, mourning the destruction of the Temple, a custom instituted in the sixteenth century by the kabbalist circle in Safed. He became known
as a "miracle worker." Even rebbes came to consult him, and R.
Aaron Rokeah of Belz advised people to visit him.

He was indefatigable in rescuing poor Jewish children from the
clutches of the missionaries, who were then very active in Jerusalem. He especially befriended a six-year-old child whom he found
abandoned and brought him up as a member of his family. At a
time when, in 1942, Field Marshal Rommel and his Afrika Korps
were at the gates of Egypt, the Rebbe assured his followers that
"the enemy will not succeed in entering the Holy Land, and the
Land of Israel will remain inviolate." When told that German
planes had bombed the Central Bus Station in Tel Aviv and that
an Italian bomber had attacked an area near the Shaare Zeddek
Hospital, the Rebbe assured his informants that the bombers
would never come back. He died at the age of 76 on 26 Iyar 1945,
on the very day World War II in Europe ended, and was buried
on the Mount of Olives.[2]

He was succeeded by his son, R. Gedalia Moshe, born 26 Iyar
1907. Ordained by R. Hayyim Soloveitchik of Brest-Litovsk and
R. Mordecai of Slonim, he married the daughter of R. David
Shlomo of Kobrin. When his father emigrated to the Holy Land,
he remained in Zwehil and, like his father, he was threatened by
the Godless *Yevsktsiya*, who tried to undermine Jewish religious
practices and rites, especially circumcision and ritual slaughter. He

2. D. Werner, *Zaddik Yesod Olam—R. Shlomo MiZwehil* (Jerusalem,
1986).

was labeled by them a "reactionary." In his attempt to perpetuate the traditional values of learning, despite the severe penalties that would be imposed on detection, the Rabbi maintained his manifold activities and recklessly continued his efforts to strengthen religious life. He was arrested, threatened with the death sentence, and finally expelled to Siberia, where he spent eight years. Arriving in the Holy Land in 1936, broken in body and spirit, he succeeded his father and died at the age of sixty-three on 24 Heshvan 1950.

He was succeeded by the sixth Rebbe, R. Mordecai II. Born on 11 Heshvan 1906, he came to the Holy Land with his grandfather and studied in the *Sefat Emet* Yeshivah. He married Esther Sheine Rachel (d. 1980), the daughter of R. Shmuel Mordecai of Neshitz-Kovel. He was the author of *Yikro D'Malko*—discourses on the Book of Genesis.[3] After serving as Rebbe for twenty-nine years, he died on 28 Shevat 1979 and was succeeded by the present rebbe, R. Avraham.

Amshinov

In his disregard for conventional prayer times as laid down in the Codes, *Orach Hayyim*, Section 89, the Rebbe of Amshinov, R. Yaakov Arye Yeshayahu Milikovsky, is not unique in Hasidism, sharing this attitude toward time with other present-day hasidic groups. It is an attitude that derives from Kotsk and Przysucha. R. Mordecai of Nadvorna (1823–1895) is reputed to have conducted the *Melaveh Malkah*, the festive meal at the termination of the Sabbath, on Sunday morning. He followed the pattern of R. Yaakov Yitzhak of Przysucha and his disciples, who maintained that "Although the Gates of Heaven are closed after the statutory times of prayer, the prayers of the *Zaddikim*, that emanate from a pure and broken heart, break through all barriers."[4] Hence, R.

---

3. Jerusalem, 1987.

4. Yitzhak Alfasi, *Bisde HaHasidut* (Tel Aviv: Ariel, 1987), pp. 236–243.

Naftali Tzvi Horowitz of Ropczyce interpreted the verse "And I besought the Lord at that time"[5] to mean that one should pray only when one is ready for prayer. For the spiritual preparation for the *mitzvah*, that is, *kavanah*, "intent" or "intention," is tantamount to a *mitzvah*. Devotion is essential to prayer, and only by means of *devekut* can we reach spiritual communion.

R. Meir of Przysucha would actually fast for two days, on the Day of Atonement and the following day. The biblical verse "Day and night shall not cease"[6] was taken by him to mean that time has been superseded. It was not until Sunday that the Amshinover Rebbe finally recited the *Havdalah* (the prayer recited at the conclusion of the Sabbath, signifying that the Sabbath is over), having extended the Sabbath for many hours, and his Grace after Meals takes more than two hours. On Mondays and Thursdays, the reading of the Law does not take place until late in the afternoon. On Hanukah the Rebbe lights the candles just before the dawn of the following day. He is a man of great spirituality, whose way of life is based on prayer.

The present Rebbe's father, R. Hayyim, a native of Slonim, was born in 1916. He miraculously evaded the Nazi Holocaust by finding refuge in Shanghai, which then became a haven for over one thousand Jewish refugees from Poland, many of them students from the *Mir Yeshivah*. On 18 February 1943, under pressure from Germany, the Japanese set up a ghetto there, though the refugees were still able to continue, to some extent, their own way of life. In response to representation by the *Vaad HaTsala* (Refugee Committee of the United Orthodox Rabbis), the United States permitted some money to be transferred to Shanghai for the support of the refugees.

The Rebbe then traveled on to Kobe with a Curacao visa in 1947. He married Hayyah Nehamah, the daughter of R. Yerahmiel Yehuda Meir Kalish of Amshinov, and was appointed principal of the Amshinov Yeshivah, *Shem Olam*, in Rehov Hapisga 22, Bayit Vegan, Jerusalem.

---

5. Deuteronomy 3:23.
6. Genesis 8:27.

The present Rebbe, R. Yaakov Arye, was born in New York in 1947 and was one-year-old when he arrived in Israel. He studied in the *Etz Hayyim* Yeshivah, which was founded in 1851 by R. Shmuel Salant, one of the few yeshivot to be established before World War One. He married Perl, the daughter of R. Avraham Eger of Lublin, who now lives in Bene Berak. They have four sons and seven daughters, two of whom are already married. The Rebbe's home in Bayit Vegan, Jerusalem, attracts many worshipers, and services take place continuously from dawn until midnight. He especially welcomes *Baale Teshuvah*.

In 1954, R. Yerahmiel Yehuda Meir Kalish (1901–27 Iyar 1976) established the Yeshivah *Shem Olam* in memory of his father, R. Shimon Shalom. Originally situated in Tel Aviv, it moved to Holon and eventually to Bayit Vegan, Jerusalem, where it was guided by the Rebbe's father. The Rebbe of Kalish, a descendant on his mother's side from "the Holy Jew," was born in Przysucha. During the Second World War, he escaped to Vilna and then to Shanghai. After the war he settled in New York. In 1958, he emigrated to Israel. His personal sufferings were masked by a smiling face and a pleasant manner. In 1984, he established a Talmud Torah that maintains a high standard of education. No more than fifteen children are allowed in one class, and at the age of four, they commence the study of the Book of Genesis. He died and was buried on Har Hamenuhot in Jerusalem.

The founder of the Amshinov dynasty was R. Yitzhak Kalish of Warka (1779–1848), who was regarded as one of the great defenders of the House of Israel and one of the most communally minded of the Polish hasidic rebbes. He was concerned with every facet of Jewish life, as well as with the economic plight of the Jews in the Holy Land, for whom he assiduously collected funds. He, together with R. Yitzhak Meir Alter and R. Hayyim Davidsohn of Warsaw, were signatories to a manifesto, dated 14 Tevet 1842, urging Jews to settle on the land. "Not only is there no trace in the Talmud of any edict against working on the land," stated the *Kol Kore* (the proclamation), "on the contrary, we find in the Talmud that many of the saintly *Amoraim* who lived outside the Land of Israel, owned lands."

His grandson, R. Simha Bunem (1851–1907), yearned to settle in the Holy Land, but obstacle was piled on obstacle. In 1887 and 1889, the Sultan Abdul Hamid put a general ban on Jewish immigration. Permission to settle was granted only after a special application, and even a permit to visit was grudgingly given. A "Red Card" allowed a maximum stay of three months, but R. Simha Bunem was not deterred. In the winter of 1887, accompanied by his wife, three sons, and two daughters, the Rabbi set out for the Holy Land. His eldest son, R. Menahem, whose wife was expecting a baby, remained in Poland. Like all Russian tourists, the party was given leave to stay for thirty days. Overstaying this period, R. Simha Bunem was arrested in Tiberias and spent five days in prison. He was freed on medical grounds and allowed to remain in Tiberias. After three months, he returned to Poland. His sixteen-year-old daughter Rachel fell ill en route and died in Warsaw soon after their return.

The Rabbi settled in Otwock, near Warsaw, but could find no peace. "If you can make a living in the Holy Land, without being dependent on charity, then by all means, settle there," R. Avraham Bornstein of Sochaczev advised him. "Do not be concerned about leaving your *hasidim* behind. Poland is not short of rabbis."

His medical adviser, Dr. Soloveitchik, pleaded with him not to undertake this hazardous journey, but his longing to return to the Holy Land did not diminish. "There in the Land of Israel, I see everything," he sighed. "Here I see nothing." In the winter of 1905, he returned on his own to the Holy Land, where he arrived on the day after *Shushan Purim*. At first he stayed with R. David Biderman of Lelov, then he settled in the *Deitsche* quarter, the German section of the city. Despite his pleading and protestations, *hasidim* flocked to him. For the last year and a half of his life, he lived in Tiberias, close to the seashore, and often visited the Yeshivah *Or Torah*, near the grave of R. Meir *Baal Hanes*. He died in Tiberias on 2 Shevat 1907, at the age of fifty-six, and was buried near R. Menahem Mendel of Vitebsk.

Slonim

Slonim stresses the study of the Torah for its own sake and the supreme importance of prayer, love and awe for the Creator, humility, and faith.[7] It believes in concentration and depth rather the accumulation of facts—a legacy of the Lithuanian Mitnaggedim and the school of R. Hayyim Soloveitchik. It nonetheless opposes the *Musar* methods that prevailed in the Lithuanian yeshivot. The Rebbe of Slonim today is R. Shalom Noah Brosovski, the son-in-law of R. Avraham Weinberg of Slonim, the author of *Birkat Avraham*.

R. Shalom Noah was born in Baranowicze in 1916, the son of R. Moshe Avraham, the head of the Jewish community of Baranowicze. His father and mother, Zivyah; his brothers Shlomo Hillel and Yaakov Yehoshua; his sister Hayyah Sarah; and all their families perished in the Holocaust.

R. Shalom Noah studied under R. Moshe Midner, and in the Yeshivah *Torat Hesed* of R. Avraham of Slonim, author of *Bet Avraham*. In 1935, he emigrated to the Holy Land and married Havah, the daughter of the Rebbe of Slonim. For two years he was the principal of the Habad yeshivah, *Ahi Temimim*, in Tel Aviv. Later he became the head of the Yeshivah *Bet Avraham*. He published the works of the rebbes of Slonim, *Bet Avraham*, *Divre Shmuel*, *Beer Avraham*, and *Zichron Kodesh*.[8] He recently published his own works, *Netivot Shalom*,[9] a collection of discourses that he has delivered in the yeshivah over the last forty years. He is active in the *Hinuch Atzmai* and is a member of the *Moetzet Gedole Hatorah* and the *Vaad HaYeshivot*. He has two sons.

---

7. Wolf Zeev Rabinowitsch, *Lithuanian Hasidim* (London: Vallentine Mitchell, 1970), p. 190.

8. *Beer Avraham*, Allegorical Commentary on the Mehilta (Warsaw, 1927); *Beer Avraham* on Torah (Jerusalem, 1970); *Yesod Avodah* (Warsaw, 1892); *Hesed Avraham* (Jerusalem, 1930).

9. Jerusalem, 1996.

Slonim is no newcomer to the setting up of Torah institutions: there was a Slonim yeshivah, *Or Torah*, near the grave of R. Meir Baal Hanes under the guidance of R. Moshe Kliers, and in Tiberias, one of the first *Bet Yaakov* schools was established in 1924. Slonim was the pioneer of girls' education in the Holy Land.

The Talmud Torah Elementary School *Emet V'Emuna* in Rehov Shmuel Hanavi has twenty-four classes and fifteen dormitory rooms, as well as a kindergarten. In all, there are over one thousand students and a large annual budget. There is a *shtiebl* of Slonim in Tiberias, going back to R. Menahem Mendel of Vitebsk and R. Avraham Katz of Kalisk. There is a Talmud Torah, *Emet V'Emunah*, established in Tel Aviv in 1983, and there are Slonim centers in Bene Berak, and *Kiryat Gat*, as well as *kollelim* in Emanuel, Betar, and Hazon Yehezkel.

The yeshivah, which was established in 1942, has now been relocated to Rehov Salant. The foundation stone for this attractive, modern, five-story yeshivah was laid in 1951 and consecrated in 1954. It accommodates over two hundred students, and there are forty graduates in the *kollel*. The yeshivah houses an excellent library of over five thousand volumes, and its *Gemilat Hasadim* free-loan society has been active since 1971. There are many students in the junior yeshivah. The yeshivah complex consists of a central synagogue, study halls for two *kollelim* for higher rabbinic studies, twelve lecture rooms, sixty-two dormitory rooms, dining rooms, and kitchens.

The founder of the dynasty was R. Avraham Weinberg (1804–1883). In 1821, he appealed for funds on behalf of the *hasidim* of the Holy Land. His book *Yesod Avodah*[10] contains letters that he wrote to his followers in the Holy Land. After the death of R. Noah of Lachowicze, most of the *hasidim* of Slonim followed R. Moshe of Kobrin, and with the death of R. Moshe in 1858, R. Avraham Weinberg became Rebbe. He was a prolific author and settled in Baranowicze, where he established a yeshivah, *Torat Hesed*. A number of his followers settled in the Holy Land, to whom the Rebbe wrote warm and encouraging letters. "The

---

10. Warsaw, 1892.

diaspora is a temporary resting place, a mere lodging place," he wrote. "But the Holy Land is the House of the Lord. You do not realize how grateful you should all be that you are residing there."

The principle of hereditary leadership, so firmly rooted in Polish hasidic life, had no guaranteed place in Slonim. R. Avraham's son, R. Michael Aaron, did not succeed his father but encouraged his grandson R. Shmuel (1850–1916) to become rebbe instead. The Rebbe maintained the traditions of his grandfather and collected funds for the Holy Land, helping to establish the *Or Torah* Yeshivah there in 1900 and a soup kitchen for the poor. His successor, R. Avraham II (1884–1933), moved to Baranowicze, visited the Holy Land in 1929 and 1933, and established *shtieblech* in Bene Berak and Tel Aviv. He was succeeded by his son R. Shlomo David Yehoshua, who died a martyr's death on 6 Heshvan 1943.

A grandson of R. Avraham emigrated to the Holy Land in 1880 and settled in Tiberias. He refused to become a rebbe but studied in the *kollel* of R. Meir Baal Hanes. For nearly half a century, Slonim *hasidim* in the Holy Land had no official rebbe. R. Avraham Weinberg, the son of R. Noah, was born in Tiberias in 1889. He visited Poland in 1906 and 1913, and studied there with his uncle R. Shmuel of Slonim. On his return to the Holy Land, he participated in the civic life of Tiberias. Elected a member of the municipality, this rabbinic scion became associate mayor in 1938. He had two daughters and five sons. In 1929, one of his five sons was killed by Arab terrorists in Tiberias; R. Shmuel works for the *Hinuch Atzmai*, R. David administers the Slonim institutions, R. Mordecai and R. Zelig both died recently.

R. Avraham refused absolutely to become a rebbe. He regarded himself as a follower of R. Mordecai (Motel) Hayyim Kislings (d. 1954), who emigrated to the Holy Land in 1935. "If you call me rebbe," he told his adherents, "I will not forgive either in this world or in the next." It was not until after the Second World War, in which all his relatives perished, that, at the age of sixty-four, he reluctantly assumed the leadership of the *hasidim* of Slonim. He was highly respected for his diligence and his learning. He spent his days in study, completing the whole Talmud twice each year, on the anniversary of his father's death in Elul and on that of his mother in Adar.

He did not accept petitions, but an exception was made before the New Year, when he accepted a composite *Qvittel*, drawn up by his *hasidim*. He settled in Jerusalem and was active in the Aguda and a member of the Council of Sages. He never entirely recovered from a car accident in which he had been involved some years before. After being rebbe for just over twenty-seven years, he died on 11 Sivan 1981 at the age of ninety-two. In his "Last Will and Testament," like the Rebbe of Amshinov, he appointed his son-in-law R. Shalom Noah as his successor. "The Torah was given in fire, and must be studied with fiery enthusiasm." This tradition is maintained in Slonim today.

A small number of his *hasidim* now follow R. Avraham Weinberg of Bene Berak. A son of R. Michael Aaron, who was a descendant of *Yesod Avodah*, he was born in 1945 and married the daughter of R. Shmuel Weinberg. They have two sons and two daughters. His in-laws are Rabbi Schneerson, the principal of the Yeshivah of Trzebina; R. Zeev Twersky, the brother of the Rachmastrivka Rebbe; R. Yehezkel Yehiel Panet, the Rebbe of Des in Bene Berak; and R. Yaakov Mendel Friedman, the Rebbe of Bohush. In 1981, on the death of his grandfather, he became Rebbe of Slonim in Bene Berak.

He, too, has established a number of institutions: a yeshivah, Gedola *Beer Avraham*, in Bene Berak, where three hundred students from the age of sixteen upward study; a junior yeshivah and a *kollel*, *Yesod Avodah*, in Jerusalem; a *kollel*, *Yeshuot Avraham*, in Bene Berak; a youth organization, *Darke Hayyim*, named after R. Mordecai Hayyim of Slonim; and a loan fund, *Hasde Avraham*, its objectives being to help mothers recuperate after childbirth and to give financial aid to needy students. He also has three *shtieblech* in Jerusalem in *Beth Yisrael*, Sanhedria and in Unsdorf, the Yeshivah *Ezrat Torah*, and is now building an imposing Slonim Center at Bene Berak, which will be made up of a large synagogue, a study hall, a mikve and a library, as well as an Institute, *Machane Emuna*, to publish the works of the Rebbes of Slonim. The Rebbe, moreover, has Shtieblech *Beer Avraham* in Borough Park, Monsey,

Williamsburg, London, and Antwerp. On 2 Tevet 1998, he visited London.

Stropkov

R. Avraham Shalom Yissachar Dov Lifshitz Halberstam is now the Rebbe of Stropkov and lives in Rehov Nisenbaum, near the Central Bus Station in Jerusalem. Born in 1946, in 1966 he married Sarah Hinda, the daughter of R. Menahem Mendel Schneebalg of Manchester. He has a small *kollel* in Mea Shearim. He edited *Yesod Likra* by R. Arye Leibish Lifshitz, the Rebbe of Opatov, who was murdered on 25 Iyar 1944. The book contains discourses and an anthology of rabbinic and hasidic scholars, as well halachic problems, all dealing with the grave of Rachel. It also contains prayers and supplications to be recited at the sepulcher.

R. Avraham Shalom Yissachar Dov, who was named after R. Avraham Shalom of Stropkov (1855–1940), the author of *Divre Shalom* on the Pentateuch,[11] succeeded R. Yehezkel Shragai Lifshitz Halberstam, a direct descendant of R. Hayyim of Zanz. A native of Stropkov, where he was born 4 Nisan 1908, he studied under his father, R. Yissachar Dov, Rabbi in Stropkov. During World War I, he lived in Budapest and subsequently settled in Ungvar. He was an expert on geneology and traced his descent to Rashi. R. Yehezkel Shragai married Miriam Leah, the daughter of R. Yitzhak Reuven Lifshitz. His wife and his six children perished in Auschwitz.

He, too, was incarcerated in Auschwitz, where he befriended the Rabbi of Klausenburg. After liberation, he became rabbi in Bamberg, Germany. As a skilled *mohel*, he circumcised hundreds of children in the Displaced Persons camps. In 1949, he settled in Jerusalem, where he was rabbi of *Shaare Yerushalayim* for twenty years. When his uncle, R. Menahem Mendel Halberstam, died childless in New York, on 7 Iyar 1954, R. Yehezkel Shragai be-

---

11. Miskolc, 1944, and Jerusalem, 1955.

came the Rebbe. In the same year, his followers established the *Bet Hamidrash Divre Menahem* in Rehov Geula in Mea Shearim.

He remarried Toba Shlager, and they had four daughters and one son. A prolific author, the Rebbe published *Divre Yehezkel Shragai*, a selection of his responsa and discourses, and also edited and reprinted some of the works of his ancestors. A man of towering intellect and an eloquent speaker, he delivered discourses in Hebrew as well as in Yiddish. His well-ordered library reflected a well-ordered mind. One 'of his treasured possession was *Avodat Kodesh* by R. Hayyim Yosef David Azulai, which was printed in Livorno in 1847, a book that was used by R. Hayyim Halberstam, his son R. Yehezkel of Sianiawa, and by R. Shalom Halberstam, and bears their signatures.

R. Yehezkel Shragai died on 6 Kislev 1994, at the age of eighty-seven.

Torah Thoughts

It is related in the Talmud (*Taanit* 25b) that once, during a drought, R. Eliezer stepped down before the Ark and recited twenty-four benedictions, but his prayers were not answered. R. Akiva stepped down after him and exclaimed: "Our Father, Our King, we have no King but Thee! Our Father, Our King, for Thy sake have mercy upon us" and the rain fell! A Heavenly voice was heard proclaiming: "The prayer' of this man (R. Akiva) was answered not because he is greater than the other, but because he is ever forbearing and the other is not." R. Akiva was a descendant of proselytes, and he had to make tremendous efforts to eliminate and overcome the unworthy sentiments that he may have inherited from his Gentile ancestors. He had to convert darkness into light. It was for this reason the R. Akiva's prayers were superior and were answered (the Rebbe of Zwehil).

We read in *Avot* (6:8): R. Shimon, the son of Menasya, said: "These seven qualities which the sages enumerated as comely for the righteous were all present in R. Juda the Prince and in his sons: the qualities of beauty, strength, riches, wisdom, honor, old age, and a hoary head. In the case of Rabbi Juda it is stated that he raised his fingers toward Heaven and said: 'Sovereign of the Universe. It is now revealed and known to you that I have labored in the study of the Torah with my ten fingers, and I did not enjoy any worldly benefits even with my little finger' (*Ketubot* 104a). Rabbi Juda, at the time of his death, raised his ten fingers toward heaven. It does not state that he lowered them, implying that his entire life was directed towards spiritual attainments" (*idem*).

And Moses said unto Aaron: "Take a jar and put in it a full omer of Manna and store it before the Lord to be kept throughout your generations" (Exodus 16:33). Twice the Torah repeats the words "and Moses said" and "as the Lord commanded you." There were two reasons why they were ordered to place a jar of manna in the Tent of Meeting. First, as a reminder of the miraculous food with which they were nourished during their forty years in the wilderness, and second, to impress the children of Israel that all sustenance comes from the Almighty (*idem*).

It is vital that we should not forget the saying of R. Yohanan ben Zakkai: "If you have learned much Torah, do not claim credit to yourself, since you were created for this purpose" (*Avot* 2:9). The acquisition of Torah should not be for motives of boastfulness and self-righteousness, nor in order to be regarded as wise. In the words of R. Akiva: "I have learned much from my colleagues but most of all from my disciples" (*Taanit* 7a). It is our duty to teach others and to make them grasp the words of the Torah (*idem*).

The section of *Taharot* (lit., "purities") follows the section *Kodashim* (lit., "holy things"). For these are the two levels of holiness and purity, based on the words of R. Pinhas ben Yair that "purity leads to separation" (*Sotah* 9:15).

The concept of holiness means cleaving to God. Those people who cleave to the *Zaddik*, who in turn cleaves to God, also merit being called holy. This high standard of sanctity and purity has not been achieved by many in our generation. It is the level of holiness where the upper part of a person's body is on the level of an angel. When a man prays, he attaches himself to his illustrious forefathers and thereby reaches a high level of holiness (the Rebbe of Zwehil).

And Joseph said unto them on the third day, "This do and live, for I fear the Almighty" (Genesis 42:18). Why did Joseph have to mention that he feared God? Because he was anxious that his brethren should repent of their crime, and it was this reference to God that led his brethren to cry out: "We are verily guilty concerning our brother in that we saw his deep misery when he pleaded with us but we would not listen. And now this misery has come upon us" (Genesis 42:21; *idem*).

"And Moses went back to God and said: "Oh, this people has committed a great sin" (Exodus 32:31). Moses was pleading with the Almighty on behalf of the children of Israel. Why, then, does he say that the children of Israel have sinned a great sin? Admitting guilt and confessing one's sin is the basis of true repentance. Moses did not excuse Israel, nor did he endeavor to condone their iniquity (Rabbi of Amshinov).

To sin against a human being is worse than sinning against God. The Almighty is omnipresent and can always be found, whereas a human being may change his abode and cannot be traced. The Almighty, however, is omnipresent and one can always find him (*idem*).

"From everyone whose heart impels him you shall take my heave offering" (Exodus 25:2). Every man who is not only ready and willing to make a monetary donation but who is prepared to offer his heart, from such an individual you should take my heave offering (R. Abraham of Slonim).

"Return them back to dust" (Psalms 90:3). First of all, remove from a human being poverty (dust), only then will he be able to repent. "Oppressive poverty deprives a man of his sense and acknowledge of his Creator" (*Eruvin* 41a; *idem*).

R. Yohanan ben Zakkai instructed his disciples: "Go out and observe which is the good way in life to which a man should cling." One of his disciples, R. Eliezer, said: "A good eye" (*Avot* 2:13). This means that a man's greatest virtue is that he should be satisfied with his portion. Jealousy is due to lack of faith. For a Jew should always believe that whatever the Almighty does is for good (Rabbi of Slonim).

8

Dynastic Revivals

The Rebbe of Talna

A close neighbor of the Rabbi of Amshinov in Bayit Vegan, Jerusa-lem, was the Rabbi of Talna, R. Yohanan Twersky, a descendant of R. David of Talna (Talnoye) (1806–1882) in the Ukraine, son of R. Mordecai of Chernobyl. R. David had a golden chair with the inscription *David Melech Yisrael, Hai Vekayam* ("David, King of Israel, lives for ever"). Born in Tulcin on 10 Elul 1906, he was seven years old when his father, R. David Mordecai (1888–1957), emigrated to New York, one of the first hasidic rabbis to settle there. He made his home on the East Side, where he established a synagogue, *Kehal Hasidim.* "In the old country," said young Yohanan at his *Bar Mitzvah* celebration, "my greatest wish would have been for material things. Here, in the United States, my most fervent desire is that I remain a Jew." When he was seventeen in 1923, he traveled to the Holy Land where he became a follower

of R. Aaron Roth. He studied in the *Ohel Moshe* Yeshivah under
R. Yitzhak Yeruham Diskin and R. Simha Bunem Werner. He
was ordained by R. Yosef Hayyim Sonnenfeld.

In 1927, his father, R. David Mordecai, visited the Holy Land,
and they returned together to the United States, where the young
man established *Zerah Kodesh,* an association of rebbes' sons in
Flatbush. He was appointed rabbi in the Romanian Synagogue in
New York. After his marriage to Zipporah Pearl, a descendant of
the Rebbe of Strettin, in 1928, he became the Rebbe of Talna in
Montreal, where in 1934, he set up a yeshivah. He had four sons
and three daughters. The Second World War brought many refugees from Nazi Europe. Many German Jews, who had found refuge in Britain, were, in 1940, sent as "Enemy Aliens" to intern-
ment camps in Canada. The Rabbi made every effort to welcome
them to his home, interceded with the authorities on their behalf,
and took care of their religious needs.

After first living in *Kiryat Moshe* and *Bet Hakerem*, he established his residence in Bayit Vegan in 1960. He founded a *kollel*
adjacent to the grave of Shimon HaTzaddik in East Jerusalem, and
also renovated the old synagogue of Talma in Safed in 1992. He
instituted the study of the Mishnah: twelve chapters were to be
studied every month, and the six orders of the Mishnah were completed in the course of four years. He died on 25 Kislev 1998, and
was buried on the Mount of Olives. He is survived by an only
daughter who married R. Yisrael Tzvi Weinberg.

Sochaczev-Radomsk

R. Shmuel Yitzhak Bornstein, who also lives in Bayit VeGan, was
born in 1961 and was orphaned when he was eight and half years
old. He studied in Ponovezh Yeshivah in Bene Berak. In 1983, he
married Rebecca, the daughter of R. Eliyahu Sternbuch of
Antwerp. They have eight children. The young Rebbe is endeav-
oring to establish a Yeshivah Ketanah, and a Yeshivah Gedolah
Bet Avraham. There are hasidic *shtieblech* in Tel Aviv and Bene
Berak. He is reprinting the erudite works of his ancestors.

His father, R. Menahem Shlomo, was a descendant of R. Avraham Bornstein (1839–1910), who is considered one of the leading
authorities of the nineteenth century. Many rabbis from far and
wide turned to him to clarify and elucidate complex legal halachic
problems. *Avnei Nezer,* his voluminous correspondence and
responsa on the four parts of the *Shulhan Aruch,* was printed between 1912 and 1934. What R. Elijah, the Gaon of Vilna, was to
the Mitnaggedic Movement of the eighteenth century, R. Avraham was to the *hasidim* of the nineteenth century. It is not surprising that R. Yaakov Arye Guterman, the rebbe of Radzymin,
eulogized R. Avraham as one of the last of the "men of the Great
Assembly."

R. Avraham was steadfast in his support of the Holy Land and
urged his *hasidim* to settle there, provided that they were able to
make a living and would not be dependent on charity. R. Yisrael
Hayyim Morgenstern of Pulawy (1840–1905), the son of R. David
Morgenstern of Kotsk, wrote a fifty-page tract/manuscript, *Shelom
Yerushalayim,* published posthumously in 1922, in which he demonstrated by means of biblical texts and talmudic dicta that it was
the duty of every Jew to participate in the rebuilding of the Holy
Land. He believed that the time was propitious. The vexing and
restrictive Turkish regulations that had debarred land purchases
and settlements had been relaxed, and Jews were now permitted
to acquire land and were even provided with police protection.
For these reasons, he urged the purchase of fields and vineyards.
In his view, it was essential for large groups to settle there, even
if they did so only because they were unable to make a living in
the diaspora.

His followers who lived in the Holy Land had to undertake
to observe all the Laws of *Shemitah.* It was up to their spiritual
leaders to see that harmony prevailed among them. He forwarded
copies of his unpublished manuscript to a number of rebbes. The
Rebbe of Sochaczev commended it, saying, "I have examined the
contents of your work and derived much pleasure from it. For
with sweet and pleasant phrases it fills the heart with love of the
Holy Land. . . . It is proper to purchase an estate in the land of
Israel, and I, too, want to do so."

In 1898, R. Avraham sent his son R. Shmuel and his son-in-law R. Meir to purchase land from the Turkish overlords. This mission was aborted, and the transaction was not completed. However, his grandson R. David did acquire property in the Holy Land in 1938.

At an Agudist conference, held on 20 Tevet 1934, R. David urged the assembly to support the *Yishuv*. "Only in the Holy Land," he said, "will the revival of Judaism take place." He visited the Holy Land in 1924 and in the winter of 1935. He made plans to settle there, but these were nullified by World War Two. When the Gestapo broke into his home, he greeted them with defiance. "I know you are going to kill me. I prefer to die in my own home and not in a cattle wagon." He was reciting the *Shema* when they shot him on 5 Kislev 1942.

On his mother's side, R. Menahem Shlomo was descended from R. Shlomo Henoch HaKohen Rabinowicz, the Rabbi of Radomsk. In his book *Tiferet Shlomo,* he wrote: "Why should the Children of Israel be impoverished and afflicted and downtrodden more than all other nations? Must the descendants of the Patriarchs be subject to the despicable Egyptians?" The spiritual leaders, too, are criticized for their apathy: "How can it comfort a father, who is languishing in prison, when his son tells him that he is making progress in his talmudic studies. Surely, the father would ask: 'What steps are you taking to have me released from prison?' "

R. Hanoch Henoch, brother of R. David, was born in Sochaczev on 14 Heshvan 1897 and in 1917 married Freidel, the daughter of R. Nathan Nahum of Krimilov, a descendant of R. Shlomo Rabinowicz of Radomsk. At the age of twenty-eight, in 1924, he settled in the Buchara District of Jerusalem and later joined his brother-in-law R. Yeshayahu Shapira in Rehov HaHida in Bayit Vegan. His father died in Poland on 24 Tevet 1926 and was succeeded by his son R. David, as R. Hanoch Henoch refused to become rebbe.

Only after his brother was killed by the Nazis could he no longer decline the rabbinate, and he became the fourth rebbe of Sochaczev, as well as the spiritual leader of the followers of the Radomsk. He befriended the Poet Laureate Shmuel Yosef Agnon and established the *Nezer* Society to reprint the works of his ancestors, which had been out of print for many years. After being Rebbe for twenty years, he died suddenly on 26 Elul 1965 at the age of seventy-six and was buried on *Har HaMenuhot*.[1] He was survived by three sons.

His youngest son, R. Menahem Shlomo, was born on 2 Heshvan 1935 and studied in the Yeshivah *Knesset Heskiyahu* in Kfar Hasidim, in Kfar Haroeh, in the Hebron Yeshivah, Jerusalem, and in the *kollel Hechal HaTalmud* under R. Michael Feinstein. He married Nina, the daughter of Daniel Mushowitz, a descendant of R. Yosef Ber Soloveitchik of Brest-Litovsk. At one time he worked in the office of the religious department of the *Keren Kayemet* and edited the periodical *HaHod*.

When his father died, he succeeded him as rebbe but continued to serve as the spiritual leader of Yad Eliyahu, Tel Aviv. He also served on the Chief Rabbinate Council of Tel Aviv-Jaffa. While on his way to visit a sick hasid of Radomsk at the Tel HaShomer Hospital, he was killed in a road accident on 27 Av 1969, leaving five young children. He was buried on the Mount of Olives, and his 8-year-old son, Shmuel, recited the *Kaddish*. A *kollel* in Bene Berak was established in his memory.

The Progeny of Biala

Ger may have "its ten thousands and Belz its thousands," but the Rebbe of Biala ministered to a hand-picked few. Yet the followers of Biala have now the choice of four rebbes in the Holy Land, for all four sons of the late Rebbe became rebbes.

The greatest number of followers give their allegience to the youngest son, R. Bezalel Simha Menahem Benzion, who acts in the dual capacity of the Rabbi of Lugano, which has a Jewish population of eight hundred, out of which only fifty families are

---

1. Yehoshua Uziel Zilberg, *Malchut Bet David* (Bene Berak: privately printed, 1991).

hasidic, and as Rebbe of Biala in Jerusalem. He also acts as a *kashrut* supervisor of the Hotel Silberhorn in Grindelwald.

Born in Siedlice, Poland, in 1935, he was one of the eight hundred sixty-one children who had received permission from the Mandatory Authorities to enter Palestine (now known as the "Tehran Children's Transport"). He arrived there on 18 February 1943 and studied in the Yeshivah of Ponevezh under R. Yosef Kahaneman, who regarded him as one of his star students. In 1958, he married Beila Bracha (Betty) (d. 1996), the daughter of R. Avraham Moshe Babad, the Agudist leader and rabbi of the *Bet Hamidrash* in Sunderland. After his marriage, he continued his studies at the *Kollel* of Gateshead, England. They had seven children.

In June 1993, one of their sons, R. Avraham Moshe, married Perl Malka, the daughter of R. Shmuel Shmelke Halpert, a member of the Knesset. The Rebbe commutes between Lugano and Jerusalem, where he established a yeshivah and a publishing firm, *Machon Ginze Mahariz,* at Rehov Sorotskin 45 in Kiryat Unsdorf. His objectives are to publish and reprint the works of the Rebbes of Biala, as well as the discourses of the "Holy Jew" that are found scattered in many hasidic works. He also controls his father's *Bet Hamidrash* in Rehov Yosef ben Matityahu in the Geula District of Jerusalem. On 10 Nisan 1997, he remarried Mrs. Steinwurzel, the widowed daughter of the Rosh Yeshivah of Bobov, New York.

His elder brother, R. Yerahmiel Tzvi Yehuda, was born in Siedlice in 1921 and was brought up by his stepfather, R. Emanuel Weltfreid, in Lodz for a time and also in the Yeshivah *Hachme Lublin.* He was brought from Poland to London by Rabbi Dr. Solomon Schonfeld in 1945 and stayed with his uncle, the Biala Rebbe, and studied in the *Mesifta* Yeshivah, London. In 1954, he married Golda, the daughter of R. Moshe Aaron Galitsky, a jeweler in Lugano, and attended the Lugano Kollel. They have eight children. In 1968, they emigrated to Israel, and he continued his studies in Jerusalem in the kollel of *Haside Vizhnitz* under the guidance of R. Mordecai Shalom Steinmetz, while his wife carried on a successful children's wear shop in the Geula District.

He styles himself as the Rebbe of Przysucha-Biala. He has a small *Bet Hamidrash* in Jerusalem and with the help of R. Shalom Hayyim Porush has reprinted *Divre Bina* by his grandfather, R. Yitzhak Yaakov of Biala. One of his sons is the scholarly R. Simha Benzion Isaac, who published an erudite work, *Piske Teshuva* on *Mishna Berurah*, in 1991. This work has received the approval of R. Moshe Arye Freind, R. Shmuel Halevi Wozner, R. Shlomo Zalman Urbach, and his uncle R. Benzion.

Another son, R. Yaakov Shalom Elimelech, is the rabbi of the Skiernewice *Shtiebl* in Haifa. R. Mendel is the principal of the Yeshivah of Ruzhin in Bene Berak, and R. Baruch Leib married Mirel, the daughter of Yeshaya Lew, the head of the Satmar Community in London, and is the Rabbi of the Biala *Shtiebl* in London. The Rabbi's daughter Havah married the Rabbi of Spinka. His other children married into the families Kopicienice, Sasov, and Sternbuch.

In Rehov Admor MiBelz, Bene Berak, lived the third son of the late Rebbe, R. David Matityahu, who was born in Siedlice on the eve of Hanukah 1929. On the death of his father he was guided by his uncle R. Nathan David of·Parczev, who at that time lived in Siedlice. In his youth, he was dangerously ill and stayed in Warsaw with his uncle R. Meir Shlomo Yehuda of Miedzyrzecz. At the outbreak of World War Two, he stayed with another uncle, the Rebbe of Koidanov in Baranowicze, and then traveled with his parents to Siberia and Turkestan.

In January 1943, after immigration permits had been obtained from the Mandatory Authorities, he was among the children who sailed to Karachi, India (now Pakistan). From there, they went to Suez, and on 18 February 1943 they reached Palestine by train. In all, they were 1,230 in number, 369 adults and 861 children who became known as the "Tehran Children". He was then befriended by his uncle, R. Tzvi Kalish, the Rebbe of Bene Berak, and studied in the Yeshivah of Ponovezh, Bene Berak. He was subsequently ordained by R. Kalish. He married Tobe, the daughter of R. Shmuel Aaron Shadrovsky of Tel Aviv, formerly of Bialistok, and when she died in 1960, leaving him with two young children, he married the daughter of R. Yekutiel Yosef Berkowitz of Bene Berak and continued his studies in the Kollel of Vlozhin, together with the Rebbe of Nadvorna.

He had a *Bet Hamidrash, Nahalat Yehoshua,* in Bene Berak and was responsible for the founding of the Yeshivah *Or Kedoshim* in Rehov Safed 14. The foundation stone was laid in 1964, and the yeshivah was completed in 1967. It was under the guidance of R. Yisrael Kalmanowitz, the son of the principal of the Yeshivah of Mir in the United States. R. David traveled regularly to South America and the United States, Austria, and London, on behalf of the yeshivah. He was a tireless fundraiser who had inherited his mother's dynamism. He reprinted his grandfather's works *Divre Bina, Yishre Lev, Tiferet Avot, Tiferet Zaddikim,* and *Avodat Halev.* He was blessed with a melodious voice, and he was a very gifted *Baal Tefillah.*

On the death of his father in 1982, he became rebbe and named his *Bet Hamidrash,* in Bene Berak, *Nahlat Yehoshua.* He also had *shtieblech* in Rehov Yerushalayim in Bene Berak and one in Jerusalem at Ohele Yosef. He was in the habit of immersing himself in the ritual bath before the blowing of the *shofar* and before the kindling of the Hanukah lights and prior to the reading of the *Megillah.*

When he visited Safed in summer 1997, he said that that was his last visit there. During the Festival of Sukkot, he made frequent allusions to death, saying that he hoped that the traditional customs of Biala would be perpetuated. During the sixth circuit on *Simhat Torah,* he said, "Let me dance my last dance."

R. David died on 24 Tishri 1997, holding his grandfather's book, *Divre Binah,* in his hand and was buried on the Mount of Olives near his father. He is survived by his sons: R. Shmuel, R. Yaakov Menahem, R. Avraham Yerahmiel, R. Pinhas Yirmiyahu, and R. Aharon, and his daughter Havvah who is married to R. Yaakov Hager of Seret-Vizhnitz, Haifa, and another daughter, married to R. Yehuda Zeev Kornreich, the Rebbe of the Biala *Shtiebl* in Bene Berak. He was succeeded on 18 Ellul 1998 by his son, R. Yaakov Menachem.

The second youngest son, R. Yitzhak Yaakov, lives in Rehov Kahaneman, Bene Berak. Born on 15 Tevet 1927, in Siedlice, he came with his younger brother on the Tehran Children's Transport in 1943. He studied in the Yeshivah *Sefat Emet,* and when his parents settled in Tel Aviv, he continued his studies at the Ponovezh Yeshivah and at *Geone Vlozhin,* Tel Aviv. In 1950, he married Miriam Sheindel, the daughter of R. Avraham Abish Kaner, the Rebbe of Wojciechov in Haifa. He was ordained by Chief Rabbi Yitzhak Halevi Herzog and by his uncle R. Yosef Tzvi Kalish of Skiernewice. He lived for a time in Haifa before establishing himself in Bene Berak.

"A pillar of prayer," "a real Sabbath Jew": this is how R. Yisrael Alter of Ger and R. Hayyim Meir Hager of Vizhnitz described the Rebbe of Biala. In his *Bet Hamidrash* in Rehov Yosef ben Matityahu, R. Yehiel Yehoshua Rabinowicz carried on the traditions of Biala. He was the sixth direct descendant of R. Yaakov Yitzhak, the "Holy Jew" of Przysucha. His father, R. Yerahmiel Tzvi (1880–1906), was the son of R. Yitzhak Yaakov of Biala who followed the doctrines of Przysucha. Protestations of piety were discouraged. Action and service, charity and lovingkindness were encouraged as the true measure of a man's sincerity.

His gifted father, R. Yerahmiel Tzvi, excelled as reader for the congregation. Once, when he was ill, his anxious mother urged his father to dissuade him from officiating at the reader's desk, but his father refused to interfere. "The entire heavenly host waits to hear the prayers of my son. How dare I stop him?" R. Yerahmiel Tzvi also recorded all the discourses that his father delivered on Sabbaths and festivals. He was an exceptionally gifted artist, who designed a most elaborate and beautiful *Shevitti* (now displayed in the Biala *Bet Hamidrash* in Jerusalem). He married Havah, the daughter of R. Arye Leibish Epstein of Ozarov, in 1898.

On the death of his father, he declined to become rebbe, and only on 8 Iyar 1906, the day of the *Yahrzeit* of his ancestor R. Yerahmiel Tzvi did he become rebbe in Siedlice. Regrettably, he lived for barely six months after this. He died at age twenty-six on 7 Heshvan 1906, leaving five young children. Their mother suffered great privations but did not stint on money for tuition fees for her children. In 1926, she eventually married, after twenty years of widowhood, R. Immanuel Weltfreind, rebbe of Przedborz, who lived in Lodz. She died of typhus in the Warsaw Ghetto.

R. Yerahmiel Tzvi's eldest son was R. Nathan David (1899–1947), who later became the rebbe in London. His second son, R. Hayyim, died very young. His daughter Alta married R. Zeev Poker, a grandson of R. Yosef Ber Soloveitchik of Brest-Litovsk, and Perl married R. Alter Perlow, the rebbe of Koidanov, who lived in Baranowicze and died in 1942. She later became famous in the Vilna Ghetto as the founder of a religious institute for women. From the valiant Perl, the women of the ghetto drew comfort and strength in those black days.[2]

The younger son, R. Yehiel Yehoshua, was born on 5 Shevat 1900 and was named after his great-grandfathers, R. Yehiel of Ozarov and R. Yehoshua of Ostrova. After the premature death of his father, he was brought up first by his grandfather, R. Arye Leibish of Ozarov, and when he died on 7 Nisan 1918, Yehiel Yehoshua lived with his uncles, first with R. Meir Shlomo Yehuda of Miedzyrezc and later with R. Aaron Menahem Mendal Guterman (1860–1934), the Rebbe of Radzymin, who was married to Matele, the daughter of R. Yaakov Yitzhak of Biala. Yehiel Yehoshua was welcome there, for his aunt had no children. The Rebbe had a mercurial temperament, and he was anxious to have an heir. "I can see my children, as I can see my fingers," he would say. In 1922, after forty-six years of childless marriage, at the age of sixty-two, he coerced his wife into granting him a divorce. This became a *cause célèbre* in Poland. He remarried in 1924 but died without issue twelve years later.

R. Yehiel Yehoshua married Beila Hannah Pesha (d. 9 Sivan 1992), the daughter of R. Hayyim Eliezer Hakohen Barenholz of Wlodova, who was a very wealthy entrepreneur. He owned large forests, a flour mill, an oil refinery, and an electricity generating plant. A hasid of R. Nathan David of Parczev, he subsidized community charities. R. Yehiel Yehoshua spent the first six years of

---

2. Menashe Unger, *Sefer Kedoshim* (New York: *Shulsinger*, 1967); p. 358.

his marriage there and in 1924 returned in Siedlice, his late father's home town, and became known as the Rebbe of Siedlice.

In 1940, during the Ten Days of Penitence, he and his family were arrested by the Russians, but, due to the efforts of his wife, managed to escape. For three days, they hid in the loft of the home of one of his friends. He fasted for that period, refusing to take bread because he had no water to wash his hands. Eventually, he and his family found refuge with his brother-in-law R. Alter Perlow in Baranowicze for ten months.

From there, he and his family were taken to Uzbekistan, Siberia, and then to Tashkent in 1941. Even in the most perilous situations, he would not modify his religious practices. In the absence of a *mikveh* (ritual bath), he would break the ice of a pond or stream with an axe and immerse himself in the icy waters. Only the resourcefulness, superhuman energy, and self-sacrifice of his formidable wife enabled the family to survive. During World War Two, all his children found safety in Israel.

After the war, the Rabbi and his wife returned to Poland but then decided to leave for Paris. With the help of Rabbi Dr. Solomon Schonfeld, who directed Chief Rabbi Hertz's Emergency Council in London, they reached the Holy Land, arriving in Tel Aviv on *Lag B'omer* in 1947. For eight years he lived in Rehov Zevulun and on 15 Tammuz 1955 moved to Rehov Yosef ben Matityahu in Jerusalem. He was no writer of books but wrote lengthy prefaces to the reprinted works of his ancestors. These prefaces were later collected in a book, *Helkat Yehoshua.*[3] He supported the work of the Aguda and *Hinuch Atzmai* and was a member of the *Moetzet Gedole HaTorah.*

He was one of the signatories of the protest proclamation against abortion and warmly supported *Kupat Rabbi Meir Baal Hanes.* He elicited financial aid for the *Keren Shemitta* to enable religious kibbutzim to keep *Shemitah* every seventh year, when the land must be left fallow and when it is forbidden to trade in the produce. He endorsed the appeal for the religious rehabilita-

---

3. Meir Yeheskel Weiner, *Helkat Yehoshua* (published privately in Jerusalem, 1983).

tion of Russian immigrants and urged his followers to vote for
the United Religious Front of the Aguda and the Poale Aguda.
He strongly opposed compulsory military service for women. He
attended the *Kenesiyah Gedolah* in January 1984.

The ardor of this frail sage was legendary and earned him the
title "servant of the Lord." He maintained the most exacting standards of piety. With every ounce of his strength he prayed, sang,
and delivered his discourses. He was "no still small voice" but fire
and thunder. On the Sabbath he acted as *Baal Keriya* (reader of
the Law). Every Thursday, young people were encouraged to visit
him, and during the summer months he studied the *Ethics of the
Fathers* with them. Like R. Yaakov Arye of Radzymin he had a
reputation as a "wonder worker." There are not many Biala
hasidim in the Holy Land, but men and women from all hasidic
denominations visited him for guidance. His friend and neighbor
R. Yisrael Alter of Ger occasionally referred *hasidim* to him.[4]

He had a number of unusual liturgical customs, such as reciting *Alenu* (It is our duty to praise) after the *Shaharit* service on
the Sabbath, in addition to repeating it after the *Musaf* (the additional service), as is universally customary. He urged his follows
to study the Talmud on Sabbath mornings prior to the service.
He followed the *Hagbahah* custom of the Sephardim, who open
the Torah Scroll before the reading of the Law in the synagogue
to enable the congregation to see the Torah script and thus testify that "this is the Law which Moses placed before the Children
of Israel." After the Sabbath service he recited five chapters of the
Psalms.

A very small *kollel* was attached to his *Bet Hamidrash*, and a
Shtiebl of Biala was established in Bene Berak. It is unfortunate
that the establishment of a dissenting *shtiebl* near his home in
Jerusalem caused this man of peace unnecessary grief. In Elul 1977,
he suffered a stroke that left him partially paralyzed, though this
did not deter him from maintaining his way of life. He died on
21 Shevat 1982 and was buried on the Mount of Olives in the

---

4. Meir Yeheskel Weiner, *HaRav HaKadosh MiBiala* (privately
printed, Jerusalem, 1982).

Polish section. He was survived by his wife, his four sons, and one daughter, Gila (1919–1996) whose husband, the industrialist Hayyim Meir Yehiel Gothelf of Tel Aviv, had lost all his family in the Holocaust and who is a real Maecenas to the Biala institutions.

Torah Thoughts

Abraham was told "Get out of your country, from your kindred, and from your father's house, for a country which I shall show you" (Genesis 12:1). Rashi, commenting on the verse, states: "For your own benefit and for your own good." This does not imply that Abraham was asked to renounce the pleasures of the world and to practice the life of a Nazarite. On the contrary, he was told to infuse saintliness into all his worldly actions (R. David of Talna).

"You shall blot out the remembrance of Amalek under the heavens" (Deuteronomy 25:19). Everything belonging to the Amalekites had to be destroyed. Amalek created doubt in the existence of God. The Hebrew word for "Amalek" is equivalent numerically to the Hebrew word for "doubt," for the children of Israel doubted the existence of God, saying, "Is the Lord among us or not?" (Exodus 17:7). Can He help us in our need? (*idem*).

"He met you by the way" (Deuteronomy 25:18). The Hebrew word for "met you" can also be translated as to "be cold." If the atmosphere is polluted, one cannot study the Torah properly (R. Abraham of Sochaczev).

"And they encamped before the mountain" (Exodus 19:2) Rashi, commenting on the verse, states that the Israelites were united as one, as one man with one voice. Only if the Jews are united are they invincible (*idem*).

It is a great thing for a Jew to acquire a habitation in the Land of Israel, especially if he can make a living there. And even if he then returns to the diaspora, it is regarded as if he were living in the Holy Land (Shem Mishmuel).

"And the priest will go outside the camp" (Leviticus 14:3). Leprosy was a direct punishment for slander and excessive pride.

The leper was excluded from the camp during the period of his confirmed leprosy, and assistance of the priest was of no avail unless the leper himself was determined to repent. The cure was entirely in the hands of the leper and in the hands of the priest (*ibid*).

"And Moses said: 'We will go with our young and with our old, with our sons and with our daughters, with our flocks and with our herds'" (Exodus 10:9). No one was to be excluded from celebrating a feast to the Lord. Without the active participation of the children, no joy can be complete (*idem*).

"When Jacob sent messengers" (Genesis 32:3). Rashi, quoting the *Midrash* (*Genesis Rabba* 75), states that they were real angels. Every time a man performs a *mitzvah*, he creates an angel in the heavenly spheres. If, however, the *mitzvah* is performed perfunctorily, without any real *kavanah*—without genuine intention—the newly created angel is defective and does not survive. All the *mitzvot* that Jacob performed were perfect and wholehearted, and all his angels survived. Hence, the *Midrash* says, "real angels, living entities, angels who survive" (*Divre Binah*).

"And these are the generations of Isaac" (Genesis 25:19). Rashi, commenting on the verse, says: Because the cynics of the time said, "See how many years Sarah lived with Abraham without becoming with child. Surely she was impregnated by Abimelech. What did the Almighty do? He made Isaac strongly resemble Abraham, so that everybody could see that Abraham was Isaac's father. And that is why the Torah states that 'Isaac was the son of Abraham.'" Why, however, should the Almighty wish to refute the cynics? The Almighty is more concerned with the welfare of the righteous than He is for Himself. He wished by all means to refute the slanderers and thereby prevent any embarrassment to Abraham (*idem*).

"This is the book of the generations of Adam" (Genesis 5:1). The Hebrew word *sefer*—book—does not always mean a volume. In Aramaic and talmudic idiom it also means a "boundary" (*Yevamot* 48b). Soldiers are given the task to guard the borders against intrusion. So a man has the duty to guard and preserve the "image of God" in which he was created (*idem*).

"Speak to the priests, the sons of Aaron and say to them" (Leviticus 21:1). The repetition of the words "say unto them"—as Rashi points out—is to warn the adults about the duty they have toward their children. It was the function and the privilege of the righteous to guide and enlighten the young. Just as an experienced physician devotes his energies to curing the sick, so it is the duty of the righteous to be concerned with the welfare of the young (ibid.).

"Let him sell it to me in your presence at its full price for a burial site" (Genesis 23:9). Generally, people are not satisfied with what they possess. "No one who loves money," says the book of Ecclesiastes (5:9), "ever has enough." Abraham, however, was completely different. He was always content with what the Almighty gave him. "For the full price" implies that he was fully contented. (*idem*).

"And the Cherubim their wings spread upwards, protecting the Ark with their wings, facing each other" (Exodus 37:9). The winged creatures are traditionally depicted as children, pointing out that the Almighty loves Israel as a father loves his children. The only pre-condition for creating harmony and concord is that "their faces face one another," that the family be united, and that there is no room for friction (*idem*).

"You stand this day before the Lord your God" (Deuteronomy 29:9). "This day" refers to the New Year when we face the Heavenly Judge. It is then vital to consider the last word of the *Sidra Ki Tavo* (Deuteronomy 29:8): "That you may make all that ye do to prosper." By specifying your pleas, you will be able to face the Almighty (R. Benzion Rabinowicz of Biala).

"Happy is the people that knows the joyful shout" (Psalms 89:16). It is not enough to know "the joyful shout," that is, to blow the *shofar*, but rather, it is the knowledge that we are able to plead before the Almighty that is joyful (Rabbi D. M. Rabinowicz).

9

From Boston to Rahmastrivka

For the last two hundred years of Hasidism, the hasidic rebbes have been known by the names of the towns or villages of Eastern Europe where they have lived. R. Horowitz is the first hasidic rebbe who is known as the Rebbe of Boston, a city in Massachusetts, U.S.A.

The flourishing Boston institutions, guided by R. Levi Yitzhak Horowitz, who commutes between Jerusalem and Boston, are to be found in Har Nof, Jerusalem. He spends six months in each locale. In his absence, the *Mosdot* are guided by his son R. Meir Alter in Jerusalem and by R. Naftali Yehuda in Boston. The dual loyalties are no problem for the Rebbe. He is an active member of the Executive of the American Aguda, as well as a member of the *Moetzet Gedole HaTorah* and fully participates in the problems and the life of the *Yishuv*. In October 1998 he opposed the Wye Agreement between Israel and the PLO Authority. "Without regard to the safety of hundreds of thousands of Jews whose lives are now put in danger, yet another 'peace agreement' has been signed by those who seek to destroy us. . . . The Government has unconditionally abandoned its ideological commitment to the territorial integrity of the totality of the Land of Eretz Yisrael."

In Jerusalem, he established a thriving center *Givat Pinhas*: two Talmud Torah centers, and three *kollelim*, specially designed for *Baale Teshuvah*, where young people formerly estranged and ignorant of Jewish observances wish to return to the Orthodox way of life. Special tuition is organized for such "returnees." They are taught that the Bible is infallible, that the Torah Laws are binding to all eternity, and not to question the authority of ancient beliefs and traditions. In Bene Berak, too, there is a Boston Talmud Torah in Rehov Perl 3.

In 1998 another *Kehillah* was established in Beitha Elit, just outside Jerusalem. It is led by R. Moshe Shimon Horowitz, the eldest grandson of the Rebbe.

The founder of the Boston dynasty was R. Pinhas David Halevi Horowitz, a direct descendant of R. Shmuel (Shmelke) Horowitz (1726–1778), who became Rabbi of Nikolsburg, Moravia, an appointment confirmed by the Empress Maria Theresa. He was noted for his signal religious devotions. To guard against oversleeping, he would endeavor to choose the most uncomfortable sleeping position. He often sat upright with his head resting on his arms, a lighted candle in his hand. When it burned low, the heat of the flame would wake him, and he would instantly resume his studies. His prayers were often impassioned improvizations.

"Alas, Lord of the Universe," he exclaimed, "on New Year's Day all the people cry out to you. But what of their clamor! They think only of their own needs, and do not lament the Exile of your Glory." He was one of the great pioneers of Hasidism in the eighteenth century.

R. Pinhas David, a relative of R. Menahem Mendel Biderman of Lelov, was born in Jerusalem in Elul 1886 and studied in Tiberias under R. Moshe Kliers and R. Mordecai Slonimer. When his father, R. Shlomo, died prematurely at the age of thirty-six, his widowed mother moved to Jerusalem, where his education was guided by R. Shmuel Salant.

He married Rebecca, the daughter of R. Aaron, the rebbe of Plaszov, Galicia, who lived in Safed. When Rebecca died in childbirth in 1904, he remarried Sara Sosha, the daughter of R. Yehiel Michael Brandwein of Stettin. Declining to become a rebbe, he was engaged in building projects, supervising the extensions of the one-floor houses in Mea Shearim. To safeguard the funds of the *Kollel* of Galicia, he traveled to Eastern Europe and took advantage of the opportunity to visit many hasidic rebbes. As an Austrian citizen, R. Pinhas David was not only liable for military service but, at the outbreak of World War One, was debarred from returning to the Holy Land. He found refuge in New York, where he arrived in Sivan 1915 and became the rabbi of the hasidic community *Reem HaHuvim* in the Brownsville section of New York.

He later moved to Boston, where he established a small yeshivah and organized afternoon Hebrew classes for boys who attended secular schools all day. He was intensively involved in the strengthening of the foundations of Torah life, particularly in the area of *glatt kosher* meat provision (literally, "smooth kosher," which indicates that the meat is kosher beyond any shadow of doubt). Besides his efforts in the development of Torah institutions, he worked to improve the observance of the Sabbath and *taharat hamishpaha* (family purity).

He visited the Holy Land in 1925 and in 1928 and was very anxious to settle there. "My right leg," he stated, "is already in Jerusalem." He relocated to New York in 1940 and lived in Bedford Avenue, Williamsburg. He died on 7 Kislev 1942. Owing to war conditions, his remains were reinterred on the Mount of Olives three-and-a-half years later.

He was survived by two sons. R. Moshe studied in the yeshivah of *Torah V'Daat* under R. Shragai Feivish Mendelowitz. In 1932, he married Leah Freidel, the daughter of R. Avraham of Zydaczov. Her stepfather was R. Meir Leifer (d. 1941), the Rebbe of Nadvorna, who lived in Cleveland and later in New York. R. Moshe succeeded his father as Bostoner Rebbe in New York. His other son, R. Levi Yitzhak, was born in Boston on 27 Sivan 1921. From 1934 to 1936, he studied in Israel in *Torah V'Yirah* Yeshivah in Mea Shearim, and on his return to the United States he resumed his studies at the *Torah V'Daat* Yeshivah and was ordained by R. Shlomo Heiman. He married Raichel, the daughter of R. Naftali Unger of Neimark, a descendant of R. Yisrael Hofstein, the Maggid of Kozienice. On her mother's side, she was the grand-daughter of R. Alter Zeev of Strzyzov.

R. Levi Yitzhak has five children: two daughters and three sons. His elder son, R. Pinhas David, born in 1944, studied in the Lakewood Yeshivah, New York, and from 1962 in Ponovezh, Bene Berak. He married Sara Beila, the daughter of R. Greenwald of Huszt. R. Levi Yitzhak became a rabbi in Boston in 1944 and settled in Dorchester. Seventeen years later he moved to Brooklyne Beacon. The Rebbe has a mastery of English as well as of Yiddish and is able to attract educated youth, students, and academics. He organizes "Sabbath programs" (*Shabbatonim*), a part-time yeshivah, and *Irgun Rofeh*, a medical liaison counseling service, which provides kosher meals for hospital patients, transportation, and, above all, moral support.

There is ample scope for him in Boston, which has a Jewish population of over two hundred thousand and is the home of temples of learning, such as the Boston University, Harvard, Brandeis in Waltham, North-Eastern, Wellesley Universities, and the Hebrew Teachers College. It is, moreover, noteworthy as a great medical center. The *Bet Yisrael* hospital, the teaching hospital of the Harvard Medical School, the Massachusetts General Hospital and the Allerton Hospital are world famous. He was able to attract students who were completely estranged from Judaism to his new center, *Bet Pinhas*, and was able to gain many "converts" in a town that has a strong Reform movement and that R. Herman Rubinowitch, of *Mishkan Tefilah*, has made a stronghold of Conservative Judaism. It is not surprising that he is known as the "Rabbi of the Colleges." [1]

---

1. Shalom Meir Wallach, *Shoshelet Boston* (Jerusalem: Har Nof, 1994); Raichel Horowitz, *The Bostoner Rebbetzin Remembers* (New York: *Mesorah Publications*, 1996).

The Rebbe of Rahmastrivka

In Rehov Sefat Emet, Jerusalem, lives R. Yisrael Mordecai Twersky, the rabbi of Rahmastrivka, who succeeded his father on 20 Kislev 1981. He was born on 7 Sivan 1929, and on 27 Av 1951, he married Sara Griwa, the daughter of R. Alexander Sender Uri. He is the spiritual guide of the Yeshivah *Meor Enayim*, "the Light of the Eyes," named after the classical work on the Pentateuch that was published by its author, R. Menahem Nahum of Chernobyl (d. 11 Heshvan 1791) in Slavuta in 1798.[2]

He was a disciple of the Besht who practiced self-denial to an almost unhasidic degree. He lived a life of self-deprivation, and his estate consisted of innumerable acts of charity. Uncompromising and often uncommunicative, this highly individualistic rebbe pursued his own course independently. The Hebrew word for repentance, *teshuvah*, was, according to his interpretation, a mnemonic for "studying, fasting, sackcloth, ashes, weeping, and mourning." The Sabbath was the center of his existence. "Honor the Sabbath as fully as you can within your means. Do so with food and drink. The Hebrew letters spelling out Sabbath are those of *teshuvah* (repentance) to indicate that he who keeps the Sabbath, even if he is an idolater, as the generation of Enoch, will be forgiven."[3] He was one of the earliest disseminators and pioneers of Hasidism in the Ukraine and was the founder of a cluster of hasidic dynasties that still flourish in the United States and Israel today.

R. Nahum's son R. Mordecai (1770–1837) took charge of the funds that were collected for the Holy Land. Their surname "Twersky" was adopted by their descendants from Chernobyl and means, in Russian, "the citizen of Tiberias." He had eight children who all became rebbes.

---

2. Arthur Green, *Menahem Nahum of Chernobyl* (New York: Paulist Press, 1982). p. 24.

3. *Sabbath* 118b.

His eldest son, R. Aaron, who died in 1872, became the head of the dynasty and president of the *Kollel* of the Ukraine. He resented the fact that the *Halukah* was supervised by R. Avraham Yaakov of Sadagora. His brother R. Yaakov Yisrael of Hornistopol openly rebelled against R. Aaron and sent out letters requesting that all money should be sent directly to him. In vain, did the other brothers, R. Yitzhak of Sqvira and R. Yohanan of Rahmastrivka, appeal to his sense of family loyalty. R. Yaakov Yisrael was unmoved. "I have found a *mitzvah* through which I could unite the whole of Israel," he reasoned. "Now they wish to rob me of this precious thing on which my spiritual welfare depends." However, when he realized that the *hasidim* were not responding, he revoked his claim. "I am putting the sword back in its scabbard," he conceded.

In the middle of the nineteenth century, a number of Chernobyl *hasidim* settled in the Holy Land, where they established a synagogue in 1875. R. Yitzhak Friedman (1805–1890) of Bohush, grandson of R. Yisrael of Ruzhin, gave limited support to the *Hovevei Ziyyon* (Lovers of Zion Society), whose aim it was to settle in the Holy Land and to use Hebrew as a living language. Dr. Karpel Lippe (1830–1913) and Samuel Pineles (1848–1928) were the guiding spirits of the society in Romania. In 1880, the rebbe was invited by the communal leaders of Galati to participate in a conference at Iasi, but his reply was noncommittal, because he felt that the proposed gathering might prejudice the struggle for Jewish civil rights, serving as a pretext for the Russian government to renege its pledges.

In Elul 1882, when the Rabbi of Bohush passed through Czernowitz, a delegation that included the historian Aaron Marcus visited him and urged him to give moral support to the movement. The Rabbi pointed out the enormous difficulties that they would have to overcome, but the *Lovers of Zion* were not discouraged. In Iyar 1887, they wrote to the Rabbi: "What can we expect from the mass exodus to America except desecration of the Sabbath and the Festivals? The Land of Israel is the only place where we can live in accordance with the Torah, and where we can rear our children in the traditional Jewish way." They assured him that they had no desire to interfere with the *Halukah*. "We want to reawaken in the Jewish heart a great love for the Holy Land, and to gather under our banner as many adherents as possible."

On 7 Iyar Avraham Mordecai Segal, the Rebbe's *Gabbai* wrote that the Rabbi was willing to encourage his followers to purchase *etrogim* (citron, one of the Four Species used during the Festival of Tabernacles) from the Holy Land. This concession did not satisfy the *Lovers of Zion*. Five days later, they wrote back, bluntly pointing out that *etrogim* by themselves would not solve any problems and that those who had settled in the Holy Land were faithful to the Covenant. And even of those Jews who had "thrown off the yoke of the Torah" in Europe, many had returned to the fold in the Holy Land.

In 1887, R. Yitzhak made it clear that he did not oppose agricultural settlements in the Holy Land. However, he felt that it was wrong to raise false hopes among Romanian Jewry since mass immigration to the Holy Land was not feasible in view of the political conditions at that time. He maintained that the best policy was gradual settlement and slow integration. He urged them to consult experts. Beril Soref, one of the rabbi's followers, was sent to explore the possibility of settling fifty Romanian Jewish families in the Holy Land.

The present Rebbe, the son of R. Yohanan, lived through the Bolshevik period. Although anti-Semitism was proscribed in Soviet Russia, there was no room for the Jewish religion. Lenin alleged that the Jews no longer constituted a people, since it was inconceivable that a people should exist without either a territory of their own or a common language.[4] The expropriation and the closing of synagogues, "in response to the demand of the masses," converted places of worship into cultural centers. The six-day week that was then introduced made Sabbath observance almost impossible. Anyone refusing to work on the Sabbath was accused of

---

4. Benjamin Pinkus, *The Jews of the Soviet Union* (Cambridge: Cambridge University Press, 1989), pp. 50 and 101.

"clericalism," an accusation that often led to arrest and trial. The Rebbe was persecuted by the Jewish section of the Communist Party, which regarded him as a "counter-revolutionary." He reached the Holy Land in 1926.

R. Mordecai (Mottel), the son of R. Yohanan, came to the Holy Land twenty years earlier. He was a skilled artisan in gold and copper, and he was involved in the Jerusalem disturbances of 1921. These were provoked by the Mufti of Jerusalem, Hajj Amin al Husseini. The military authorities gave the Arabs a free hand while arresting Jewish defenders. The third son of R. Mordecai, R. Menahem Nahum (1870–1936), the son-in-law of R. Zeev Urbach, succeeded him. Six years prior to his death, he appointed his two sons to succeed him, R. Avraham Dov (1865–1945), who was known for his knowledge of Jewish philosophy, and R. David (1872–1951), the son-in-law of R. Avraham Joshua Heschel of Sqvira. This unique dual rabbinate was blessed by harmony.

The Rebbe supervises the Yeshivah *Meor Enaim*, which was established by his father in 1903. Originally, only a few young men studied in his father's *shtiebl*. In 1976, the *yeshivah* moved to a spacious building, at 34 Rehov David Yelin, and has ninety students under the spiritual guidance of R. Menahem Nahum Twersky. The building also accommodates a *kollel* with twenty-eight students. Encouraged by the success of the yeshivah, the Rabbi established a Torah center in Rehov Mirsky, Jerusalem, in 1989. In order to raise funds, he visited London in December 1996.

Torah Thoughts

"After the Lord your God shall you walk" (Deuteronomy 13:5). R. Nahum of Chernobyl used to welcome and befriend every Jew. He treated an ordinary Jew with the same cordiality that he would show toward a *Zaddik* and justified his conduct by quoting the verse in Deuteronomy that one has to follow the ways of the Lord. In the words of the Talmud, "Is it possible for any human being to imitate the ways of the Lord? which means that we should follow God's attributes. As He clothes the naked, so should you clothe the naked. As He visits the sick, so should you also visit the sick. As He buries the dead, so should you bury the dead" (*Sota* 14a). Similarly, in our liturgy for the High Holy Days, we read that the Almighty "does good to the just as well as to the evil." For I firmly believe in the words of the Prophet Isaiah (60:21) that "your people, all of them righteous, will possess the country forever" (R. Nahum of Chernobyl).

"And Naftali," said Moses in his farewell address: "Oh, Naftali, satisfied with favor" (Deuteronomy 33:23). "Who is rich?" asked Ben Zoma. "He who is happy with his lot" (*Avot* 4:1). Moses blessed the tribe of Naftali that they should be satisfied with their portion (*idem*).

R. Nahum of Chernobyl spent his life collecting money for the "redemption of captives." One day he was temporarily in prison, and an old man whom he had never seen before knocked on his cell and said to him: "Do not regard your imprisonment as an intolerable burden or as a punishment. You are being imprisoned so that you should personally experience the fate of prisoners, and what they are going through. To alleviate their lot is just as important a *mitzvah* as the redemption of captives, a *mitzvah* to which you devote your life" (*idem*).

Why do the *hasidim* present "petitions" to the rebbe and ask him to pray that they should earn their "daily bread"? Tradition describes the tribes of Issachar and Zevulun as partners. Zevulun was engaged in commerce, enabling the tribe of Issachar to devote its time to study. Hence, Jacob in his farewell blessings gives precedence to Zevulun over Issachar. If Zevulun is unsuccessful in their business ventures, he would blame Issachar for not devoting his entire energies to study and prayer. Giving the rebbe a *Qvittel* (petition), is a gentle reminder to him that he, too, has to concentrate his energies on study and prayer (R. Yohanan of Rachmanstrivka).

10

A Lithuanian and Romanian Legacy

Stolin-Karlin

The Rebbe of the Stolin and Karlin *hasidim* is R. Baruch Meir
Halevi Shochet, who was born in New York in 1955. His mother,
Feiga, was the only daughter of R. Yohanan. She married Ezra
Shochet, and her son was one-year-old when his grandfather died.
In March 1975, he married his first cousin Rebecca Shochet and
officially became the Rebbe of Karlin and Stolin. The marriage
ended in divorce in 1977. One year later, he got married again, to
Hayyah Miriam Steinwurzel, the daughter of R. Moshe David, the
principal of the Bobov Yeshivah. The Rebbe has one son, David
Yehoshua, from his first marriage and ten children from the second. He has a clear mind, a sense of organization, and a decisive
personality. Despite his checkered matrimonial life, he is a rebbe
with a mission. His efforts and tenacity are not without effect.

The roll of students in the Central Institutions of Karlin and
Stolin, *Bet Aharon V'Yisrael*, is more than two thousand. It em-

braces a rabbinical college, seven *kollelim*, a yeshivah high school, a *Yeshivah Ketanah*, elementary school, school for girls, teachers' seminary, kindergartens, dormitories, a fund to assist the needy, a society for visiting the sick, a kitchen that provides nearly one thousand meals daily, evening classes, and a hostel for Russian immigrants. There are six places of worship in Jerusalem, one in Betar Elat and another in Givat Zeev. The total budget is over fifteen million Israeli shekels per annum.

The father of the dynasty was R. Aaron, who died at the age of thirty-six in 1772 and was known as "R. Aaron the Great." He founded Hasidism in Lithuania, the stronghold of the *Mitnaggedim*. A great innovator and an ascetic, he practiced ritual immersions and fostered humility, self-effacement, and the avoidance of dissension. Like his namesake Aaron the High Priest, "he loved peace, pursued peace, loved his fellow men, and brought them near to the Torah."[1] He advised every one of his followers to shut himself up in solitude in a special room for one day of each week and to spend the time in fasting, repentance, and the study of the Torah. His Sabbath melody *Yah Echsof Noam Shabbos* ("Lord, I yearn for the Sabbath delight") is still the favorite melody in the hasidic courts of Novominsk, Koidanov, Kobrin, and Slonim. His elder son, R. Yaakov, and his family, as well as his son-in-law R. Avraham Hasid, settled in the Holy Land.

His son R. Asher Perlow (1765–1822) made his home in Stolin, hence his followers became known as the Karlin and Stolin *hasidim*. A group of Karlin *hasidim* settled in the Holy Land, where they established a *shtiebl* in Tiberias, in the very house used by R. Menahem Mendel of Vitebsk at the end of the eighteenth century. The building was renovated several times and later became known as *Mesifta De'Rabbi Yohanan*. The rebbes of Karlin regularly appealed to the public, especially to their *hasidim*, to support Jewish settlements in the Holy Land. During the second half of the nineteenth century, there were small groups of Karlin *hasidim* living in Safed and Jerusalem. There was also a *kollel* that was guided by R. Moshe Dov, the son of R. Aaron, a brother of

---

1. *Avot* 1:12.

R. Aaron Perlow of Stolin. Later, it was guided by R. Mordecai Sheftel Wahrhaftig.

R. Asher II, who was known as "the young rabbi," died, having been rabbi for only one year, during a plague in Drohobycz on 17 Sivan 1872. His only son, Yisrael, born on 10 Kislev 1868, was four years old. The story of *HaYenuka MiStolin* ("the child rebbe of Stolin") was unusual in the history of hasidic masters. *Hasidim* traveled long distances to the town of Stolin, in the province of Pinsk, Byelorussia, to see and admire this prodigy, almost worshiping him as he grew from boyhood to manhood. People sought his blessing and his advice, clothing his childlike utterances with profound meanings. At his *Bar Mitzvah* in 1881, he officially took over the leadership of the *hasidim*.

As an adult, the *Yenuka* more than fulfilled the hopes and aspirations of his youth. He became a father to his followers, a wise and erudite counselor and a tower of strength to the community in an age fraught with physical peril and economic distress. The Rebbe used to send special emissaries to collect funds for the Karlin *Kollel* in the Holy Land, and all emissaries from the Holy Land found a welcome in his house. With his knowledge of Russian and German, he was able to intercede with governmental authorities on behalf of the community and individual members. He conducted the *Melaveh Malkah* with musical accompaniment. He and his three sons formed a quartet and performed pieces of liturgical music. He financed many families, enabling them to make their home in Palestine.

He died in Bad Homburg at the age of fifty-two, on the second day of *Rosh Hashanah* 1921, and was buried in Frankfurt-on-Main. He was survived by four sons and two daughters. His fourth son, R. Moshe, who perished in the Holocaust, twice visited the Holy Land in 1933 and 1937 and established a *shtiebl* in Tel Aviv. Through his contact with members of the Jewish Agency, a number of hasidic families were able to settle there. R. Yisrael's successor and son R. Avraham Elimelech visited the Holy Land twice between 1922 and 1939 and kept up a regular correspondence with his followers. He was killed by the Ukrainians in the Pinsk Ghetto on 14 Heshvan 1943.

The youngest son of the *Yenuka*, R. Yohanan, rabbi in Lutsk in Volhynia, his wife, and two daughters joined the partisans, with whom they spent one year. They were later deported to Siberia, where his wife and elder daughter died. After the liberation, the Rebbe and his surviving daughter, Feigele, returned to Poland and, after staying in the Feldafing Displaced Persons Camp in Germany, finally reached the Holy Land in 1946. He first lived in Haifa for a short time. He then moved to New York in 1948, where he established a yeshivah, *Bet Yisrael*, and published *Bet Aharon Ve'Yisrael*, a liturgical compendium of the rites and customs of Karlin.[2] He revisited Israel for *Rosh Hashanah* 1955 and died on 21 Kislev 1956, at the age of fifty-one, shortly after his return to New York. His remains were interred in Tiberias on 18 Adar II. The only survivor of the dynasty was his grandson Baruch Meir, who was born in the United States in 1955, one year prior to the Rebbe's death.

Orphaned of their mentor, many *hasidim* of Karlin persuaded R. Moshe Mordecai Biderman, the Rebbe of Lelov, to become their leader and assume the title of "Rebbe of the Lelov and Karlin *hasidim*," which he did on 15 Av 1962. They declared: "With God's help, and on behalf of the Karlin *hasidim* in the Holy City of Jerusalem and all the cities of our Holy Land and the Diaspora, we hereby undertake to regard you as our Master, Teacher, and Rebbe—our divinely appointed leader. We trust that you will guide the Holy Congregation in the way of the Holy Forefathers of the Karlin-Stolin dynasty. We pray to Him that dwells on high, that we may all be granted to advance, together with our Rebbe, to meet our righteous Messiah."[3]

A number of *hasidim* who lived in the old *Yishuv* of Jerusalem, in Haifa, Tel Aviv, and the United States, and the members of the *Bet Aharon* Yeshivah, however, dissociated themselves from this arrangement. Instead, they pledged their allegiance to the second *Yenuka* and declared themselves willing to wait for Baruch

2. New York, 1952.
3. Wolf Zeev Rabinowitsch, op. cit, pp. 229–30.

Meir Halevi Shochet to grow up in years, in wisdom, and in scholarship, so as to become the twentieth-century counterpart of the *Yenuka* of Stolin. The present rebbe, by his energetic revival of Karlin-Stolin institutions in Israel and the United States and efforts for Jewish revival in the former Soviet Union, has more than justified the confidence of his followers.

Boyan—A Scion of Royalty

Boyan, a town near, Czernowitz, became a hasidic center with a grandiose court. The founder of the dynasty, R. Yitzhak Friedman (1850–1917), was the president of the *Kollel* of Vohynia, covering the region of Podolia, Kiev, and Kherson. He was known among the *hasidim* as *Pahad Yitzhak* ("the fear of Yitzhak"), due to his great reverence and fear of the Almighty.

He was a descendant of R. Yisrael Friedman of Ruzhin (1797–1851), whose six sons established hasidic dynasties in different towns, each attracting large followings and adding new luster, new richness, and new depth to the hasidic constellation. For more than 150 years, Ruzhin and Sadagora were focal centers—cities of refuge for *hasidim* in Eastern Europe. These rebbes were virtually the exilarchs of Hasidism. They dressed elegantly, their residences were palatial, their coaches were drawn by four horses, they employed a large retinue of servants as was befitting descendants of the House of David, from which they claimed descent.

The Ruzhin dynasty had close associations with Jerusalem, especially with the synagogue *Tiferet Yisrael* or *Bet HaKnesset Nisan Bak*, established with the help of the Rebbe of Ruzhin who wanted to settle in the Holy Land. He became a Turkish citizen, and his passport was stamped "Native of Jerusalem." "There will come a time when nations will drive us out of their lands," he predicted. "How strange that after such a long-drawn-out exile the redemption should take place under such humiliating circumstances."

One hundred years before the Balfour Declaration, the Rabbi prophesied: "As in the time of Ezra, a government will arise which will permit the Jews to return to the land of their fathers. The nations will realize that despite all persecutions and massacres, the only way to get rid of us will be to send us to the Land of Israel."

Like Maimonides and Nahmanides, R. Yisroel believed that the Redemption would take a natural course and would be neither miraculous nor supernatural. He realized that only mass *Aliyah* could transform the country. "If I alone settle in the Holy Land, they will ask me 'why did you not bring your followers with you?' What answer can I give to such a question?" He maintained that the deliverance of Israel will take place even before Israel's repentance. He regarded R. Menahem Mendel of Vitebsk and R. Avraham of Kalisk as its trailblazers.

One of his *hasidim*, Yisrael Bak (1797–1874), became a pioneer in Hebrew printing in the Holy Land. After printing twenty-six books in Berdichev, he settled in Safed in 1831. The first book he printed one year later was *Siddur Sefat Emet*, a prayer book that was endorsed by the Safed rabbinate. Two years later, he was joined by his wife, five daughters, and his son Nisan and other families from Berdichev and Odessa. His printing press grew, and he soon had a staff of thirty. He became friendly with Sir Moses Montefiore, then on his second trip to the Holy Land, who acted as *sandek* to his grandson Shmuel in 1839.

During the Peasants' Revolt against Muhammed Ali on 8 Sivan 1834, his printing press was damaged. He himself was attacked and physically injured, and he remained lame for the rest of his life. Three years later, his son-in-law perished in the earthquake that rent Safed on 24 Tevet 1837. Yisrael Bak spent the year 1840 in Cairo, seeking, in vain, compensation for his losses from Ibrahim Pasha. He moved to Jerusalem in 1844, where, for twenty-two years, he enjoyed the monopoly in printing Hebrew books. The first book he printed in Jerusalem, in 1847, was *Avodat Hakodesh* by the kabbalist and bibliographer Hayyim Yosef Azulai. By 1883, nearly 130 Hebrew books had been printed by the Bak family.[4]

In 1843, Sir Moses Montefiore sent him a new printing press, and the printer gratefully recorded on the title page of each book

---

4. Shoshanah Halevi, *The Printed Hebrew Books in Jerusalem during the First Half of the Century* (Jerusalem, 1963), pp. 4–12.

he printed "The Gift of Sir Moses and Lady Judith." On the frontispiece was an engraving of the Western Wall, the Temple Mount, and the Mount of Olives. It became the printer's mark for all Bak's books printed in Jerusalem. In 1863, he also established in Jerusalem a Hebrew newspaper, *Havazzelet*, which became the organ of the *hasidim* in the Holy Land. It was maintained by Bak's son-in-law I. D. Frumkin and by his son Gad Frumkin.

Printing was only one facet of Israel Bak's activities. In 1837, he acquired from the Pasha of Acre land that he farmed on Mount Yermak, six miles west of Safed. Bak inspired Sir Moses Montefiore and other European philanthropists to found agricultural colonies. Later, his son Nisan Bak (1815–1889) visited R. Yisrael Friedman of Ruzhin, who sent him to London to see Sir Moses. The latter was to be entreated to persuade the Turkish government to permit fundraising for the Holy Land in Russia. In 1845, Sir Moses sent Nisan, Mordecai ben Zalman, and Yitzhak Rozenthal of Danzig to Caterham, near Preston, England, to study the art of weaving. When Sir Moses subsequently opened a weaving workshop in Jerusalem, there was friction between the Gentile expert and the local Jewish workmen. Sir Moses replaced the Gentile expert with a Jew, Shlomo Elbow, but the change of personnel did not improve the situation, and in 1858, the weaving venture came to an end.[5]

In 1843, Nisan Bak told R. Yisrael that the Tsar of Russia was planning to buy a site near the Western Wall and erect a monastery there. Quickly, the Rabbi raised the money to enable Bak to acquire this strategic piece of land. Legend has it that when Tsar Nicholas I heard that he had been out-maneuvered by the Rabbi, he allegedly exclaimed: "That Jew always blocks my path." But the difficulties were not over. The burial place of a sheik was discovered, and it took delicate diplomacy, including the intervention of the Austrian Consul, to have the remains reinterred in another locality. Small wonder that R. Yisrael felt he was not des-

5. A. R. Malachi, "Le'Toldott Bet Ha-Arigah Shel Montefiore B'Yerushalayim," in *Abraham Weiss Memorial Volume* (New York: Abraham Weiss Jubilee Committee, 1964), pp. 441–459.

tined to see the erection of the synagogue in his lifetime, and that his son would have to build a house "for my name." [6]

In 1699, Juda Hasid Segal (1660–1700), the fiery *Maggid* of Szydlowiec, who was probably associated with the Shabbatean movement, left Grodno with 120 people. He was said to indulge in asceticism, and his associates were known as the "Holy Society of Juda Hasid." He, like his disciples, wore a white shroud, and as they traveled to Altona, Frankfurt, and Vienna, their number grew to 1,300, of whom many died en route. No more than a few hundred of them eventually reached the Holy Land on 14 October 1700. Unhappily, Juda died five days after arrival. His followers purchased a site in Jerusalem on which they planned to erect a synagogue and forty homes. The new settlers borrowed heavily from the Arabs, who, in November 1701, attacked them and destroyed the synagogue.

This synagogue, known as the *Hurva Yehuda Hasid*, remained a ruin from 1701 until the foundation stone of the chief synagogue of the Ashkenazi community was laid on 7 Nisan 1857. The synagogue was dedicated on 24 Elul 1864. It took nearly eight years to build and became the foremost synagogue of Jerusalem. Its completion inspired Bak to persevere in his efforts to erect a hasidic synagogue. In a public proclamation he pleaded that "it is already twelve years since we acquired a site to erect a magnificent structure." He was financially backed by R. Avraham Yaakov Friedman of Sadagora and by the family of Ezekiel Reuben Sassoon. When the Emperor Franz Joseph, on his way to the ceremonial opening of the Suez Canal, visited Jerusalem on 14 November 1869, he noticed the unfinished building. "Where is the roof of the synagogue?" asked the Emperor. "Your Excellency," replied Nisan, "even the synagogue is happy to welcome you, and has taken off its cap in deference to your Majesty." The Emperor took the hint and donated one hundred franks to complete the structure.

The beautiful synagogue, a fine example of Ottoman architecture, with its thirty windows facing the Temple Mount and the

---

6. 2 Samuel 7:13.

twelve-windowed dome, was consecrated on Shabbat *Nahamu* (Sabbath of Comfort) 1870. It was known as *Tiferet Yisrael* (in honor of R. Yisrael of Ruzhin) or *Bet HaKnesset Nisan Bak* (Nisan's synagogue), for Nisan was its first *Gabbai*. The synagogue also had a ritual bath in its basement. Together with fifty-seven other historic synagogues, it was destroyed by the Jordanians on 19 Iyar 1948. The Jordanians also vandalized the Scrolls of the Torah and the synagogue's very valuable library.

In 1875, another Jewish neighborhood outside the Jerusalem walls, near the Damascus Gate, was built by Nisan Bak, and it was known as *Kiryat Ne'emana*, or Nisan Bak's neighborhood. Only half of the planned number of houses were actually built, and in 1884, a synagogue called *Bet Shmuel BeZeharia* was built with the help of the philanthropist Kalonymus Kalman Wollrauch of London.[7]

The Rebbe of Boyan today is the peripathetic R. Nahum Dov Brayer, a grandson of R. Mordechai Shlomo. His mother, Bluma Malka (d. 1998), the only daughter of the Rebbe, married Dr. Menahem Mendel Brayer, professor of the Graduate School of Jewish Education of Yeshiva University, New York. He has two doctorates, one in Hebrew literature, and one in clinical psychology. He contributed a learned article on "The Rebbes of Romania and Hungary and the Land of Israel" to the work of Shimon Federbush *HaHasidut VeZiyon*.[8] His eldest son, Yigal Yisrael, became an aerospace engineer, working for NASA.

The younger son, Nahum Dov, who was born in New York in 1959, studied in Jerusalem in the Yeshivah of Ruzhin and married Shoshanah, the daughter of R. Zusya, the son of R. Avraham Yehoshua Heschel, the rebbe of Kopicienice. They have eight children. After an interregnum of fifteen years, he became Rebbe on Hanukah 1984, and he, like the Rebbe of Boston, regularly commutes between Israel and the United States, where he lives in East Broadway, New York, in the building that was once the home

---

7. Yehoshua ben Arye, *Jerusalem in the Nineteenth Century* (Jerusalem: Yad Yitzhak ben Zvi, 1986), p. 117.

8. Jerusalem: Mosad HaRav Kook, 1983, pp. 190–246.

of his grandfather. In Betar, a small town located between Jerusalem and Tel Aviv, he has established a boys' center, a synagogue, and a *kollel*. The path he follows was marked out for him by his grandfathers. Thanks to his affability, he has won the confidence of his followers.

The youngest son of R. Yitzhak of Boyan was the present Rebbe's grandfather, R. Mordecai Shlomo Friedman. Born on 30 Tishri 1891, he married Havah Hayyah, the daughter of R. Shalom Yosef of Miedzeborz, on 18 Sivan 1908. During World War One, he, in common with so many other rebbes, lived in Vienna. On the death of R. Yitzhak on 17 Adar 1917, three of his sons made their homes in different towns: R. Menahem Nahum in Czernowitz, R. Shalom Yosef in Leipzig, R. Avraham Yaakov in Lvov, and R. Mordecai Shlomo remaining as rebbe in Vienna.

In 1927, he settled on the Lower East Side in Manhattan. He was president of the "Association of Rebbes" and actively involved in the Aguda. He fréquently visited the Holy Land and was very anxious that his visits should coincide with *Lag B'Omer* (the thirty-third day of the Counting of the Omer, which is observed as a minor holiday). He loved to participate in the annual pilgrimage to the little town of Meron in Upper Galilee, near Safed. On this day, men and women, Ashkenazim and Sephardim, *hasidim* and *Mitnaggedim*, Sabras and Yemenites, converge on the white-domed tomb of R. Shimon bar Yochai and his son R. Eliezer. On an elevated pillar stands a large stone basin filled with olive oil. Devout pilgrims immerse kerchiefs of silk and pieces of embroidered cloth in the oil. At the stroke of twelve, the *Hadlakah* (bonfire) is lit as a signal that the celebrations have begun. By tradition, the honor of kindling the bonfire belongs to the rebbes of Boyan.

He supported the extension of the Yeshivah *Tiferet Yisrael*, in memory of R. Yisrael of Ruzhin in Jerusalem. At first, only a few students studied in the temporary premises of the *Batei Orenstein* under the spiritual guidance of the hasid of Boyan, R. Yehoshua Heschel Brim (d. 1986). A native of Jerusalem, he studied under R. Zalman Meltzer and guided the yeshivah for over three decades.

With the encouragement and support of the Rebbe, the foundation stone for a magnificent yeshivah building was laid on 15

Shevat 1964, and the building was completed on 15 Av 1967. The yeshivah attracts students from the United States and England. R. Shlomo Friedman of Tel Aviv has formed an association for its support. He launched an appeal, signed by nine rebbes of the Ruzhin dynasty, then living in Tel Aviv and the United States. As a result, the campus now consists of three buildings: a *kollel* for study for the rabbinical diploma; a junior school, *Tiferet Menahem*; and a girls' school, *Bet Havah*, with a roll of three hundred. It also houses an invaluable library, with many rare books that have been professionally catalogued. The Rebbe of Boyan died in 1971 and was buried in Israel.

Torah Thoughts

"Learn from this that the Lord your God was chastising you, as a man chastises his son" (Deuteronomy 8:5). A father can discipline and punish his son, but he resents it if this is done by a stranger. Similarly, God disciplined the Israelites: "the clothes on your back did not wear out and your feet were not swollen all these forty years" (ibid., Verse 4). The Almighty did not tolerate other nations harming the Israelites (*Divre Torah*, Rebbe of Chernobyl).

"And know this day, and lay it to your heart that the Lord He is God in Heaven above and upon the earth beneath" (Deuteronomy 4:39). If a man becomes cognizant that there is a God Who controls the universe, no other knowledge is necessary (*idem*).

"And he dreamt that there was a ladder planted on the ground with its top reaching to heaven" (Genesis 28:12). If a Jew stands firmly on earth, then his head can reach the heavens above (*idem*).

"Frequent fasts, ascetic practices, and ritual immersions are measures employed by the evil inclination to distract you from study and prayer, to make you pray with a weakened body and a confused mind. Read *Reshit Hochmah* [by the sixteenth-century moralist R. Elijah ben Moses Vidas] and carry out all that is written in it, except the self-mortifications and fasts prescribed in it. And then it will be well with you" (*idem*).

"I stand before the Lord and you" (Deuteronomy 5:5). According to R. Mordecai of Chernobyl, a man who truly wishes to become attached to the Almighty must first eliminate putting himself before all, as this is a sign of self-importance and creates a division between man and man (R. Mordecai of Chernobyl).

"The most terrible thing that the evil inclination can achieve is to make a Jew forget that he is the son of a king" (R. Shlomo of Karlin).

There are three periods that affect a human being in his life: the day of his birth, his wedding day, and the day of his death. It is vital that these crucial periods should all be of the same spiritual quality (R. Yitzhak of Boyan).

11

Bene Berak
A Miniature Torah Town

The greatest concentration of *hasidim* in the Holy Land is to be found in Bene Berak, five miles (eight km) from Tel Aviv. Already mentioned in the Bible,[1] it is associated with the mid-first-century scholar and martyr R. Akiva, one of the key figures of rabbinic Judaism, who established a distinguished academy at Bene Berak.

In addition to *Kiryat Vizhnitz*, *Shikkun Yoel* of Satmar, and *Zichron Meir* (in memory of R. Meir Shapiro), and the housing estates of the Poale Agudat Yisrael, Bene Berak is the home of more than forty hasidic rebbes. Before the outbreak of World War Two and in the immediate postwar period, Tel Aviv was the city of refuge, not only for the descendants of Ruzhin, but of other rebbes, too. Today, Tel Aviv is almost without rebbes, the rebbes of Tel Aviv, with very few exceptions, having moved to Bene Berak.

---

1. Joshua 19:44.

Bene Berak has over two hundred synagogues and *Bate Midrashim*; one hundred fifty *shtieblech*; seventy *hadarim*; two hundred yeshivot, and *kollelim*; *Bet Yaakov* schools; girls' seminaries; six *Baale Teshuvah* centers; and twenty-six specialized women's institutes. There are no less than twenty *shtieblech* of Ger, six of Belz, and there are few hasidic dynasties that are not represented by a *shtiebl*. The town crier announces and ushering in of the Sabbath. The sound of the bugle informs all the residents of Bene Berak of the arrival of the Queen Sabbath. The proportion of children in Bene Berak is higher than elsewhere. Bene Berak is one of the poorest cities in Israel, with forty-five percent of its residents living below the poverty line.

"Nowadays, yeshivah students should not live in shacks and eat like beggars," declared R. Meir Shapiro in the 1930s. "I will build a palace for them." At Lublin, the one-time seat of R. Shlomo Luria, R. Shapiro erected his "palace"—one of the finest prewar buildings in interwar Poland. It was six stories high and had one hundred twenty rooms and a huge auditorium. R. Shapiro's example was followed by R. Yosef Shalom Kahaneman (1881–1969), a disciple of R. Yisrael Meir Hakohen Kagan, the *Hafetz Hayyim* (1838–1933). R. Kahaneman came to the Holy Land in 1940 after making every effort to save his family and his students. He built the Yeshivah of Ponevezh with space for a thousand students in the magnificent hilltop quarter of Bene Berak and made it the largest and most influential yeshivah in Israel, covering an area of two hundred square meters. It has a huge auditorium, graced with an Italian Renaissance Ark, magnificent student lecture halls, and the Sherman Library.

The Bene Berak telephone directory devotes three full pages to enumerating local yeshivot. The municipal contribution for the Bene Berak Talmud Torah centers was 1.5 million New Israeli shekels in 1996, when, out of 141,000 inhabitants, 77,955 were under the age of nineteen. Bene Berak is one of the very few towns in Israel where all roads are closed to public and private traffic on the Sabbath and Holy Days. It has a tangible religious atmosphere even on weekdays. The streets, named after R. Akiva, Ben Zakkai, R. Ashi, Sefat Emet, and Noam Elimelech, are crowded by *hasidim* in their distinctive attire. It is as if an East European *shtetl* of the nineteenth century had been transplanted to the Middle East of the twentieth century. Bene Berak, covering an area of seven thousand *dunams*, is also an industrial urban center, with over one hundred fifty factories and numerous workshops. It is a town with a soul. There are innumerable welfare agencies, covering every possible eventuality, from hospitals to old-age homes, from convalescent homes for the ailing to rest homes for mothers after childbirth.

The dream of establishing this new hasidic townlet was conceived by R. Yitzhak Gerstenkorn (1891–1962), in the hasidic *shtiebl* of Skierniewice in Nalevka 43, Warsaw (he was later the mayor of Bene Berak from 1924–1954). Born in Warsaw, the son of R. Petahya, a hasid of R. Yisrael Yitzhak Kalish of Skierniewice, he often accompanied his father on visits to the Rebbe. He studied in Lida, in the yeshivah of R. Yitzhak Yaakov Reines (1830–1915), the founder of the Mizrachi, in whose yeshivah secular studies were taught side-by-side with the traditional talmudic and rabbinic studies. He continued his studies in Radin under R. Naftali Tzvi Trop (1871–1929).

After his marriage to Sarah, the daughter of R. Yitzhak Weinberg of Siedlice, he engaged in business. His commercial ventures were frustrated by the newly emergent Polish State, which adopted administrative measures specifically calculated to incapacitate the Jews and to dislodge them from the economic life of the country. There was also the pernicious "Polonization" policy that was rigorously applied to the Jews. Anti-Jewish boycotts had assumed formidable proportions under the auspices of the first anti-Jewish "Green Ribbon League," which was later continued by the Endeks.

In 1921, R. Yitzhak formed a society, *Bet Venahala* ("home and inheritance"), with the aim of establishing a new religious settlement in the Holy Land. He was greatly encouraged by R. Aaron Menahem Mendel Guterman, Rebbe of Radzymin, and R. Avraham Mordecai Alter, Rebbe of Ger. He, accompanied by two members of the society, visited the Holy Land in Adar 1922, and together with the Geula Society he acquired one thousand forty-four *dunams*. The foundation stone of Bene Berak was laid on 11 Tammuz 1924, and his family, joined by thirty other Polish Jewish families, settled there eventually.

During the Fourth *Aliyah* that reached Palestine between 1924 and 1928, the country experienced an economic slump. Not only was there a sharp drop in the number of immigrants, but also a number of enterprises engaged in construction went bankrupt. R. Yitzhak traveled on fundraising missions to the United States and South Africa, and established a bank to help the new settlers. By 1937, Bene Berak had a population of four thousand.

He attended the Agudist conventions, *Kenesiyah Gedolah*, in Vienna in 1922 and in Marienbad in 1937, as well as the Fourteenth, Fifteenth, and Twentieth Zionist Congresses. Apart from his mayoral duties, he engaged in literary work and published two volumes on the development of Bene Berak and other works.[2]

At the invitation of R. Yitzhak, R. Yosef Tzvi Kalish (1885–1957) became spiritual leader of the new settlement. R. Kalish was the son of R. Shimon of Skierniewice (1857–1927), who was known as "R. Shimon the Merciful." A descendant of R. Yitzhak of Warka, R. Yosef Tzvi Kalish married Golda Bluma, the daughter of R. Yaakov Yitzhak Rabinowicz of Biala. When his father-in-law died on 23 Adar 1905, he lived in Warsaw for some time. He then succeeded his father as rabbi in Karczev. In 1936, he became rabbi of Bene Berak. A tall, handsome man with a flowing white beard, he endeared himself to *hasidim* of all denominations. It was one of his customs to kindle two lights on the eve of the Sabbath, a duty most Jews delegate to their wives. He interpreted the biblical verse "I seek for my brothers" to mean that it is the duty of every rabbi to create a spirit of harmony among his followers. He died on 1 Adar 1957 and was buried in Tiberias.

R. Gerstenkorn was succeeded as mayor by Reuven Aharonowitz (1903–1975), a hasid of Ger who came to the Holy Land in 1934. He was mayor for fifteen years. Other personali-

2. D. Tidhar, *Encyclopedia L'Halutze HaYishuv*, vol. 2 (Tel Aviv: Sifrat Rishonim, 1944), pp. 935–936.

ties who participated in the work of the townlet were Yehuda Meir Abramowitz, a former student of the Yeshivah *Hachmei Lublin*, who came to the Holy Land in 1935; Shmuel Weinberg, who was the city treasurer; R. Moshe Schreiber, who came to the country in 1940; Shimon Siroka; and R. Moshe Orenstein. The Chief Rabbi of Bene Berak was R. Yaakov Landau (1893–1986), a native of Russia, who was ordained by R. Yozef Rozin (1858–1936), known as the "Rogachover Gaon." He was an adherent of R. Shalom Dov Ber Schneersohn of Lubavitch. When he died at the age of ninety-three, he was succeeded by his son R. Moshe Yehuda Leib.

In 1998 the Central Torah List comprising a combination of Aguda and Degel HaTorah gained seventeen out of the twenty-five seats, with the Mayor, R. Mordechai Karlitz, who received eighty-seven percent of the vote. The Election followed almost two years in which a Committee appointed by the Ministry of the Interior maintained the City.

Kalev

At Haranowitz Street in Bene Berak is the Kalev World Center, a building erected at a cost of $4½ million (U.S.) and dedicated on 26 Av 1993.

The center is controlled by the white-haired, cherubic figure of R. Menahem Mendel Taub, who is singleminded and has a keen eye for detail. He never forgets his struggle to stay alive in the ghettos and concentration camps or the fate of European Jewry under the heel of the Nazi murderers. He is the most innovative rebbe in Israel. Kalev is hardly a mass movement. The Rabbi's success lies in his individual approach and in his creativity. He bubbles with new ideas, many of them wholly original. Almost every day, he comes up with new plans for strengthening religion in the State of Israel.

He has dedicated a new center, *Mishkan Kalev*, in Tiberias (near *Kiryat Shmuel*). He is also planning a center in Jerusalem and the establishment of a *Bet HaMidrash* near the grave of Shimon bar Yochai in Meron. Apart from the late Rebbe of Lubavitch, no other rabbi controls so many activities. No door remains closed to him. He is welcome even in the nonreligious kibbutzim, army camps, factories, and hospitals. He has a gift of endearing himself to the young and is capable of inspiring lasting loyalty and affection in those who know him.

On 15 Shevat 1973, he launched an educational drive named *Bar B'Rav D'Had Yoma*, one-day scholar scheme, which is a phrase borrowed from the Talmud that stated that one of the teachers, R. Idi, used to spend three months on his journey and one day at the school. Hence, he was called "one-day scholar."[3] The rabbi feels that the study of the Torah is central to Jewish life and that its study is among the precepts "the fruit of which a man enjoys in this world, while the stock remains for him in the world to come."[4] As so many Jews neglect Torah study, the rabbi feels that at least one day should be entirely devoted to the study of the Torah, which is a positive duty of the highest importance. He felt that the *Moreshet Yehudit* program has not fulfilled its promise. There are many Israelis who have never seen a *Sefer Torah*; neither do they know the meaning of *Kiddush*, nor can they find the *Shema* in the prayer book. He does not limit his activities to Bene Berak but travels, literally, from Dan to Beersheva to provide every area with facilities for Torah education. So far, more than six hundred thousand people have participated in this program. He regards these gatherings as a suitable forum for the propagation of the Jewish way of life. His talks are enthralling and keep his audiences hanging on his every word. He is a great communicator and finds a relevant hasidic story for every occasion.

Another program, *Keter Shabbat*, is designed to enhance the observance of the Sabbath. From time to time, the rebbe and his entourage leave Bene Berak to spend Sabbath in different parts of Israel. "I hate political parties," he says, "but I love Jews." He has a missionary spirit, and he feels that he has the ability to redeem people. "Together we dance, we pray, we sing, we partake of the

---

3. *Haggigah* 5b.
4. *Peah, Mishnah* 1.

Sabbath meal, and we give discourses. Then everybody is bound to feel the sanctity of the Sabbath," which he calls the *lebedige took* ("the lively day"). He does not approve of Orthodox Jews creating their own ghettos. He maintains that the Torah is the heritage of the entire congregation of Israel. Every Jew has a part in it, and no Jew is exempt from studying it. He has already visited two hundred fifty settlements where he created a Sabbath atmosphere. He continues to stress that the Sabbath is a day of physical rest and spiritual joys and that its observance has been the most distinguishing feature of Jewish life.

The rabbi maintains a network of six *kollelim* where the students are expected to help him further his educational schemes. Some of them are engaged in examining *Mezuzot* and have discovered that many of those checked are not valid, as they contain printed and not the handwritten text of the first two paragraphs of the *Shema*. Some *Mezuzot*, surprisingly, have been found to contain the Priestly Benediction or assorted prayers.

In his *kollelim*, study goes on for twenty-four hours each day on a rota system, divided into regular four-hour shifts. For the very young there are *Gadi* centers, with branches in Jerusalem, Haifa, and Rishon LeZion. The centers have lending libraries, and prizes are offered to those who master sections of the *Mishnah Berura*, the legal Code of the *Hafetz Hayyim*. The Rebbe also provides special study facilities for Russian immigrants. His fund *Yad Kalev* (Kalev food and clothing program) supplies shoes and food, such as wine, eggs, oil, and potatoes, to needy families and students.

In 1987, the rabbi ordained that the phrase of the *Shema* "Hear O Israel, the Lord our God, the Lord is One" should be recited not only, as is customary, in the statutory services morning and evening, but also after the recitation of *Aleinu* (it is incumbent upon us), the prayer used at the conclusion of all services, morning, afternoon, and evening, throughout the year. Reciting the opening sentence of the *Shema*, he felt, would serve as a constant daily reminder of the martyrdom of the Holocaust and be a tribute to the invincible spirit of the Jews, and remind people that they must never be oblivious that two out of every three European Jews perished in the Holocaust.

The Rabbi recalled that when he was incarcerated in Auschwitz, he noticed a very timid young boy who kept himself apart and continuously murmured to himself. The rabbi eventually befriended him, gave him some food, asked him what his name was and why he was muttering. The child told him that his name was Yitzhak Weining from Warsaw, and that when the Nazis tore him away from his widowed mother, her parting words to him were: "My child, you are very young. There was no opportunity in the ghetto to teach you about your faith. The only thing you do know is the *Shema*. So, please, I beg of you, remember, that wherever you are, always recite the *Shema*."

The Rabbi recorded his own personal experiences:

The Nazis, apart from destroying twelve thousand Jews in the crematoria daily, felt that this "production rate" was insufficient for their plan for the Final Solution of the Jewish people, and resorted to additional and more primitive methods. The prisoners had to dig themselves a large grave, and the Germans would line them up and shoot them, so that their bodies would fall straight into the grave. I was standing at the edge of an open abyss surrounded by Germans who were shooting and throwing us into the pit. I cried out *Shema Yisrael*, and then added a prayer: "Holy Father in Heaven, in a few seconds I shall return my soul to You. You can do wonders and nothing is impossible for You, even here and now. If I come out of this hell alive, I will continue to recite *Shema Yisrael* with my fellow-Jews whenever and wherever the occasion presents itself."

The rebbe is thus fulfilling his vow. He came close to death on a number of occasions. To him the Holocaust is not a "literature of silence" or a "literature of the unspeakable" but a "literature of martyrdom."

Another idea of the Rabbi is *Yom Taanit Dibbur*, which requires that once a year everyone should devote one day to reflect on the injury we perpetrate by talebearing and calumny. *Lashon hara* ("the tongue of evil"), slander, trafficking in evil reports or rumors, he felt, should be strictly avoided. He quotes rabbinic authorities, such as the *Hafetz Hayyim*, who held that refraining from talebearing is preferable to fasting.

Recently, the rabbi established a *Shema Yisrael* Institute, whose aim it is to publish an encyclopedia recording Jewish martyrdom. So far, five hundred stories have been collected. In the last fifty years there has been an upsurge in Holocaust study. Thousands of books have been written on the suffering of the Jews and on their spontaneous opposition to the Nazi butchers. The rebbe feels that the works of Menashe Unger, Moshe Praeger, and Isaac Levin are not enough and that more information of the sacrifices of the many Jews who gave their lives, at that time, for the observance of the *mitzvot* should be made available.

The Rabbi is fond of telling the story of an incident that happened in the Auschwitz concentration camp, where there was an electrically wired fence. Any inmate who dared approach it would either be shot by the Gestapo who manned the watchtower or would be electrocuted by the fence. One Jew, before the festival of Pentecost, noticed that a torn page of the Festival Prayer Book, containing part of the *Akdamot*, the eleventh-century, ninety-verse Aramaic poem that is recited in the synagogue on the morning of the festival prior to the Reading of the Law, was lying next to the fence. Anxious to retrieve the page and oblivious of the mortal danger, he approached the fence and was killed instantly.

The Rebbe's proposed encyclopedia will contain photos, entries, written testimonies, and stories hitherto untold of *Kiddush HaShem*, in the *Shoah*. For this purpose a voice-mailbox has recently been installed so that people can call in and leave their names and telephone number and a brief synopsis of their story. People whose stories have been selected for printing will then be contacted for an interview. Today, a group of experts, editors, and historians are working on the material, preparing it for publication.

R. Menahem Mendel, the present rebbe, was born in Marghita in Romania in 1924. His father, R. Yehuda Yehiel, rabbi in Rosla for forty years, died on 19 Av 1938. During World War One, he lived in Marghita for eight years. R. Menahem Mendel was barely fifteen when war broke out and, to use his own expression, he "went through the seven fires of *Gehenna*." He was imprisoned in several concentration camps, including Belsen and Auschwitz.

Together with the rabbi of Klausenburg, R. Halberstam, he was taken to the Warsaw ruins after the liquidation of the ghetto. His mother, the daughter of R. Moshe David Ashkenazi, a descendant of R. Tzvi Ashkenazi, known as the Haham Tzvi (1660–1718), had died on 3 Iyar 1940, leaving eight children. She was so highly esteemed that her coffin was brought into the synagogue where eulogies were delivered.

In Grosswardein, R. Menahem Mendel married Hannah Sarah Shifrah, daughter of R. Pinhas Shapiro, rabbi of Kechnie. His mother-in-law was the daughter of R. Meir of Crasznov, a descendant of the rabbi of Nadvorna. Every day, every hour, R. Menahem Mendel faced a fearful death. On one occasion, death was so imminent that he made his confessions and prepared to die. At the very last instant, an SS officer drove up to conscript workers and took him to another labor group. After two harrowing years, he was liberated on the last day of the war. His wife had been sent to different concentration camps, and six months after the war, it transpired that she had also survived and lived in Sweden. They were eventually reunited. His father-in-law, however, perished on 3 Sivan 1944. His experiences in the concentration camps have had a profound impact on all his actions.

Through the intervention of his brother-in-law R. Shalom Yissahar Dov, the Rabbi traveled from Sweden to the United States and settled in Cleveland, Ohio. He believed that he had been spared for a special reason—to revive Judaism in the free world. In the hometown of the late R. Hillel Silver, a center of Reform Judaism, the Rabbi set up a *Bet 'Hamidrash*, a *mikveh*, and an educational center. He brought with him a religious fervor that was foreign to the Jews of Ohio. Americans who had never experienced Hasidism found in him a friend in need. Later, he moved to New York, where he published *Zofnat Paneah*[5] (discourses on the Torah and Festivals by his father-in-law).

After fifteen years in the United States, the Rabbi longed to settle in the Holy Land. On the verse of Isaiah "Hark! one calleth:

---

5. Jerusalem, 1964.

'Clear ye in the wilderness the way of the Lord' " [6] he commented: "Now that Eastern Europe has been turned into a wilderness, and its soil drenched with the blood of six million Jewish dead, Jews are summoned to return home and rehabilitate the Holy Land."

He settled at first in Rishon L'Ziyon, a town in the Judean coastal plain, founded in 1882 by Russian pioneers. There he established a *Kirya* on 7 Adar 1967. The *Kirya* has one of the most beautiful synagogues in the State of Israel. The five chandeliers are made up of 613 lamps—equivalent to the 613 Commandments listed in the Pentateuch. Each lamp has been fashioned like a miniature Scroll of the Torah. As a visible reminder of the glory that was Kalev, two bricks of the original synagogue in Hungary were placed in a prominent position on the Eastern Wall.

Hasidic *shtieblech* are generally devoid of artistic embellishments, relying for their atmosphere on the ardor of the worshipers rather than on the artistry of the decor. The Rebbe's synagogue is a noteworthy exception. "This is my God, and I will glorify Him," [7]—a verse that is interpreted to mean that precepts should be observed in a manner that is aesthetically pleasing.

The four walls of the synagogue present a pictorial history of Judaism. The south wall depicts the tent of Abraham, the binding of Yitzhak, the dream of Yaakov, the giving of the Ten Commandments, Aaron the High Priest, and the City of Hebron. These are flanked by David's Citadel and a symbolic representation of six tribes, Dan, Naftali, Gad, Asher, Yosef, and Benjamin.

On the west wall are scenes showing the life of Jonah, the Prophet Elijah, the exploits of Samson, the division of the Red Sea, the crossing of the River Jordan, the sun standing still at Gibeon, and Daniel's exploits. The lower panels illustrate the Six Days of Creation. The north wall features the burning bush, King David and his harp, Yitzhak musing in the field, and the fiery furnace mentioned in the Book of Daniel. The lower panels show the tribes of Reuben, Simeon, Levi, Juda, Issahar, and Zevulun.

---

6. Isaiah 40:3.
7. Exodus 15:2.

The east wall, with its impressive Ark, has representations of the Western Wall of the Temple. The painter was a local artist, Yaakov Epstein, whose sheer inventive resourcefulness more than compensates for lack of creative originality. In 1967, the Rabbi planned a project at Toheret (near Kfar Habad), with one thousand housing units. R. Aaron Rokeah of Belz told him encouragingly: "Rabbi of Kalev, Rishon LeZiyon is waiting for you. You are destined to achieve great things there." However, after living there for some years, he missed the true Torah environment and gravitated to Bene Berak.

It is here that the songs of Kalev are now heard, for his melodies express a longing for Zion and the Redemption. In this respect he follows the traditions of his ancestor R. Yitzhak Eizig (1751–1821) of Kalev (Nagy Kalo) in Northern Hungary. It was a young shepherd's love song that caught the fancy of the Rebbe: *Royz, royz, vi vayt biztu? Vald, vald, vi groyz biztu? Volt di royz nisht azoy vayt geven, volt der vald nisht azoy groys geven.* ("Rose, rose, how far away are you? Forest, forest, how vast are you? If the rose were not so far away, the forest would not seem so vast.") He substituted *Shechinah* (Divine Presence) for "rose" and *Galut* ("exile") for "forest" and created a song that inspired and consoled generations of *hasidim*. He sang the tune to the following words: "Holy Spirit, how far away are you? Exile, Exile, how long are you? If the Holy Spirit were not so distant, then the Exile would not seem so long."

"Father in Heaven," he once said, "You must be my father, I have no other God beside You. Show me the green pasture where I may feed my flock." The simple faith of this untutored shepherd inspired R. Leib Sara's, a contemporary of the Besht, and made him a shepherd of men. He took the young Yitzhak Eizig to R. Shmelke Horowitz of Nikolsburg for guidance. Later R. Yitzhak Eizig established his court in Kalev in his native Hungary, where he lived for forty years. He never lost the common touch and would often interject Hungarian words into his dialogues with the Almighty. Thousands of Hungarian *hasidim* sing his song: *Szol a kakas mar* ("The Cock Crows"), and according to R. Hayyim Halberstam, the ministering angels join in the refrain.

The Rebbe's contemporaries held him in high esteem. "The light that emanates from his Passover Seder," remarked the "Seer of Lublin," "illumines the whole world."

His burial place became a place of pilgrimage: "From the synagogue to the cemetery where the *Zaddik* is buried," said R. Naftali of Ropczyce, "you feel the atmosphere of Jerusalem." The Hebrew spelling of *Kalev* is an accrostic of the verse in Psalms "The Lord is nigh unto all them that call upon Him, to all that call upon Him in truth." [8]

Torah Thoughts

"And the rain fell upon the earth forty days and forty nights" (Genesis 7:12). There was thus a continuous flood for forty days. What is the significance of forty? The Talmud states (*Sota* 2a), "Forty days before the creation of a child a *Bat Kol* (a voice descending from heaven and offering guidance on human affairs) comes forth and proclaims that the daughter of A is intended as a partner for B." Marriage partners are thus pre-ordained even before the birth of a child. It is said of the generation of the Flood that "all flesh had corrupted their way upon the earth" (ibid., Verse 6:13), thus destroying family morality, which is the basis of civilized society. They were therefore punished by a Flood that lasted for forty days (Rabbi M. M. Taub).

"And Isaac prayed to God on behalf of his wife" (Genesis 25:21). Rashi comments that he was "facing his wife." He stood in one corner and prayed while she stood in another corner and prayed. The Patriarch Isaac said to God: "Look at my wife, Rebecca. She was the daughter of a wicked father, Bethuel, and a sister of an iniquitous brother, Laban. She lived in an immoral environment, and yet she remained completely uninfluenced by it. She stood apart among her contemporaries" (*idem*).

---

8. Psalms 145:18.

"And Aaron did so . . . He set up the lamps to the front of the lamp-stand" (Numbers 8:3). Rashi, quoting the Siphri, states, that "this is in praise of Aaron." He did not deviate from what he was bidden. Why should Aaron, the High Priest, of all men, deviate from that which he was instructed to do? But Aaron was so overcome with religious enthusiasm that he might have exceeded his specific instructions. He, however, restrained himself and performed his duties exactly as instructed (*idem*).

"Now these are the names of the children of Israel who came unto Egypt with Jacob" (Exodus 1:1). Rashi states that "although Scripture has already enumerated them by name while they were still living in Canaan when they went down to Egypt (Genesis 46:8–27), it again enumerates them when it tells us of their deaths, thus showing how dear they were to God, that they are compared to the stars." It is a well-known fact that generally the righteous are not fully appreciated while they are alive. Hence, the Talmud states (*Hullin* 7b) that "the righteous are more powerful after death than in life." During his lifetime, the Prophet Elisha had to exert himself by both action and prayer in order to revive the dead (2 Kings 4:33), while, after death, a mere touch revived a dead man. The stars are always there, but they are only visible to the human eye in the darkness of the night. Similarly, the righteous are appreciated when they are no longer on this earth (*idem*).

12

The Singing Rabbi and His Neighbors

Both Modzitz (Demblin, Modrzyc) and Kuzmir (Kazimierz) occupy high places in the history of hasidic musicology. What Habad did for the philosophy of Hasidism, Modzitz did for its music. Even in the Valley of the Shadow of Death, as so many Jews trod the fearful path that led to the crematoria, where a multitude of *hasidim* perished, even then the songs of Modzitz sustained them. It was then that R. Azriel David Pastag, a hasid of Modzitz, composed a triumphant melody that was a passionate affirmation of an undying faith. He sang and many sang with him: "I believe, with a perfect faith, in the coming of the Messiah and though he tarries, I will wait daily for his coming."

The rebbes of Modzitz endorsed the idea of the *Zohar* that the Heavenly Gates are firmly shut except to song and dance. Modzitz melodies have captivated the hasidic world. The rebbe-composers could not read music, and, originally, the melodies were not even written down. Nonetheless, literally by word of mouth, they were carried far and wide. The rebbes composed melodies for the Sabbath liturgy, for *El Adon* (God, the Lord over all works), *Yismah Moshe* (Moses rejoiced), for the Sabbath morning service, and *Yismehu* (they that keep the Sabbath and call it a delight, shall rejoice) for the Sabbath *Musaf Amida*.

They also composed songs for the *Seudah Shlishit* (the third meal), when *hasidim* spend many hours long after the end of the Sabbath, singing such melodies as *Bene Hechalah* (members of the sanctuary), composed by R. Yitzhak Luria, and *Yedid Nefesh* (beloved of the soul) by R. Eliezer Azkri, as well as melodies for the *Melaveh Malkah*, for festivals, Psalms, weddings, and other happy occasions. Some of the melodies were without words, employing only vocalized syllables, such as *bim bom* and *aha aha* or *dai dai* or *yam bam*. As R. Shneur Zalman of Liady stated, "Melody is the outpouring of the soul. Words interrupt the stream of emotions. For the songs of the souls, at the time they are swaying in the high regions, to drink from the well of the Almighty King, consist of tones only, dismantled of words."[1]

Echoes of this hasidic music are still heard today on the Israeli radio, *Kol Yisrael*, in kibbutzim, and at hasidic gatherings. One soaring melody, *Ezkerah Elohim Ve'Hemaya* (When I Remember This, O God, I Moan), composed by the Rebbe's ancestor R. Yisrael is an elaborate musical composition containing thirty-two short melodies.

On *Lag B'Omer* 1995 the Rebbe of Modzitz, R. Yisrael Dan Taub, moved from Tel Aviv to Bene Berak and made his home at Revov Habbakuk. A son of R. Shmuel Eliyahu Taub, he was born in Warsaw in 1928. His mother, Rebecca Zlata, was a descendant of R. Yehiel Michael of Zloczov and of R. Avraham Yehoshua Heschel of Opatov. In 1936, at the age of eight, he came with his parents to the Holy Land where he studied in various yeshivot. He married Malkah, the daughter of Shmuel Shiderowski, originally from Bialystok, later a leader of the Aguda

---

1. Velvel Pasternak, *Songs of the Hasidim* vol. 2 (New York: Tara Publications, 1971), pp. 1–14; David Sztokfisz, *Demblin–Morzyc Book* (Tel Aviv: Irgune Demblin, 169), pp. 221–237.

in Tel Aviv. For three years, he served as a member of the rabbinate of Tel Aviv/Jaffa and became Rebbe only after the death of his father in 1984.

He enlarged the Yeshivah *Imre Shaul*, which was founded by his father in 1981. The Rebbe's son R. Hayyim Shaul, the son-in-law of the Rebbe of Alexander, is in charge of the yeshivah. There are *shtieblech* of Modzitz in Tel Aviv and in Jerusalem. The rebbe is a person with warm and winning ways. He inherited the love of music from his father and is a very gifted musician, with many melodies to his credit. Like his ancestors, he maintains that he does not feel any delight in the Sabbath unless he produces a new melody, and that one melody can express more than a thousand words. In addition to being a very prolific composer, he enjoys the role of being a *Shliah Tzibbur* (reader), and he delights his followers with innovative renderings. He steers clear of confrontations.

R. Shmuel Eliyahu was born in Lublin on *Rosh Hodesh Adar* 1906, studied in Warsaw, and was ordained by the members of the Warsaw rabbinate, R. Shlomo David Kahane and R. Tzvi Yehezkel Michelson, rabbi of Plonsk. In 1921, he married the daughter of R. Hayyim Moshe Kohn. In 1935, accompanying his father, he settled in the Holy Land and lived very modestly in Rehov Kfar Giladi in Tel Aviv. After his father's death, he succeeded him as rebbe and moved to Dizengoff Street, where he had a *Bet Hamidrash*, a ritual bath, and a bakery for *matzot shemura*.

Although he had become an Israeli, the Rebbe observed some of the customs of the diaspora, such as *Hakafot* (circuits) on the night of Shemini Atzeret. "If our fellow-Jews outside the Holy Land are celebrating," said the Rabbi, "we should, nay, we must, participate in their joy." He dedicated the sixth circuit of the *Hakafot* (*Ozer Dalim*, "who supports the poor") to the memory of the six million Jewish Holocaust victims. The lights of the synagogue were dimmed and mournful melodies were chanted. The Rabbi refused to despair over the state of religion in Israel. "Conditions today," he maintained, "are better than they used to be." In 1982, he established a small yeshivah, *Imre Shaul*, for exceptional students. He died on 4 Iyar 1984 and was buried on the Mount of Olives.

The present Rabbi's grandfather was R. Shaul Yedidia Elazar, who was born in Ozarov on *Hoshanah Rabbah* 1887. He was a tenor of great dramatic power, and he believed that only melodies that emanate from the heart can reach the heart, which is possible only when the heart is overflowing with the love of God. He quoted the *Zohar* [2] that all God's creatures recite melodies in heaven and on earth, and that there are mansions in heaven that can only be opened through songs. He, too, stamped his influence on hasidic music.

He occupied rabbinic positions in Rakov, near Kielce (1917). When his father died in Warsaw on 13 Kislev 1921, he became rebbe and moved to Karczev and finally to Otwock. He established a yeshivah, *Tiferet Yisrael*, in memory of his father. Music-loving *hasidim* as well as *Maskilim*, and even Gentiles, flocked to Otwock to listen to the compositions of this untutored genius who is reputed to have composed over seven hundred melodies. He visited the Holy Land in 1925, 1935, and 1938. During his first visit, he was received by the British high commissioner, Sir Herbert Samuel (later Lord Samuel). He strongly opposed the British White Paper (the MacDonald Paper) of 1939, which stated that in the subsequent five years only seventy-five thousand Jews would be admitted to the Holy Land and that after that period, no more Jewish immigrants would be allowed to enter without Arab agreement. The Rabbi bitterly denounced this as a "breach of faith" with the Jewish people, because it left Palestinian Jewry at the mercy of the Arab majority and closed the country to Jews fleeing Nazi persecution.

On the day the Second World War broke out, he urged his fellow-rebbes who were his neighbors in Otwock to escape. His plea fell on deaf ears; only R. Shimon Kalish, the Rebbe of Amshinov, took his advice. Narrowly escaping the Nazi clutches, the Rebbe of Modzitz left Otwock and spent the first Sabbath of his journey in Chelm. He then made his way to Vilna, which was occupied by the Russians on 18 September 1940 and which thus became a temporary haven for twenty-five thousand Polish Jews.

---

2. *Zohar*, Genesis, *Hayye Sarah*.

The Rabbi felt that the establishment of the Soviet regime offered no permanent safety and did not eliminate future Nazi threats. With this in mind, he obtained an exit visa that enabled him to travel to remote parts of the Soviet Union. After a train journey lasting one month, he reached Vladivostok, then traveled on to Kobe in Japan and on to San Francisco. He arrived in New York in 1951 and settled in the Williamsburg Section of Brooklyn.

He visited a number of towns in the United States and Canada and, despite his traumatic experiences, did not lose his creative genius, nor could anything crush the music in his soul. He could not, however, resist the call of the Holy Land. On *Rosh Hodesh Tammuz* 1947, he arrived in Israel and settled in Tel Aviv. He suffered from advanced arteriosclerosis and died within six months, at the age of sixty-one, on 29 November (16 Kislev) 1948, the very day on which the United Nations recommended the establishment of a Jewish State. On the advice of the Hazon Ish, despite the precarious conditions then prevailing, he was buried on the Mount of Olives in Jerusalem and was eulogized by his son.

The Rebbe was the last person to be buried on the Mount of Olives before it was taken over by the Jordanians. There was not even time to erect a tombstone over his grave. This was finally done after the Six-Day War when the Old City was recaptured by the Israelis.[3]

Alexander

"Everything needs *mazal*," says the *Zohar*.[4] "Even the Scroll in the Ark." This adage applies to the Rebbe of Alexander in Bene Berak. While Ger is rebuilding its lost empire, Alexander remains a mere shadow of its former glory. The *hasidim* of Alexander are now numbered in hundreds and not in thousands.

---

3. Yehuda Nathan, "Shaul Yedidya Elazar Taub," in *Torah Luminaries* (New York: *Mesorah Publication*, 1994), pp. 76–87.

4. *Zohar, Nasa* 134.

A century earlier, the town of Alexander, or Aleksandrov, near Lodz, was the home of the Danziger family. There were few Polish towns without one or two Alexander *shtieblech*. As the kabbalists in the Holy Land gravitated to Safed, so *hasidim* in Poland turned to Ger and Alexander. While Ger lured the scholars, Alexander drew the *baalei batim* (householders, the merchants). As Ger was "the spiritual fortress" that guarded Warsaw, so Alexander dominated Lodz, which was in prewar days the most prosperous town in Poland, the textile capital of Eastern Europe. Only Warsaw had a larger Jewish population. There were 230,000 Jews residing in Lodz prior to the outbreak of World War Two. Many of the owners of the cloth mills were *hasidim* of Alexander who lived in palatial residences that are now used as civic buildings and museums. "The Manchester of Poland" had some thirty-five Alexander *shtieblech*.

The Rabbi of Alexander today was born Avraham Menahem Tieberg but, in order to perpetuate the dynasty, has changed his surname to Danziger. Born in Lodz in 1921, he studied in the home of his grandfather, R. Bezalel Yair (1865–1935), the son of R. Yehiel, under whose leadership the dynasty grew in influence and prestige. R. Avraham Menahem came with his parents to the Holy Land in 1934 and studied under the rabbi of Trzebiana. In 1942, he married Esther Leah, the daughter of Hanania Yosef Halpern, a hasid of Lubavitch. He has seven children, three sons and four daughters. He became rebbe on 28 Adar 1973, on the anniversary of the death of his grandfather, R. Bezalel Yair. The Rebbe is a member of the *Moetzet Gedole HaTorah* and is highly respected for his mastery of talmudic and rabbinic law. Like all rebbes of Alexander, he stresses the need for continual striving to achieve perfection, modesty, and humility, which are the most important attributes conducive to the fear of God and the love of one's neighbor.

The Rebbe has enlarged the yeshivah. It is noteworthy that already in 1928 an Alexander Yeshivah was opened in the Bet Yisrael district of Jerusalem. The yeshivah in Bene Berak was at first housed in Rehov Petahya and, in view of the increasing number of students, a new building in Givat Rokeah is in the process of completion. It is guided by the Rebbe's eldest son, R. Yisrael Tzvi Yair. His other son, R. Eliezer Yitzhak, is in charge of the *kollel, Emunat Moshe,* which also serves as a study center for laypeople. Nor are the very young neglected; a children's paper, *Karmenu,* is published regularly. There are now Alexander *Shtieblech* in Borough Park, New York, and Antwerp.

The Rabbi's publishing house is reprinting the works of the rebbes of Alexander: *Yismah Yisrael,* a homiletical work on the Pentateuch, which was originally printed in Lodz in 1911; *Akedat Yitzhak,* by R. Yerahmiel Yisrael Yitzhak; *Tiferet Shmuel,* by R. Shmuel Tzvi; and a commentary on the Passover *Haggadah.* The publishing house is engaged in collecting the discourses, responsa, and letters of R. Yehiel, which are dispersed in many diverse publications. It also produces a periodical, *Karmenu,* containing *novellae* written by students, biographical studies on the rebbes of Alexander, and *Kobbetz Torani Kerem Bet Shmuel* dedicated to halachic discussions and talmudic problems.

The present Rebbe's father, R. Yehuda Moshe Tieberg (1898–1973), was born in Plavno, south of Lodz. On his maternal side, he was descended from R. David Dov Taub, the author of commentaries on the Talmud. He studied under R. Yehiel Halevi Halstok of Ostroviec, who described him as a great talmudist, well-versed in the Law. He was known as the *Illui* (talmudical prodigy) of Lodz. His work *Hashuvah Letovah*[5] was acclaimed by his colleagues.

He married Esther Perel, the daughter of R. Bezalel Yair of Lodz. One of his sons, R. David Tzvi, died on 3 Kislev 1936. R. Yehuda Moshe initially refused to become a rebbe and worked for a time as a diamond cutter. He eventually became a member of the hasidic *bet din* under Rabbi Shur. However, the Rebbe who lived in Alexander, R. Yitzhak Menahem Mendel, his three sons, and seven sons-in-law perished in Treblinka on 23 Elul 1942. In his "Last Will and Testament," he requested that his household effects be sold and the proceeds of the sale be used for charitable causes in the Holy Land.

---

5. Piotrokov, 1933.

Then R. Yehuda Moshe became Rebbe. He settled in Bene Berak and traveled to the United States to raise funds for his institutions. Commenting on the *Mishnah* "Wander forth to a home of Torah,"[6] he said: "Travel abroad to collect money so that you may establish in your home a home for the Torah."

Considerable rivalry existed in interwar Poland between the followers of Ger and Alexander. There were arguments over the appointments of rabbis, slaughterers, and communal officials. In Israel, however, there is no rivalry. As the Rebbe of Alexander says: "After the Holocaust, dissension completely disappeared."

R. Yehuda Moshe was the author of *Emunat Moshe* on the Pentateuch and the Festivals, published in four volumes by his son. In his "Last Will and Testament,"[7] written on 8 Heshvan 1951, he stated that he did not bear any grudge against those people who opposed or spoke unfavorably about him. He knew that they meant well. He very much recommended his only son as a worthy successor who, in addition to being an outstanding scholar, had the merit of being descended from great luminaries.

Chernobyl

Chernobyl, a town on the River Pripet, Ukraine, where in 1986 the nuclear power explosion produced more fallout and radiation than the atomic bombs of Hiroshima and Nagasaki combined, was the home of R. Menahem Nahum, known as "Nahum the Great" (d. 1797). He was a disciple of the Besht, and "his words," said R. Levi Yitzhak of Berdichev, "were the words of the living God." He urged his followers to rise from their sleep at midnight, for that was the time when the Holy One, Blessed be He, was most accessible. He urged them to do acts of lovingkindness, for good deeds and Torah go hand in hand. It was his belief that only one

---

6. *Avot* 4:18.

7. *Emunat Moshe* (Bene Berak: Mehon L'Hazuot Sefarim, 1976), p. 373.

who resides in the Holy Land is entitled to be called a *Zaddik*.[8] All his descendants proved to be tireless in mustering support for the Holy Land. His devoted disciple R. Avraham Dov Ber of Ovruch (d. 1840) settled in Safed and revived the hasidic settlement.

Dr. Eliezer (Louis) Loewe, secretary to Sir Moses Montefiore, records that in 1839 the Rabbi invited him home. "He is one of the most scholarly and precious persons that I have ever met. He works for the Community without drawing any salary from communal funds, but he was also dispensing charity. From ten to fifteen people always eat at his table every day."[9] On 1 January 1837 an earthquake shook the region, and two thousand Jews, half the population of Safed, perished and a great many people were seriously injured. Of the eight hundred and fifty to nine hundred *hasidim* who had lived in Safed, some three hundred were killed. The Rabbi appealed to Sir Moses for help, "to enable the poor of Safed to till the soil and become shepherds." In spite of the dangers, he categorically refused to leave. He told his followers:

"We must remain here, no matter what befalls us, in order to maintain this old settlement and to save the synagogue."[10] The *hasidim* remained in Safed and repaired the Jewish Quarter.

The Rebbe of Chernobyl in Bene Berak today is R. Menahem Nahum, the son of R. Meshulam Zusya Twersky. Born in Jerusalem on 22 Shevat 1942, he studied in the Yeshivah *Etz Hayyim* and then in the Yeshivah of Belz under R. Shalom Brender and under R. Moshe Sterenbuch (now *dayan* of *Eda Haredit*), Jerusalem. He studied with phenomenal ardor and diligence. In 1961, he married Nehamah Miriam, the daughter of R. Elhanan Halpern of London, a grandson of R. Shmuel Engel of Radomysl, who was

---

8. *Or Enayim Likkutim Beshallah.*

9. A. Rivlin, *HaAretz* (8 Sivan 1938); Samuel Klein, *Toledot HaYishuv HaIvri BeEretz Yisrael* (Tel Aviv, 1935), p. 231.

10. Avraham Yaari, "Letters from Safed in 1835," *Sinai* 28 (1951): 338–345; Montefiore, Sir, *Diaries of Sir Moses and Lady Montefiore*, vol. 1, ed. L. Lowe (Chicago, 1890), p. 162.

one of the great hasidic scholars of the interwar years. The Rebbe has ten children, six daughters and four sons (Mordecai, David, Aaron, and Arye).

The Rebbe is completely devoid of worldly ambition and is essentially a private man who shuns the limelight. He lives a frugal existence, content with very little, but is held in great esteem not only by his *hasidim*, but also by other *hasidim* who consider him a saintly person. He has achieved a lot in a short time and does not lack drive or determination. He is a man of discernment but on occasion appears to be somewhat remote. He recites the whole book of Psalms on Sabbath morning prior to the service. His yeshivah, *Tiferet Meshullam Zusya*, has over two hundred students. He has *shtieblech* in Jerusalem and Ashdod.

R. Meshulam Zusya was the son of R. Hayyim Yitzhak of Chernobyl-Leovy and Rachel Devorah, a granddaughter of R. Yitzhak Yeshaya Halberstam of Czeszow. Meshulam Zusya was born on the second day of Elul 1917 in Musir, near Kiev; he accompanied his father to Kiev (now the capital city of the Ukraine) in 1923. His father's was the only *Bet Hamidrash* open in Kiev, which then had a population of 175,000 Jews, one of the largest number of Jewish inhabitants of any town in Russia. R. Hayyim was exiled to labor camps in Siberia, was released, and, on his release, returned to Kiev. Before the outbreak of World War Two, he was once again arrested. He fasted the whole of Passover, refusing to eat *hametz* in prison. He died in Siberia on 24 Nisan 1943.

R. Meshulam Zusya, too, was imprisoned and on his release lived in Homel, Kursk, and Vitebsk. He studied in the underground yeshivah of Habad, *Torat Emet*, which, in order to avoid discovery by the Bolsheviks, had to move from place to place. Despite everything, he retained his cheerfulness and optimism and never experienced feelings of despair or discouragement. In 1934, at the age of sixteen, he was eventually permitted to leave for the Holy Land, where he was befriended by R. Nahum and R. Zeev, the Rebbes of Rahmastrivka. In 1936, he spent some time in Poland studying with his grandfather, the Rabbi of Czeszow Cracow. In 1939, he was expelled by the Polish authorities, and he returned to the Holy Land, where for eighteen years (1941–1959) he lived in Jerusalem and married the daughter of R. Yaakov Mordecai Brandwein of Strettin.

After the death of his father and grandfather, he became the Rebbe of Chernobyl in Bene Berak in 1959. In keeping with the tradition of Chernobyl, he rarely gave discourses. At his Sabbath *Tish* the Rebbe remained silent. The *hasidim*, too, were silent, yet the atmosphere was such that their silence was superior to others' discourses. The *hasidim* pointed out that the High Priest in Temple times, on entering the Holy of Holies on the Day of Atonement, did not utter a word. Only on his departure did he recite a short prayer. Speech is a physical attribute, but to remain silent is a spiritual constraint. The Rebbe had no set times for visitors. His door was always open to all. He was blessed with unlimited patience. He would daily recite the whole Book of Psalms.

He died on 17 Heshvan 1988 and is survived by two daughters and five sons, some of whom are now living in the United States.

Torah Thoughts

"And for every matter of law-breaking . . . whereof one says: 'This is it,' the cause of both parties shall come before God" (Exodus 22:8). The worst trespass is if the sinner regards himself as important or as a superior being (R. Israel of Modzitz).

"And ye shall take a bunch of hyssop and dip it in the blood" (Exodus 12:22). Even when you reach a low state, if you are united and ready to sacrifice your life for Judaism, you can still be elevated (*idem*).

We say in the Grace after Meals: "Let us not be in need of the gifts of flesh and blood." Why not use the phrase "gifts of man"? But if a person is in dire need and asks for gifts or favors from his own kith and kin, the response is often insensitive and unfavorable, hence, his flesh becomes as blood (R. Ezekiel of Kuzmir).

"And the servant ran to meet her" (Genesis 24:17). In the words of Rashi, when Eliezer, Abraham's servant, saw the miracle that the waters rose in the well at Rebecca's approach, he ran to meet her. As Eliezer already witnessed this miracle, why did he subsequently have to test her, saying, "So let it come to pass that the damsel to whom I will say, 'Let down thy pitcher, I pray thee, that I may drink', and she shall say, 'Drink and I will give thy camel to drink' " (ibid., Verse 14). The answer is that Eliezer was aware that one good attribute is superior to a hundred miracles (*idem*).

"And Abraham passed through the land" (Genesis 12:6). In the words of Rashi, "he entered at one boundary and left at another." Abraham was not satisfied with merely viewing the country's physical conditions. To him, the spiritual aspect of the country was more important (R. Taub of Modzitz).

The main purpose of the transmigration of souls is to rectify some omissions of one's previous earthly existence. A man can live a lifetime without being aware of what he has to rectify or amend. If, however, he encounters some difficulties in the performance of certain *mitzvot*, he then has a clear indication of the true purpose of his reincarnation (R. Shmuel of Zwolyn).

The Rebbe of Kalev's melody of the song "By the rivers of Babylon we sat and wept" (Psalms 137:1) has its origin in a shepherd's tune. Many melodies that were originally chanted by the Levites in Temple times have been lost and are now in exile and have to be redeemed from the Gentiles (*idem*).

"And Moses turned unto the Lord and said: Oh, this people have sinned a great sin, and have made themselves a golden calf" (Exodus 32:31). Adam ate of the forbidden fruit in the Garden of Eden (Genesis 3:12), and then blamed Eve. Moses, however, fully admitted Israel's sin. He felt that it was within a man's power to repent, by changing his ways and returning to God. "For God does not delight in the death of the wicked, but He is pleased if the wicked turn from evil and live" (Ezekiel 33:11) (*Nehmod Mizahav*).

The worst result of their slavery in Egypt was that the children of Israel became accustomed to slavery (R. Hanoch Heinoch of Alexander).

The *Midrash* (*Leviticus Rabba* 9:3) states that "courtesy precedes the Torah." Hence, a love of the Almighty should grow out of courtesy and not exist only because we are commanded to feel it. Jacob praised Juda that he "stooped down: crouched as a lion" (Genesis 49:9). This metaphor alludes to the fact that Juda, despite his transgression with the childless widow Tamar. (Genesis 38), had the courage to confess his sins, saying: "She is more righteous than I" (Genesis 38:26). His act of contrition entitled him to rise up (*idem*).

"And the people they had acquired in Haran" (Genesis 12:5). Rashi tells us that Abraham throughout his life converted the men and Sarah converted the women. What then became of all these converts? The Torah tells us that only seventy persons arrived in Egypt (Exodus 1:6). However, when Abraham died, the proselytes did not give their allegiance to his successor, Isaac, as they regarded him as inferior to his father. Not having a spiritual guide, they eventually reverted to their former idolatrous ways (*idem*).

13

Dissent in the Movement

Mahnovke

It is one of the ironies of history that R. Elijah, Gaon of Vilna, who himself was called the "hasid," became one of the bitterest antagonists of Hasidism. Mystic though he was, the Gaon failed to discern in Hasidism a new and momentous phase in the evolution of Jewish mysticism. In taking isolated thoughts out of context, the Gaon misunderstood and distorted the movement. For nearly four decades, there was internecine war between *Mitnaggedim* and *hasidim*. It took a long time before the *hasidim* and the *Mitnaggedim* learned to coexist and to allow each other the freedom to worship as each saw fit.

Though the struggle between the *Mitnaggedim* and the *hasidim* was over, from time to time in the nineteenth and twentieth centuries "civil wars" broke out within the hasidic movement itself. It is paradoxical that a movement that hoped to foster close fellowship between hasid and hasid was often marked by jealousy

and division. Rival factions exchanged recriminations and occasionally even excommunicated each other.

There were undignified exchanges in the beginning of the nineteenth century between R. Shneur Zalman of Liady, the founder
of Habad, and R. Avraham Katz of Kalisk, who wished to create
his own fundraising establishment. There was also the undignified controversy between R. Baruch of Miedzeborz (1757–1810),
the grandson of the Besht, and R. Shneur Zalman, who was
accused, when he traveled to raise funds for the poor, of "trespass-
ing" on R. Baruch's territory. Theological differences were intensified by clashes of personality.

R. Nahman of Braclav, the great-grandson of the Besht, was a
volcanic and complex individual. Paroxysms of despair alternated
with bursts of ebullience, a pattern that continued throughout his
brief but tempestuous life. He, too, alienated R. Baruch, who was
by nature quarrelsome and could not tolerate R. Nahman's novel
ideas. Rigorous, indeed, were the standards that R. Nahman set
for the *Zaddik*, for the role of the *Zaddik* was of transcendent
importance. R. Nahman believed that only through the *Zaddik*
could a man attain understanding of the Divine. The *Zaddik* could
perform miracles in Heaven and on earth. Thus, for the hasid to
visit his rebbe occasionally was not enough, for close communion between the two was essential. So exalted was R. Nahman's
concept of the *Zaddik* and so exacting were his standards that few
of his contemporaries passed muster.

It was R. Nahman's habit to castigate his fellow *Zaddikim* and
to call them hypocrites. R. Baruch could not tolerate R. Nahman's
remarks: "When Satan saw that it was difficult to lead the world
astray, he appointed a number of *Zaddikim* in various locations
to help him in his work." [1] When R. Nahman moved from
Medvedivka Zlatopolye, two miles from Shpole, he aroused the
antagonism of R. Arye Leib (1725–1812) of Shpole, known affec-
tionately as the "Shpole Zeide" (the grandfather of Shpole). Repeatedly, the older *Zaddik* clashed with the turbulent newcomer.

---

1. *Likkute Etzot* (Warsaw, 1875), p. 7.

R. Arye Leib regarded R. Nahman as irresponsible and presumptuous, seeking to destroy from within what the Gaon of Vilna had failed to destroy from without. "This is not the way a *Zaddik* should conduct himself," he remarked. "Nor is this manner in which a *Zaddik* should converse." The mantle of the Gaon of Vilna had fallen on the octogenarian of Shpole. "Curse Nahman," urged the Sage of Shpole, losing much of the serene benevolence that characterized his life, "and I will assure you a portion in the World-to-Come."

After R. Nahman's death, his leaderless *hasidim* became known as the *toite hasidim* ("dead *hasidim*") and were vilified and persecuted by R. Moshe Tzvi of Savran (d. 1839), who stigmatized them as "sinners who caused others to sin." He warned his followers not to intermarry with them: "A hasid of Braclav should not instruct your children" and "A *shohet* of Braclav is disqualified from *Shehita*."

In the third part of the nineteenth century, R. Hayyim Halberstam of Zanz became the great accuser and declared "war" against the Sadagora dynasty. The reason for the quarrel is vague; perhaps it was that the royal lifestyle of the Sadagora dynasty was so alien to him. "They are rebels . . . . Their scribes are apostates. One must not use their *tefillin* and *Mezuzot*. . . . It is forbidden to eat the meat slaughtered by them." On 4 Nisan 1869, Nisan Bak and forty-nine other *hasidim* issued an *isur* (prohibition), known as *Mishpat Katuv* (written judgment), forbidding people to obey the dictates of the Rebbe of Zanz. This *isur* was proclaimed at the Western Wall in Jerusalem and repeated in Safed and Tiberias. The day after *Shavuot* 1869, the followers of R. Hayyim Halberstam publicly excommunicated Nisan Bak and his followers. For seven years this "civil war" raged through Galicia, dividing families and splintering communities. These were the seven lean years of Hasidism.

In the twentieth century, R. Hayyim Elazar Shapira was embroiled in a bitter controversy with R. Yissahar Dov Rokeah of Belz. In the interwar years, there was the rivalry between the *hasidim* of Ger and Alexander. Nor has the post-Holocaust period seen harmony in the world of Hasidism. There is, for example, the dissension of the *M'lochim*, the splinter group formed by R. Hayyim Avraham Dov Ber Levin Hakohen of Lubavitch.[2]

When R. Yissahar Dov Ber of Belz formed his own independent community in Jerusalem, it not only aroused the ire of the *Eda Haredit* but also had repercussions in New York. There is still animosity between R. Eliezer Menahem Schach of Bene Berak and the Lubavitch movement. Nor is Satmar free from friction. Feige Teitelbaum, the widow of the old Rebbe, has many adherents who are dissatisfied and have formed a rival establishment known as *Bene Yoel*. Other Satmar dissidents are R. Yehiel Michael Leibowitz, the Rebbe of Nikolsburg, New York, and the group of R. Menahem Mendel Wachter.[3]

The rebbes of Alexander and Kalev in Bene Berak have their counterparts in New York in R. Yehiel Mendel Singer and R. Moshe ben Menahem Taub, respectively. There is also a "Cold War" between R. Moshe Yehoshua Hager of Vizhnitz and his son R. Yisrael, and his brother R. Mordecai Hager of Monsey. There is internal friction in the dynasties of R. Arale's grandchildren, Ashlag, Biala, Lelov, Nadvorna, Slonim, and Spinka. Belz like Ger, Lubavitch, and Alexander, has always followed one Rebbe. There is no room for splinter movements, and the younger son or younger brothers submit to the hegemony of the chosen rebbe, unlike in other dynasties, such as Chernobyl, Nadvorna, Spinka, and Biala.

When R. Aaron Rokeah of Belz died, a number of his followers wished to give allegiance to R. Yaakov Yosef Twersky (1900–1968), the rebbe of Sqvira, then residing in the United States. The majority of *hasidim*, however, were willing to wait until the rebbe's young nephew Yissahar Dov Rokeah reached maturity. When he eventually became rebbe, discord was simmering beneath the surface, and he had to contend with some bitterness from a number of dissidents. Some of the older *hasidim* had misgivings

---

2. Jerome R. Mintz, *Hasidic People*, op. cit., pp. 53–59.

3. David Landau, *Piety and Power* (London: Secker & Warburg, 1993), p. 223.

about him, and they maintained "that the countenance of R. Aaron Rokeah (the Rebbe of Belz) was like that of the sun, and the face of R. Berele was like that of the moon."[4] A number of opponents "rebelled" against the new Rebbe, including R. Yisrael Yaakov Klapholz (1910–1988), the personal attendant of the late Rebbe of Belz, the head of the yeshivah in Bene Berak, and a popular writer on Belz; a small number of *hasidim* in Jerusalem, Antwerp, and Williamsburg; and a lively hasidic circle in London, with the support of Eliasz Englander, a son-in-law of the late Getzel Berger. The spirit of dissension affected the Bethune Road Center in London, which no longer accepts R. Berele Rokeah as its spiritual mentor.

"When you are drowning," goes the Yiddish expression, "you clutch even at a straw." After the death of the Rebbe of Mahnovke, who died childless, the rebels gave their allegiance to R. Joshua Twersky. Born in Tel Aviv in 1948, the son of R. David, a scion of a prestigious dynasty, he lives quietly in Jerusalem and never became rebbe. He has no pretensions to rabbinic or talmudic brilliance. R. Joshua studied in Sqvira, U.S.A., and married Gittel, the daughter of R. Shalom Michalowitz. They have thirteen children, seven sons and six daughters, five of whom are married. Devoid of charisma, not renowned for his scholarship, he is dependable and modest and seems utterly bewildered by the devotion that so many followers are showering upon him, which he feels to be utterly undeserved.

R. Joshua succeeded R. Avraham Yehoshua Heschel Twersky, known as the Rebbe of Mahnovke. Born on 24 Adar 1895, he was a descendant of R. Nahum of Chernobyl. It was his father, R. Yosef Meir (d. 29 Av 1917) who settled in Mahnovke. R. Avraham Yehoshua Heschel married Havah, the daughter of R. David Aaron Twersky of Zarik and granddaughter of R. Avraham the Maggid of Turisk, in 1921.

He refused the post of "chief rabbi" of Moscow, which he regarded as a "puppet" position, a public relations exercise by the

---

4. *Bava Batra* 75b.

Soviet regime that was intended to present to the world a picture of religious tolerance in Russia. He refused to accede to its demands, was interrogated and pressured by the KGB, and exiled to Siberia for three and a half years. Returning from Siberia, he first lived in Kolno and then, from 1958 to 1968, lived in Moscow. It was only on 15 Shevat 1965 that he moved to Israel, settling first in Tel Aviv and then in Bene Berak, where he established a small *kollel* and yeshivah. He was deeply concerned with the plight of the new immigrants from Eastern Europe, many of whom visited him and to whom he was Known as the Rebbe of the Proletariat. He was elected to *Moezet Gedole HaTorah* and participated in the work of the Aguda.

Unlike most hasidic rebbes, he recited instead of chanting *Lecha Dodi* ("Come my Beloved"), composed by R. Shlomo Halevi Alkabetz, which is sung at the Sabbath Eve Service. His most treasured possession was a *Sefer Torah* that he alleged had belonged to R. Israel Baal Shem Tov. He would only use the Scroll on *Shabbat Mevorchim* (the Sabbath when we announce the New Moon). This Scroll of the Law was taken out of Russia in a diplomatic pouch.[5] Suffering from urinary and kidney infections, he died on the Day of Atonement 1989 and was succeeded by his sister's grandson, R. Joshua, the head of Yeshivah *Mahzike Lomde Torah*.

The Royal Rebbe

Bene Berak now houses most of the Torah Institutions of R. Avraham Yaakov Friedman, the Rebbe of Sadagora-Ruzhin. He is gradually relinquishing his palatial home in Rehov Pinkas 41 in North Tel Aviv and is moving to Bene Berak, where he already has a three-story yeshivah building, *Bet Yisrael*. Over one hundred boys aged from thirteen to sixteen study there. It was originally located in Rehov Bene Berak, Tel Aviv, and in 1957 moved to

---

5. Gavriel Munk, "Remembering the Mahnovke Rebbe," in *Torah Luminaries* (New York: *Mesorah Publications*, 1994), pp. 105–113.

Rehov Ezra, Bene Berak. There are four kindergartens, a *kollel*, a *Keter Yisrael*, a Talmud Torah *Knesset Mordecai* in Rehov Yoel, editorial offices, and a publication society, *Knesset Mordecai*, for the printing of the works of his ancestors. A periodical, *Mesilot*, containing discourses of the Rebbe and biographical material, is regularly published.

The center is under the auspices of the Rebbe, and secular subjects, even computer studies, are included in the curriculum. The Rebbe also has a *Bet Hamidrash*; a *Talmud Torah*; a yeshivah, L'Zeirim; and five *kollelim* in Kiryat Sadagora in Jerusalem. He is one of the spiritual guides of the Yeshivah *Tiferet Yisrael*.

Born in Vienna on 5 Elul 1928, in 1953, he married Feiga Zipporah, the daughter of R. Yosef Arye Feldman of Tel Aviv, a descendant of R. Meir Schiff, known as *Maharam Schiff*, a German talmudist of seventeenth century. For two decades (1953–1973) he lived in New York, and on his return to Israel, he became the head of the Yeshivah in Bene Berak. On becoming rebbe in 1979, he made his home in North Tel Aviv and had his residence above the newly built and handsomely appointed synagogue. He has a valuable library of over fifteen thousand volumes, including rare works and autographed letters of R. Yisrael Friedman of Ruzhin, as well as manuscripts of the Chernobyl and Karlin dynasties and autographed letters of R. Hayyim of Zanz. As is customary in Ruzhin, he prays by himself in a room attached to the synagogue. While he is hidden from the congregation, he can hear every word of the service.

He enjoyed living in Tel Aviv because it is the only town in Israel that has neither a church nor a mosque, but he now feels that he can achieve more in Bene Berak, where so many of his followers reside. He possesses a superior intellect and has a very pleasant personality. Though a talmudic scholar, he is gentle and unpretentious. He is a father to his followers, not only lending a sympathetic ear to his *hasidim*, but also supplying practical and continuous aid and solving many of their personal and financial problems. His abundant energy, drive, and hard work have galvanized his institutions. He is very active in the Aguda and is a member of the presidium of the *Moetzet Gedole HaTorah*, where he makes his views heard.

He, like the rest of the Aguda, is dissatisfied with the status quo, agreed between David Ben Gurion, then chairman of the Jewish Agency, and the religious parties on 19 June 1947, which laid down that the legal day of rest in the Jewish State should be the Sabbath; that all necessary measures be taken to guarantee that every state kitchen intended for Jews be kosher; that the personal status of Jews be adjudicated by the rabbinical courts; and that full autonomy be given to every trend in the educational system.

The Rabbi feels that a redefinition of the "Law of Return" should be undertaken. Under the present Law of Return, every Jew has the right to come to Israel unless he has been guilty of offenses against the Jewish people or is liable to endanger public health or security. Many immigrants from Poland and the former Soviet Union have non-Jewish spouses and sons who have not been circumcised. Many have undergone "conversion" by a *Bet Din* set up by the Immigration Department of the Jewish Agency with the participation of the Chief Rabbi of Vienna, and the Rabbi feels that these authorities were not qualified to perform this function. He asserts that the Law of Return, which provides the automatic right to citizenship for those who can prove that they are Jews, should be amended to conform with the strict religious code of *Halachah*, which stipulates a Jewish mother or conversion by an Orthodox rabbi as the sole qualifications for Jewish identity. He strongly objects to the "fictitious conversions" by the special *Bate Dinim* and the Conversion Ulpan who carry out conversions with the minimum degree of bureaucracy.

He welcomed the April 1997 Conversion Bill, granting the Rabbinical Courts the sole jurisdiction over conversions performed in Israel. He felt, however, that this amendment does not go far enough. Secular Israeli law, as it now stands, permits Gentiles who underwent a Reform conversion ceremony outside Israel to live in Israel under the framework of the Law of Return and be recognized as "Jews."

Nor is he satisfied with the provisions of the 1948 Act that established the Sabbath and the Jewish Festivals as official days of rest. He urges the government to legislate for the cessation of all nonessential services, especially buses, trains, and airplanes, from sundown on Friday to sunset on the Sabbath. Public transport operating in Haifa on the Sabbath is to him a matter of great concern. Similarly, he is unhappy with the 1951 Act that ruled that every employee was to have at least thirty-six hours of leisure each week, because this did not specify that these hours were to include the Sabbath, and with the September 1948 Law that made women subject to conscription. True, the government agreed to exempt Orthodox girls who applied for exclusion on religious grounds. It was stipulated that such girls would be assigned agricultural or social welfare tasks, but in 1971, the Israeli Cabinet decided to introduce a volunteer service for these Orthodox girls. The Rebbe feels that there should be total exemption without any reservation. He was distressed when the Israeli Supreme Court consisting of eleven judges ruled in December 1998 that exemption from Compulsory Military Service enjoyed by thirty thousand Yeshivah students was illegal and must be stopped.

He endorsed the view of the deputy housing minister, R. Meir Porush, that the State should pass a Law prohibiting missionary activities and close mission schools. In 1997, he was disturbed that thirty-three Georgian immigrants were baptized in Tel Aviv on a Sabbath. He favors the prohibition of pig breeding and major changes in the Anatomy and Pathology Act of 1953, which permits postmortem operations without the prior consent of the deceased or his family, requiring only that three doctors sign a certificate of necessity. He opposes this Act because he considers the mutilation of the dead to be a desecration. He also opposes archaeological digs in sensitive areas, especially where there were burial grounds in the past.

He favors increased child allowances for large families and more funds for religious educational institutions, in view of the high Orthodox birthrate and school enrollments. He points out that the hasidic community has suffered from discrimination in the provision of public housing. Only 6.4 percent of the one hundred thousand housing units available were allocated to *hasidim*, and the budget allowance for the Jerusalem hasidic community does not reflect the size of the population.

The Rebbe has two daughters: Havah Yutta Hadassah lives in Israel and is married to R. Shmuel Zanvel Scharf, a grandson of R. Shmuel Akiva Schlesinger of Strasburg, who is now in charge of the *Bet Hamidrash Sadagora* in Bene Berak; and Elishevah, who married R. Pinhas Shapira and lives in the United States. Sadagora does not always follow the tradition of marrying into hasidic dynasties; more often its adherents marry spouses from lay hasidic families. His only son, R. Yisrael Moshe, born in New York in 1956, was ordained by Rabbis H. D. Padwa, Y. J. Weiss, S. Wosner, and M. Fainstein. In 1978 he married his second cousin Sarah, the daughter of Hayyim Moshe Feldman, a son-in-law of the late Getzel Berger of London and a hasid of Vizhnitz. In 1993, R. Yisrael Moshe opened a *Bet Hamidrash, Or Yisrael*, in northwest London for the *hasidim* of Ruzhin and Sadagora.

R. Avraham Yaakov's father was R. Mordecai Shalom Yosef Friedman. He was born in Sadagora on 17 Kislev 1896. When his father, R. Aaron, died at the age of thirty-six on *Hol Hamoed Sukkot* (19 Tishri) 1913, R. Mordecai Shalom Yosef, at the age of sixteen, became Rebbe in Sadagora. He married Mirel, the daughter of R. Israel Shalom Yosef of Medziborz. At the outbreak of World War One, he settled in Grenadier Strasse, Vienna, which had the third largest Jewish community in Europe, after Warsaw and Budapest. To keep in touch with his scattered followers, he traveled regularly to Przemysl and Czernowitz. The outbreak of World War One found him there, and he hastened to return home, but to avoid desecrating the Sabbath, he broke his journey at Oswiecin. The train continued without him and was wrecked on the way.

The Rabbi hated his brief sojourn in Oswiecin. He related that when the voluntary exiles R. Elimelech Lejask and his brother R. Zusya of Annopol arrived there, R. Zusya said to his brother: "We cannot stay here, Jewish blood is being spilled. I sense it, and I feel it." This was in 1773. Nearly one hundred seventy years later, Oswiecin (Auschwitz), thirty miles west of Cracow, became the site of the largest Nazi concentration camp, where approximately 1.5 million Jews perished.

He was active in the Aguda and attended all its conventions in Vienna and in Marienbad, and he was a member of the *Moetzet Gedole Hatorah* and of *Keren Hatorah*. He was one of the signatories of a special appeal to support Torah institutions. Among the other signatories were R. Yisrael Meir Hakohen of Radin and R. Abraham Mordecai Alter of Ger. The Rebbe was in constant touch with Jacob Rosenheim, the Aguda leader, and R. Yehuda Leib Zirelsohn, the rabbi of Kishinev.

"Black clouds are covering the sky and whoever is able, let him go to the Holy Land," the Rebbe urged. He implored his *hasidim* to settle in the Holy Land, but of the three thousand followers to whom he specifically addressed himself, only thirty took his advice, among them Joel Lieber, who became a noted chocolate manufacturer in the Holy Land. A number of his followers settled in Shechunat Tzvi, near Netanya, and were among the founders of the Aguda settlement *Mahne Yisrael*. The Rabbi himself visited the Holy Land in Iyar 1933, participated in the *Lag B'Omer Hadlakah* at Meron, and also met Rabbi A. I. Kook.

When Engelbert Dollfuss became chancelor of Austria in 1932, the Rabbi realized that nothing could halt the Nazi infiltration. He moved to Przemysl, where many hundreds of *hasidim* turned up on Friday nights to listen to his discourses. There he established a yeshivah, *Meshivat Nefesh*, whose students later studied in *Yeshivat Hahme Lublin*. An additional attraction was the cantorial renderings of Cantor Levi Rosenblatt, the brother of the famous Yosele. The Rabbi saw the writing on the wall, which was not difficult to read. The Nuremberg Laws and the economic boycott were sinister auguries of what was to come. His forebodings regarding the fate of his Austrian followers soon proved to be justified. By September 1938, some sixty thousand of the one hundred ninety thousand Jews of Vienna were dependent on communal help, and Hermann Goering announced the avowed Nazi policy of making Vienna "Jew-free" within four years.

On 10 Adar 1939, he settled in Rehov Bezalel, Tel Aviv, and became active in the Aguda. Yet despite his identification with the Aguda, he disliked party political machinations. "I am here," he told an Aguda gathering, "to see that there are no party politics."

He was particularly concerned with the education of the young, especially the Tehran children, and at one gathering he offered his gold watch toward the financing of their education. He was one of the few hasidic rabbis present at the induction of R. Isser Yehuda Unterman as Ashkenazi Chief Rabbi of Israel in 1964. Unlike many of his rabbinic colleagues, he celebrated *Yom HaAtzmaut*, Israel's Independence Day, each year. In 1967, he went on a fundraising mission to the United States and dedicated his *Bet Hamidrash* in Tammuz 1971.

The Rabbi disliked longwinded discourses. "He who gives us the ability to speak, also gives us the ability to refrain from speaking." His comments had sparks of originality. On the fourth benediction of the *Amida* of the Sabbath Morning Service, *Yismah Moshe* ("Moshe rejoiced"), where it says "In his hand, he brought down the two tables of stone on which was written the observance of the Sabbath," he commented that the Decalogue[6] contained ten precepts, so why is the reference in the *Amida* confined to the observance of the Sabbath? Because when Moses returned to the camp after forty days and beheld the people who had been in Sinai worshiping the Golden Calf, he felt that they were unworthy of the Divine Tablets of the Law. "He cast the Tables out of his hands and broke them beneath the mount."[7] The Tables were shattered, with only one fragment remaining intact—namely, the Fourth Commandment, which stresses the observance of the Sabbath.[8]

The Rabbi has not fulfilled his dream of establishing a *Kirya* to perpetuate Sadagora. His two sons, R. Yisrael Aaron and R. Avraham Yaakov, lived in New York. "The Rabbi of Klausenburg had an easier task," said the Rabbi, referring to the difficulties of his role. "Most of his followers in the United States settled there after World War Two and their roots were shallower. It was comparatively easy for them to settle in the Holy Land. My *hasidim*,

6. Exodus 20:1–26; Deuteronomy 5:7–19.
7. Exodus 32:19.
8. Exodus 32:15–20.

however, have lived in the New World for many years. It is hard for them to uproot themselves."

To maintain contact with his followers, he regularly traveled to the United States and England. "This generation is doubly orphaned. Both the shepherd and his sheep have perished," he lamented. "It is not good for sheep to be without a shepherd. It is equally bad for a shepherd to be without sheep." He died on 29 Nisan 1979 and was buried in Nahalat Yitzhak, Tel Aviv. He was succeeded by his son R. Avraham Yaakov.

Ashlag

R. Yosef, son of Rabba, a talmudic sage, said of his illustrious father that he was most particularly concerned with the law relating to ritual fringes.[9] This dedication to a particular religious precept calls to mind the special attention that R. Ashlag devotes to the *ketubah*.

A whole tractate of the Babylonian and Palestinian Talmud is devoted to the *ketubah* (plural *ketubot*)—the marriage contract. It is written in Aramaic, the *lingua franca* of the Near East since the eighth century of the Common Era. It outlines the economic responsibility of the husband to the wife in the event of her divorce or widowhood. According to the Talmud, it is forbidden to live with a wife for even one hour without a *ketubah*.[10]

In many localities it is the rabbi who prepares the *ketubah* prior to the wedding ceremony. The text is usually printed nowadays, and the officiant merely fills in the names of the bride and bridegroom, the date and place of the marriage. R. Ashlag was surprised when he examined a number of *ketubot* and found innumerable errors. The Hebrew names of the bride and bridegroom were spelled incorrectly; even the date of the marriage was inaccurate. He feels that many rabbis do not know how to fill in a *ketubah*

---

9. Tractate *Shabbat* 118a.
10. *Bava Kamma* 89a.

correctly. He has made it his life's task to arouse the attention of rabbis to pay greater attention to this problem.

R. Simha Avraham Halevi Ashlag lives in Bene Berak. Born in 1948 in Tel Aviv, he was educated in the Yeshivah Etz Hayyim and was ordained by his father. He married Hayyah, the granddaughter of R. Yitzhak Meir Weinstock.

For seven years he was rabbi in Bet Gamliel (between Yavne and Rehovot). He is qualified *Shohet*, a highly skilled scribe and renowned for his circumcisions. He has five sons and four daughters. He has an inquiring mind, and his instinctive empathy with those in trouble secures him wide respect and affection. He has a small *kollel* and a Talmud Torah.

He is a grandson of R. Yehuda Leib Ashlag, who was the colorful founder of the dynasty. Born in Warsaw on 5 Tishri 1885, he was educated in the hasidic yeshivot of Poland and was ordained at the age of nineteen. He was a disciple of R. Meir Shalom Rabinowitz (d. 1909), the rebbe of Kaluszyn, and of his son R. Yehoshua Asher (d. 1938) of Parysow, as well as of R. Yissachar Dov Rokeah of Belz. In 1906, R. Yehuda Leib married Rivka Rosa, the daughter of R. Yosef Meir Abramowitz, and for a time acted as *dayan* in Warsaw.

He attributed his vast knowledge of Kabbalah to an unidentified tutor, with whom he studied for three months. In his youth he wrote a number of esoteric religious poems that have never been published. He also composed melodies for the Psalms. He was so poor that his compositions were written on scraps of paper. He was particularly concerned with the observance of the Festival of Sukkot and on one occasion, when the necessary *Arba Minim* (Four Species) were scarce and costly, his wife sold her jewelry to pay for them.

In the winter of 1922, he emigrated to the Holy Land, where he studied at the *Etz Hayyim* Yeshivah. Later, he established a *kollel*, *Itur Banim*, in the Old City of Jerusalem. In 1924, he became Rabbi in Givat Shaul, a suburb of Jerusalem. From 1934, he lived in London for two years, first in the home of R. Yosef Lew and then in the home of the late Yosef Margulies in Dunsmure Road, Stamford Hill, London (now the hasidic *Shtiebl* of Sqvira). During that time, he studied the large collection of kabbalistic manuscripts in the British Museum (now the British Library). Many of these priceless documents have never appeared in print, a fact so distressing to him that he resolved never to write a new book unless he was sure it would be published.

In 1934, he lived for a short time in Rehov Ben Petahya, Bene Berak, where he was befriended by the Hazon Ish. He returned to Jerusalem and in 1936 began to publish a periodical called *Kuntres Matan Torah*, but it lasted for only a few issues. In these journals he propounded the daring theory that there was no contradiction between Judaism and socialism. It is not clear whether the publication was shut down because of its novel views or because it lacked an official license. In Jerusalem he established a small circle of kabbalists. Students who could not afford a minimal sum for tuition were expected to help to sell his publications. Among the students were his brother-in-law R. Yehuda Tzvi Brandwein, David Minzberg, R. Yosef Weinstock, Moshe Yair Weinstock, and R. Yeshaya Horowitz, a grandson of R. Eliezer Mendel Biderman of Lelov. These esoteric *shiurim* began one hour after midnight and lasted throughout the night. In 1943, when Rommel was about to invade Egypt, he moved to Tel Aviv. "I am moving there," he said, "to stop Rommel."

He felt that Kabbalah was a neglected subject. Just as Gershom Scholem introduced Jewish mysticism to the secular world, so R. Ashlag reintroduced it to Jewish scholars. Like R. Yitzhak Yehuda Yehiel Safrin (1806–74) of Komarno, R. Ashlag believed that the survival of Israel depended on the study of the *Zohar* and that Israel's troubles were due to its neglect. He quoted the words of R. Elijah, the Gaon of Vilna, that the Redemption will take place only through the study of the Torah and especially of the Kabbalah. "To study hasidic works without the *Zohar*," he maintained, "is like studying the commentary of Rashi without the Pentateuch." He stressed again and again that the study of Kabbalah should not be restricted to an elite but should be accessible to young and old, scholar and unlearned. Even at the tender age of nine, a child should begin to study mysticism. A teacher was an asset but not indispensable. Indeed, it was better to study the Kabbalah without a teacher than not to study at all.

He began work on his twenty-two-volume magnum opus, *Ha-Sulam* ("The Ladder") in Heshvan 1943 and finished it in 1954. Many of his disciples attempted to dissuade him, crying, "We are in the midst of a terrible war. The Nazis are battering at the gates of Egypt. There are shortages of food. What relevance has such a work these days?" He had a ready reply: "Sword and slaughter come to the world because people fail to study the holy *Zohar*." Eighteen volumes of his commentary appeared in his lifetime, and three appeared posthumously. His work is a running commentary as well as a translation of the *Zohar* in Hebrew. It received high praises from R. Yosef Hayyim Sonnenfeld; R. Avraham Mordecai, Alter of Ger; R. Mordecai Rokeah, the brother-in-law of the Rebbe of Belz; R. Mordecai Shalom Yosef Friedman of Sadagora; and from the well-known kabbalist of Jerusalem R. Hayyim Shaul Duwayk Hakohen.

R. Ashlag celebrated the conclusion of his great work on 18 Iyar 1954 at Meron, the burial place of R. Shimon Bar Yohai, the author of the *Zohar*. "I am incapable of finding the right words with which to thank God for enabling me to conclude this task," he said. He constantly urged Torah scholars and principals of yeshivot to encourage their students to devote time to the study of the *Zohar*, for example, one page a day, or at least extracts from the *Zohar*. "Redemption surely depends on the study of Kabbalah," he maintained. "If people neglect the study of mysticism, then poverty, war, despoliation, will come to the world." His work *The Ladder*, for all its undeniable strength, lacks hasidic fervor. There is greater insight and moral warmth in *Tiferet Hahanochi* [11] by R. Gershon Hanoch Leiner of Radzin.

A steady stream of books testifies to R. Ashlag's industry and meticulous scholarship. Among his published works were *Panim Me'irot* and *Panim Mesbirot*, a double commentary to the *Etz Hayyim* by R. Hayyim Vital, and *Talmud Esser Sefirot* on the kabbalistic doctrines of R. Yitzhak Luria.

R. Ashlag died on *Yom Kippur* 1954. His last words were from the Book of Psalms: "With long life will I satisfy Him and make

---

11. Warsaw, 1900.

Him behold my salvation." [12] He was buried on Har HaMenuhot in Jerusalem. At the suggestion of David Ben Gurion, an *Ohel* (a stone sepulcher) was erected over his grave. His voluminous works gave an impetus to the study of Kabbalah and were reprinted several times in England and in Israel.[13] His brother-in-law, R. Yehuda Tzvi Brandwein (1903–1969), Rebbe of Strettin also known as the Rebbe of the *Histadrut*, completed Ashlag's unfinished commentary on the *Zohar* and called it *Maalot HaSulam*.

He was survived by four daughters and five sons. His second son, R. Shlomo Binyamin was born in Warsaw on 5 Tevet 1914, and at the age of twelve accompanied his father to the Holy Land. He married Liba, the daughter of R. David Aaron Hauser, a hasid of Sochaczev, in 1932, and they had two sons and two daughters. He lived for a time in Haifa, where he was a *dayan*, then in Tel Aviv, and finally in 1955 he settled in Bene Berak and took over his father's *Bet Hamidrash* in Shadal 4. His ornate and spacious *Sukkah* was renowned. He succeeded his father and maintained a *kollel*, *Ateret HaTalmud*. He died on 7 Kislev 1984 and was also succeeded by his second son, R. Yeheskel Yosef Ashlag, who established a *Bet Hamidrash* in Bene Berak.

R. Shlomo Binyamin's older brother, R. Baruch Shalom, established a rival *shtiebl* in Rehov Ibn Ezra in Bene Berak. Not much love was lost between the two brothers. Each claimed to be his father's heir, and two decades have not healed the rift between them. R. Baruch Shalom lived for a time in Manchester, England, and was one of the tutors of R. Solomon Sassoon. He died on 5 Heshvan 1989.

Torah Thoughts

"So that you can tell your sons and your grandsons what I have wrought upon the Egyptians" (Exodus 10:2). The Torah uses the

---

12. Psalms 91:16.
13. *Sefer HaZohar Al Hamoadim*, ed. Yeheskel Yosef Halevi (Bene Berak, 1992), Appendix, pp. 1–7.

singular "you can tell" first, and then the plural "you may know."
This implies that only one who is convinced can influence others. We read in the Talmud (*Berachot* 6b) that "If one is filled with
the fear of God, one's words will be heard," meaning that by the
manner one tells a story, one can implant in others true faith in
the Almighty (the Rebbe of Mahnovke).

"And it came to pass because the midwives feared God, that
he made them houses" (Exodus 1:21). God built up their families
and increased their prosperity. Why does Scripture use the term
lahem (them)? and not the feminine *lahen*. The Talmud (Sabbath
49a) records that the Roman government once proclaimed a ban
against the Jews, forbidding them to don *tefillin*. One rabbi, R.
Elisha, put them on and went into the street. When a Questor
saw him, R. Elisha fled, thereupon the Questor gave pursuit and
overtook him. Elisha then removed them from his head and held
them in his hand. "What have you got in your hand?" the Questor
demanded. "The wings of a dove overlaid with gold," the rabbi
replied. He was thereafter known as "Elisha, the man of the
wings." Similarly, in the merit of the self-sacrifice that the midwives imposed upon themselves to safeguard the lives of the children, not only were they rewarded, but the children also were
saved (R. Abraham Jacob, Rebbe of Sadagora).

"And he smote the Egyptian and hid him in the sand" (Exodus 2:12). The Sages of the *Midrash* argue as to the method by
which Moses slew the Egyptian. Different methods are discussed.
Some say he slew him with his fist, others with a clay shovel, and
there is the view that he pronounced God's name (*Shem
HaMeforash*) against him (*Midrash, Exodus Rabba* 1:29). There seem
to be three methods of defeating an enemy: by sheer physical force;
by arousing popular sentiment against the injustice that has been
committed; the most effective way, however, is to use God's name,
the *Tetragrammaton*, which was only pronounced by the High
Priest in the Holy of Holies once a year (*idem*).

"And he was there with the Lord forty days and forty nights,
he did neither eat bread or drink water" (Exodus 34:28). In
Deuteronomy (9:18) it is stated, "And I fell before the Lord forty
days neither did I eat bread nor drink water." Similarly, in the

case of the Prophet Elijah (1 Kings 19:8), it is stated that he arose and did eat and drink and went on by the strength of that meat forty days and forty nights until he reached Horeb, the Mount of the Lord. Why does the Torah stress the problem of food? Surely, on a spiritual pilgrimage, the need for material things does not arise? Moses, however, differentiates between the First Decalogue and the Second Tablets. He shattered the First Tablets in righteous indignation when he beheld the people dancing before the golden calf. Then, however, the Divine Presence was removed from him and he was less elevated when he fashioned the Second Tablets, hence the reference to bread and water (*idem*).

"If he came by himself, he shall go out by himself" (Exodus 21:3). Just as a human being comes into this world free of sin "by himself," so should he endeavor that his exit (when he dies) should similarly be without sin (R. Shlomo Hayyim of Sadagora).

"And all the people perceived the thunderings and the lightnings and the voice of the horn and the mountain smoking. And when the people saw it they trembled and stood afar off" (Exodus 20:15). What is the meaning of "they stood afar off"? Surely, the entire world is full of His glory? The belief in God should not depend on "signs and miracles." When the Israelites witnessed the "thunderings and the lightnings," they realized that they were still "far off," they still had not reached the true stage of faith (R. Abraham Jacob of Sadagora).

In the "Grace after Meals" we say: "Those who fear him, shall lack nothing," which means that those who truly fear the Almighty shall lack nothing. They are satisfied with their lot (*idem*).

"And if the road is too long for you, so that you are not able to carry it, because the place is too far from you" (Deuteronomy 14:24), really means that if the yoke of the Torah is too difficult for you to carry, it is because you have distanced yourself from God, Who is also called *Hamakom* ("the Place"). The only remedy is that "you shall turn it into money" (ibid., Verse 25). The Hebrew word *kesef* (money) can also be translated as "longing"—by desiring to serve the Almighty, you will be able to bear willingly the yoke of the Torah (R. Yehuda Leib Ashlag).

"The Lord loves those, who hate evil" (Psalms 97:10). It is not enough to proclaim the love of God, it is equally essential to hate evil, for "the fear of the Lord is to hate evil" (Proverbs 7:13). Man by himself is powerless to eliminate the evil that prevails in the world. "The Almighty preserves the souls of the saints who hate evil" (ibid., Verse 10). He preserves them by delivering them from the hands of the wicked (*idem*).

14

Trees with Many Branches

Spinka

The *gematria* (numerical value) of the Hebrew letters of the town "Spinka" (Szaplona or Sapanta), a town in Marmaros in Carpathian Russia, is equivalent to that of the Hebrew word *esh* (fire), say the *hasidim*. For seventy years, until the outbreak of World War Two, this small town near Sziget was the home of a dynasty that attracted laborers and scholars. The Spinka following in Hungary was second only to that of Belz. It combined the mysticism of Zydaczov, the scholarship of Zanz, and the fiery worship of R. Uri of Strelisk, known as *Ha-Saref*. Today, Spinka lives and flourishes in *Eretz Yisrael*, and the dynasty is represented there by rebbes in Jerusalem and Bene Berak, and in the United States—in Williamsburg, New York, and in other localities.

The Rebbe in Rehov Dunolo, Bene Berak, R. Yisrael Hayyim Weiss, was born in New York on 5 Shevat 1955 and studied there

in the Wiener Yeshivah. In 1973, he emigrated to Israel and continued his studies in the Yeshivah of Spinka. Two years later, he
married Havah, the daughter of R. Yerahmiel Tzvi Rabinowicz,
the Biala-Przysucha Rebbe of Jerusalem. He has a large family and
became Rebbe in 1988. He has *shtieblech* in Jerusalem, Petah
Tikvah, and Rehovot. He maintains a yeshivah, *Mesifta Bet
Yitzhak*, for boys between twelve and sixteen, a Talmud Torah,
and a *kollel*, *Ner Avraham*, in memory of R. Avraham Abish
Weiss. His monthly budget is more than $70,000, one-third of
which is subsidies from the government. He is a very affable and
nonpolitical man. He follows the traditions of Spinka by wearing
not only a *kittle* but also a *tallit* on *Seder* nights. He lights candles
on Friday night, which is normally the prerogative of the mistress of the house. He follows the special liturgy of the Spinka
family, for the *Hakafot*, the processional circuits on *Shemini Atzeret*
and *Simhat Torah*. On the Sabbath, he only speaks Hebrew.

Spinka is a comparative latecomer in the hasidic constellation.
The founder, R. Yosef Meir Weiss, the son of R. Shmuel Weiss,
Dayan of Munkacz, was born on 18 Adar 1838. His mother, the
daughter of R. Tzvi Hirsch of Drohobycz, died when he was sixteen years old in 1854. He studied in Ungvar under R. Meir
Eisenstadt, known as *Maharash Esh*. When R. Meir died in 1852,
he continued his education under the latter's son R. Menahem,
and then in the yeshivah of R. Shmuel Shmelke Klein in Huszt,
the author of the *Zeror HaHayyim* novellae on talmudic tractates,[1]
who predicted that "he would one day be a famous *Zaddik*." His
personal life was beset by sorrow. In 1854, he married the daughter of the wealthy Mordecai of Borsa, a descendant of R. Meir of
Przemyslany. His wife died three years later in the summer of
1857. He then returned to Munkacz where he married the daughter of R. Meir. In 1868, she, too, died, leaving him with two young
daughters.

On *Lag B'Omer* 1870, he married for the third time, Perl, the
widowed daughter of the wealthy Ezra Yaakov Bash of Spinka,
who was a devout hasid of R. Hayyim of Zanz. R. Yosef Meir

---

1. Hakdamot Likkute Torah Ve'Shas (Munkacz, 1876).

was influenced by R. Shalom Rokeah of Belz, R. Hayyim Halberstam of Zanz, and above all by R. Yitzhak Eizig Eichenstein of Zydaczov. "I do not know why the Rebbe of Spinka continues to visit us," said R. Yitzhak Eizig. "He certainly does not need to acquire the fear of God from me. In Spinka the heavens shine more brightly than in Zydaczov." After the death of his mentor, the Rebbe of Zydaczov, on 9 Sivan 1873, he became Rebbe in Spinka and attracted many *hasidim*.

He became known as a "miracle worker." "Master of the Universe," the Rebbe would pray, quoting the words of the *Musaf Amidah* for Festivals, "bring together our scattered ones from amongst thē nations, and gather our dispersed people from the ends of the earth. Lead them to Zion, and only then will they serve You with a perfect heart." He died on 6 Sivan 1909 at the age of seventy-one, and on 6 Iyar 1972 his remains were reinterred in Petah Tikvah, near his son R. Avraham Abish who had died at the age of twenty-five. Throughout his life, he did not publish any of his works except a preface to his Rebbe's work *Likkute Torah* and a ritual for *Hakafot*.[2] His son posthumously published his erudite writings on mysticism, as well as homiletics and his responsa, under the title *Imre Yosef*.[3]

His only son, R. Yitzhak Eizig (1875–1944), named after the Rebbe of Zydaczov, established a yeshivah, *Bet Yisrael*. He married Miriam, the daughter of R. Yissachar Ber Eichenstein of Verecki. "I need not be ashamed of my son-in-law," said R. Yissachar Ber. "He can hold his own among all the rabbis." During the first World War, R. Yitzhak Eizig lived for a time in Budapest and then in Munkacz, but in order to avoid the antagonism of R. Hayyim Elazar Shapira, he moved to Selische, near the Czechoslovakian border. R. Yitzhak Eizig was known as a *Matmid* par excellence. The Talmud was his constant companion. His love of learning was an all-consuming passion, and his life was

---

2. Sziget, 1897.

3. *Imre Yosef*, Genesis (Sziget, 1910); Exodus (Munkacz, 1911); Leviticus and Numbers (Sziget, 1913); Deuteronomy (Seini, 1927); *Imre Yosef* on Festivals, part 1, (Varanov, 1929); part 2 (Baranov, 1931).

an act of worship. "Holy Creator," the Rabbi would often implore, "have compassion on me. My only desire is to serve You."

He was known for his kindliness and would not begin his prayers unless he had distributed all his money to charity. When he had no more money of his own to give to the poor, he would borrow money for this purpose. "First I study the Laws relating to loans," he remarked, "then the Laws pertaining to charity." His favorite phrase was: "May you be granted salvation from heaven." Despite his various rabbinical preoccupations, he never failed to deliver his daily discourse to the students of the yeshivah.

R. Yitzhak Eizig corresponded on halachic problems with R. Yitzhak Elhanan Spector (1817–1906), rabbi of Kovno, with R. Shalom Mordecai Hakohen Schwadron of Brzezany, and with R. Hayyim Hezkiahu Medini (1833–1905) of Hebron, the author of *Sede Hemed*, a talmudical encyclopedia. Though Selische had now become his residence, he did not sever his links with Spinka. Twice each year, on the *Yahrzeits* of his father (on 6 Iyar) and of his mother (on 3 Shevat), he made the pilgrimage to this home-town to renew his ties with his followers. It was there that a ye-shivah, *Bet Yosef*, was established under his son R. Naftali Tzvi. Selische was only fifty kilometers from the Polish border, and after the outbreak of World War Two, many Polish Jews escaping the Nazi inferno found refuge in the Rabbi's house. To accommodate the ever-increasing flow, he built a bunker where they could hide in comparative safety. The Hungarian authorities soon became aware of what was happening. He was arrested and reprimanded for harboring aliens. "I cannot ask a fellow-Jew for his passport," was his answer. He was released, and his prison experiences did not deter him from continuing his rescue operations.

The Rabbi had many opportunities to leave Eastern Europe. He was offered a certificate to enable him to enter the Holy Land. His relative R. Yissachar Dov Bergman of New York procured an American visa for him, and he also received a permit to enter England. But the aged Rabbi could not bear to abandon his followers and family. Conditions rapidly deteriorated. On the day after Passover 1943, twelve thousand Jews were crammed into a ghetto, and transports to Auschwitz began. The third transport left on *Rosh Hodesh Sivan*. A hasid implored him: "Rabbi, pray for a miracle. We are traveling to our death." "Do not be afraid," the Rabbi comforted him. "We are going to welcome the Messiah. The Messiah is in chains in Rome: it is our duty to redeem him."

Throughout the fearful journey, he sang over and over again the words from the Sabbath morning service: "Purify our hearts, to serve thee in truth and in thy love and favor." The Rabbi, his wife, Rachel Leah, his sons R. Yisrael Hayyim and R. Avraham Yakir, and nine members of the Rebbe's family arrived in Auschwitz on 13 Sivan. With the biblical phrase "Fire shall be kept burning upon the Altar continually,"[4] he met his Maker on 13 Sivan 1944. Thirty-one members of his family perished under the Nazis. Like his father, he did not publish any books in his lifetime. After the liberation, his grandson R. Yaakov Yosef returned to Selische, where he found the manuscripts of R. Yitzhak Eizig. The manuscript was in a very bad condition, as it had been exposed to rain and snow, which had left many pages torn and illegible. It was a herculian task to prepare it for publication. He eventually published these works, which contained responsa on the four orders of the *Shulhan Aruch* as well as homiletical discourses, under the name *Hakal Yitzhak*, since the Hebrew word *Hakal* is equivalent to one hundred and thirty-eight, the numerical value of the name Eizig.[5]

The third Rebbe of Spinka, R. Yaakov Yosef, the son of R. Yisrael Hayyim, was the only member of the family to survive the Holocaust. Born in Spinka on 12 Nisan 1916, with his mother, Havah Sarah, the daughter of R. Eliezer Rubin, the Rebbe of Sasov, dying in childbirth, he was brought up by his father and grandfather. In 1936, he married the daughter of R. Alter Menahem Mendel of Borsa. During World War Two he was trans-

---

4. Leviticus 6:3.

5. *Hakal Yitzhak*, Genesis and Exodus (New York: Agudat Haside Spinka, 1952); Leviticus, Numbers, and Deuteronomy (New York, 1954); Responsa (New York, 1966); Commentary on the *Passover Haggadah* (Jerusalem, 1964).

ferred from camp to camp, each time narrowly missing death, though his wife and three children perished. One Saturday evening, he left his hut in order to "sanctify the moon." At that moment the camp was attacked by Allied bombers and the entire barracks destroyed. He was captured then by the Russians, who refused to believe that he was fleeing from the Nazis and prepared to execute him. A Russian officer who happened to be passing by asked him the meaning of a *mishnah* from the tractate *Berachot*. The Rabbi's ready explanation established his identity and saved his life.

After the war, he returned from Dyhernfurth to Borsa in Transylvania and lived for a time in Arad. A year later he settled in Crown Heights, New York, where he remarried and established a *Bet Hamidrash* and a yeshivah. Despite his growing popularity, he dreamed of living in Israel, which he visited frequently. In 1955, he settled in Bene Berak. He kept in touch with his American *hasidim*, and just as his grandfather visited Spinka, so he regularly visited New York.

The Rabbi felt that spiritual improvement must precede material improvement. On Friday night, he did not deliver discourses because, as the rabbis of Zydaczov believed, "No one should give a discourse unless he has heard it directly from the Almighty. The discourse should be for the edification of the speaker as well as of the listeners." Instead, the Rabbi told tales of *Zaddikim* whose *Yahrzeit* fell in the course of that week. The Rabbi was selective in the choice of students for his yeshivot in Bene Berak and Jerusalem. He also maintained a school in Acre.

In 1969, he acquired twenty-five *dunam* in Petah Tikvah and made elaborate plans to establish a *Kirya*, but because of technical and administrative problems, these plans have still not left the drawing board. The greatest catastrophe of his life was the death in 1972, of his twenty-five-year-old son R. Avraham Abish, the principal of the yeshivah of Spinka, who left two young daughters. To perpetuate his son's memory, a *kollel*, *Ner Avraham*, was established. He lost another son, R. Yitzhak Eizig who was killed in a road accident on 4 Shevat 1984. "What can I say," said the Rebbe, "except that I accept the yoke of the kingdom of Heaven

in love." The Rebbe died during *Hol Hamoed* Pesach 1988, and
was survived by three sons who became rebbes.

In Rehov Hosea, Bene Berak, lives another Spinka rebbe, R.
Moshe Elikum Bria, born on 13 Sivan 1936, in Karlsburg, Romania. On 20 Shevat 1953, he married Esther Leah, the daughter of
R. Hayyim Eliezer Breitman of Arad, Romania. His father was
R. Nahman Cahane of Spinka. R. Nahman, born on 2 Heshvan
1905, the son of R. Hayyim (1861–1904) of Sziget, became rabbi
of Spinka in 1885, despite the opposition of R. Yomtov Lipa
Teitelbaum, who regarded Spinka as part of his empire. Until the
day of his wedding, he studied with his father, R. Tzvi Hirsch
Cahane, the son-in-law of R. Yitzhak Eizig. In 1924, R. Nahman
married the daughter of R. Yaakov Yisrael Vishurun Rubin, the
rebbe of Szaszregen, a descendant of R. Naftali of Ropczyce. He
obtained his rabbinical diploma from R. Yaakov Gottlieb of
Miskolc, Hungary, and of R. Tzvi Hirsch Kunstlicher, rabbi in
Hermanstadt in Transylvania, and became rabbi of Spinka in 1928.

During World War Two, he lived in different Romanian ghettos and afterward became rabbi of Cluj. He sent his four children
as "illegal immigrants" to the Holy Land, where he joined them
in 1951. For a time he lived in Bene Re'em, the first *Moshav* of
the Poale Agudat Yisrael. In 1957, he settled in Bene Berak, where
he had a *Bet Hamidrash* and a small *kollel*. On Friday evenings,
the rabbi gave three discourses, two before the meal and one after it. He did not belong to any political party but, nevertheless,
participated in a number of protest demonstrations. He died on
16 Tishri 1976, survived by two daughters and five sons. He was
succeeded by his son R. Moshe Elikum Bria.

R. Nahman's brother was R. Yosef Meir Cahane, who made
his home in Jerusalem. He was born in Spinka in 1910. He studied under his maternal grandfather, R. Baruch Rubin of Gerela,
and was ordained by R. Yosef Elimelech of Ungvar. In 1930, he
married the daughter of R. Yitzhak Teitelbaum of Husakov, near
Przemysl, and for the first three years of his marriage he lived in
the house of his father-in-law. He then became rabbi of Seredna,
near Ungvar, and two years later moved to Radvanka, a suburb
of Ungvar, where he, too, became known as the Spinka rebbe.

He was the first of the Spinka dynasty to reach the Holy Land in 1941. He made his home in Jerusalem and established a *kollel* for thirty students in Rehov Salant. He died on 8 Shevat 1978 and was succeeded by his son R. Mordecai David Cahane. The other grandson of R. Yitzhak Eizig, R. Shmuel Tzvi Horowitz, survived Auschwitz, and in 1948 he established a *Bet Hamidrash, Bet Yitzhak* in Williamsburg, New York.

The Rebbes of Nadvorna

"There is no town without a rebbe of Nadvorna," say the *hasidim.* Nadvorna puts Spinka in the shade: sons, brothers, sons-in-law, all became rebbes. In Jerusalem, they are represented by R. Tzvi Hirsch Rosenbaum of Kretchneff, R. Levi Yitzhak Leifer, and R. Yehiel Leifer. In Bene Berak lives R. Yitzhak Eizig of Zutzke, R. Nathan David Rosenbaum, R. Yaakov Yissachar Ber, R. Yosef Leifer, and R. Meir, known as the Przemyslaner. In Hadera lives Rebbe R. Asher Yeshayahu Rosenbaum, and in Rehovot, there is R. Menahem Zeev Rosenbaum of Kretchneff; in Ashdod is R. Mordecai Issachar Ber Leifer of Pittsburg; in Safed, R. Aaron Yehiel Banya; in Kiryat Gat, R. Yisrael Nisan; in Jaffa, R. Zeidel Rosenbaum, Rebbe of Bishkov. In New York lives R. Yosef Meir (son of R. Meshullam Zalman); R. Shalom Leifer in Brighton; R. Asher Mordecai of Strozhniz, R. Yosef of Kalush, R. Aaron Moshe of Huszt, R. Meir of Mosholov, and R. Meshullam Zalman Leifer in Brooklyn; R. Meir Isaacson in Philadelphia, and R. Yitzhak Eizig Leifer in Cleveland-Raanana.

In Bene Berak lived R. Hayyim Mordechai Rosenbaum who was born on 24 Iyar 1903. He was the eldest son of R. Itamar. His mother Malka was the daughter of R. Asher Yeshaya, a descendant of R. Naftali of Ropczyce. He was a gregarious and big-hearted Rebbe. In 1922 he married the daughter of R. Eliezer Zeev of Kretshneff. After living with his father-in-law, he settled in Seret. He visited the Holy Land on *Rosh Hodesh Adar* 1936. After miraculously surviving the Holocaust, he came to Israel in 1948. He lived in Jerusalem near the Mandelbaum Gate before moving to Jaffa and then to Bene Berak in 1962. One of his sons Ezekiel, whom he sent on an illegal transport *Knesset Yisrael*, died on 3 Kislev 1947. "I sent my son to study in the earthly academy," lamented the Rabbi, "but he was taken to the Academy 'on High.' " The Rebbe died on 15 Tevet 1978 and was buried on the Mount of Olives next to his father. He was survived by six sons, who all became rebbes.

He was succeeded by his son, R. Yaakov Yissachar Ber, born in Seret, Romania, in 1930, where his father was then rabbi. He came to Israel on his own in 1946 and studied in the yeshivah of R. Yosef Tzvi Duszinsky. In 1950, he married the daughter of R. Moshe Hersch, the rabbi of Arad. In 1952, he erected, with the financial help of Meir Rosenthal of Frankfurt-am-Main, a magnificent building on a twenty-*dunam* site in Rehov Ezra and Rehov Hazon Ish. It houses a yeshivah, *Maamar Mordecai*, for two hundred and fifty students; a Talmud Torah, *Tiferet Mordecai*, for 400 students; *kollelim*; and a *Bet Hamidrash* that is the largest hasidic synagogue in Bene Berak. He is nonpolitical and has cordial relations with the *Eda Haredit* and the Aguda. He receives visitors every day from 4 P.M. until late at night. He rises at 6 A.M. when he prays with the students of the yeshivah. Rabbis, rebbes, *dayanim*, and doctors come to him for guidance and advice.

The *grand seigneur* of the dynasty, whose branches have spread far and wide, was R. Itamar Rosenbaum, who lived in Yad Eliyahu in Tel Aviv. The progenitor of a large family, he lived alone in an apartment attached to his *Bet Hamidrash*, attended by his faithful warden. Ailing and frail, he was a cheerful, friendly man who made every visitor feel at home. R. Itamar was born in Mihaileni, Romania, in 1886 and was a descendant of R. Meir of Przemyslany, of R. Tzvi Hirsch of Nadvorna, and of R. Mordecai of Nadvorna. R. Mordecai was an ascetic: "I must train my body to be satisfied with whatever I eat." He would pray for hours on end. "I am sorry to keep you waiting," he once told his followers, "but you know that I am not playing cards or visiting the theater."

There were then no hasidic yeshivot in Romania. He studied under his father, R. Meir of Kretshneff (Craciunesti), and under private tutors when such were available. There is a story that his father was very concerned about the lack of suitable tutors and fervently prayed on New Year's day for Divine help in this matter. His prayer was answered with Divine promptness. "Are you the teacher for whom I have been praying all the morning? Has the Almighty answered my prayer so quickly?" asked R. Meir. "Would that all your prayers be fulfilled, as this one has been," replied the teacher.

R. Itamar married Malkah, the daughter of R. Asher Yeshayahu of Kolbuczov, near Rzeszov, and, after living during World War One in Vienna and Marmaros, settled in Czernowitz, which he described as a "golden city." All were welcome in his home; other hasidic rabbis visited him regularly. He liked to drop in on his colleagues without prior notice. "When I long to see someone, I do not wait for an invitation." Even the mitnaggedic Rabbi Benzion Katz encouraged people to consult R. Itamar: "Listen to him. He does not speak empty words."

He was a proud and loving father. "If you have such children, you need never sigh," a rabbi told him. As a rabbi, he was very conscientious. "Contrary to popular opinion, being a rebbe is not the easiest way to make a living," he once said.

> First of all, even a rebbe has a Jewish heart. It is difficult to listen day after day to tales of woe. Furthermore, to give advice is a tremendous and onerous responsibility. Often the problem is a question of life and death. It is no less difficult to advise people on monetary matters when a man's life savings depends on this advice. A rebbe's position is less defined than a doctor's. The physician knows the patient's symptoms, but the rebbe has only the patient's petition (*Qvittel*) in front of him. He needs the *Urim* and *Tummin* (a Divine oracle) to provide the right guidance.

King Carol's new government declared Romania's intention of joining the Axis, renouncing the British Guarantee of April 1939. He withdrew Romania from the League of Nations and threw himself into Hitler's sphere of influence. On 9 August 1940, the King decreed his anti-Semitic racial laws on the Nuremberg model.

On 11 October 1941, all the fifty thousand Jews in the city were confined in a small area consisting of a few side-streets. Despite the efforts of Wilhelm Filderman (1882–1963), the most important Jewish leader who worked with Marshall Antonescu to protect the lives of the Jews threatened by Nazi racial policies, the Iron Guard, under Nazi influence, re-established a Romanization office to transfer goods, factories, and businesses from Jewish owners to Romanians. During the Festival of Tabernacles (12 October 1941), the deportations to Transnistria began, R. Mordecai Friedman of Boyan and R. Eliezer Hager being among them. R. Itamar was among the twenty thousand Jews who were left behind, having been issued with a special permit-certificate that "they were useful for the economy." Early in February 1944, Czernowitz came under the control of the German army. The Rebbe, his family, and only two thousand other Czernowitz Jews survived the Holocaust.

After the war, he wanted to settle in the Holy Land but could not obtain the necessary permits from the British authorities. He then settled in Washington Heights, New York, where he attracted many followers. He often officiated at the Reader's desk and read the Law. "I read it," said R. Itamar, with a twinkle in his eye, "like all other hasidic rebbes, neither in correct Hebrew, nor in accordance with the musical notations. We do not fast as often as the Lelover Rebbe, nor do we sing like the Rebbe of Modzitz, but we do our best to our fellow-Jews." He did not approve of rebbes who become involved in politics. "I belong to the party to which my father, of revered memory, belonged—the Party of the Lord." He was a quietly spoken man with strong convictions.

He deplored R. Yoel Teitelbaum's anti-Israeli activities. When a hasid of Satmar told the rebbe that R. Yoel was the Messiah, he retorted: "If you were to say that R. Yoel is a great scholar, I would agree. I would also endorse the view that he is a *Zaddik*, a giant among men. But to assert that he is the Messiah, this is ridiculous and preposterous. How could we face the world with him as the Messiah?" He explained the influence by means of which R. Yoel wields such power over such large masses of *hasidim*. "The owner of a Fifth Avenue store is not necessarily superior intellectually to a shopkeeper in the Bronx. The former was just lucky, and fortune smiled upon him." He found it incomprehensible that the Rebbe of Satmar forbade his followers to visit the Western Wall. "If he lived in Israel," said R. Itamar, "he would visit the Wall. Only in heaven is it known who is a genuine rabbi." However, he endorsed the Satmar Rebbe's view that television is "Satan's domain" when watched excessively and indiscriminately. Radio-listening did not appeal to him either. "Bad news, I do not want to hear. Good news I will get to know in any case."

Naturally, he would have liked to see a revival of religion in the Holy Land, especially in Tel Aviv. "A Torah-true city would be an ornament for the entire world." He was not optimistic about the revival of interest in Hasidism in Israel and in the diaspora. "In by-gone days most people were observant, now it is only a tiny minority. It is unlikely that a tiny minority will transform the lives of the majority."

R. Itamar found it hard to explain the dissension and disputes among *hasidim* before the Holocaust. "There was once a rabbi who cried bitterly when told that his opponent had died. The informant expressed surprise. "But, Rabbi, while he was alive, you criticized him, rebuked him, and even excommunicated him. Why do you weep now that he is no longer alive?" "How little you understand," lamented the Rabbi. "My opponent had a haughty soul and only my attacks and criticism sustained him, acting as an antidote to his pride. Were it not for me, he would have died a long time ago."

Death held no terror for him as he advanced in years. "I am not afraid of death, but I do not like the preliminary lodging arrangements." His greatest joy was the fact that he had lived to see children, grandchildren, and great-grandchildren studying the Torah, and that his sons were now rebbes in different localities. On 22 Sivan 1973, surrounded by his children, his grandchildren, and his great-grandchildren, R. Itamar was gathered to his fathers.[6]

---

6. Shlomo Rozman, *Roshe Golat Ariel,* part 1 (Brooklyn: *Zichron Kedoshim*, 1975), pp. 101–120.

R. Yitzhak Eizig was born on 21 Tevet 1906 in Czernowitz and studied under R. Binyamin Katz, the Rabbi of Czernowitz, and under the erudite R. Yitzhak Shapira. During the First World War, the family lived in Vienna. In 1926, he married Hannah, the daughter of R. Nathan David HaKohen Hollander of Galicia. Later, R. Yitzhak Eizig became Rebbe in Zutzke, near Czernowitz.

During World War Two, in the summer of 1941, the Rebbe and his family were deported to Balta, near Odessa, in the region of Transnistria, which was handed over to Romania by the German conquerors. Over ten thousand Jews were confined there in a ghetto and put to forced labor "for the public good." It was controlled by the Romanian gendarmery, and many Jews perished from starvation, typhus, and dysentry. The Rebbe secretly constructed a large bunker, in which forty-five Jewish refugees were hidden. On one occasion, he was arrested and a noose put round his neck prior to his being hanged. He was miraculously saved by a Romanian officer at the last minute. On 15 March 1944, the Soviet Army liberated Transnistria, and the Rebbe and his family were allowed to return to Czernowitz. He then moved to Prague.

He emigrated to the United States and lived in New York, first on the East Side, then in Borough Park for the following sixteen years. He was always preoccupied by the strict observance of the Sabbath, and every Friday would walk the streets of Borough Park, pleading tearfully with the nonobservant shopkeepers to close their premises and to observe the Sabbath. This is significant, because this *mitzvah*, more than any other, absorbed the heart and soul of the Rebbe. There is hardly a discourse in which he does not touch upon some aspect of the seventh day.

On his father's death, he took over his *Bet Hamidrash* in Tel Aviv, and in 1981 he moved to Bene Berak. The Rebbe plays the violin at every *Melaveh Maklah* and during the eight days of Hanukah. He had inherited this instrument from his ancestors, who held the belief that with this violin the family would welcome the Messiah.

In 1985, the Rebbe established *Mifal Shone Halachot*, which encourages young men to study thoroughly the Codes and the *Mishnah Berurah*, the laws of the Sabbath. Written examinations are held monthly, and monetary prizes of over ten thousand U.S. dollars are awarded. The Rebbe also maintains a *kollel*, *Beer Mayyim Hayyim*, consisting of selected young men who, apart from talmudic studies, are urged to avoid *lashon hara* (tongue of evil). The Rebbe endorses the rabbinic view that slander, talebearing, and evil talk are worse than the three cardinal sins of murder, immorality, and idolatry. In this respect he emulated R. Yisrael Meir Kahan, known throughout the Jewish world as the *Hafetz Hayyim*. This was the title of his famous book, published in 1873, based on verses 13 and 14 of Psalms 34: "He who desires life . . . keep thy tongue from evil and thy lips from speaking guile." His most important work was the *Mishnah Berurah*, a commentary on the Code *Orah Hayyim*, a standard work of reference, though he is known as the *Hafetz Hayyim* after his work on the laws of talebearing, gossip, and slander.

Over ten thousand U.S. dollars annually are spent by the Rebbe on *Mifale HaHesed*, an organization that provides basic necessities of food for the festivals, especially for Passover to the needy. His network, *Shiure Torah VeYehadut*, sends out fully trained Orthodox women to secular and nonreligious girls' schools and seminaries to disseminate basic principles of Judaism. "Some of the girls do not know even the *Shema* or the Blessing for lighting the candles for the Sabbath," he explained.

The Rebbe is the author of a 552-page book, *Hazniyut VeHaYesha*,[7] which deals with modesty in women's clothing. He contends that women's dresses should have sleeves reaching their hands. Like R. Arale Roth, he lays down strict rules on head-covering. This book was welcomed by R. Elazar Menahem Shach, R. Yaakov Landau of Bene Berak, and R. Yitzhak Grunwald of New York. One of his pamphlets stresses that on the Sabbath, it is forbidden to open any receptacle other than a tin of sardines.

The Rabbi's wife died on Purim 1984. She was survived by two daughters (since deceased) and by three sons: R. Meir is the Rabbi of the Sephardi Community in Caracas, Venezuela; R. Yisrael is

---

7. Bene Berak, 1984.

Rebbe of Stanislav in Monsey; and R. Nathan David is the principal of a yeshivah in Bene Berak. Though the Rebbe is reserved and quietly spoken in private, in public he becomes enchantingly loquacious, especially on his favorite topic—the Sabbath.

He has many grandchildren and over forty great-grandchildren. Despite his advanced age, he undertook a fundraising tour of the United States and England in March 1997.

Ozarov

Ozarov, a small village located west of the river Vistula, east of Opatov, was transplanted to Bene Berak on the first day of Shevat 1997, when the foundation stone for a new Ozarov-Chentchin Torah center was laid in Rehov Hazon Ish. The structure will house a synagogue, a study hall for a *kollel*, and a publishing house to disseminate Ozarov writings. The present Rebbe, R. Tanhum Binyamin Becker, was born in Milwaukee, Wisconsin, U.S.A., in 1950 to Miriam, the daughter of R. Moshe Yehiel Epstein, and R. David Eliyahu Becker, a student of R. Raphael Shapira of Volozhin and of R. Shimon Shkop. R. David Eliyahu was rabbi in Milwaukee for forty years. He died on 25 Iyar 1979 and was buried in Bene Berak.

R. Tanhum Binyamin studied at first in Lakewood, New York, then in the Mir and Ponovezh yeshivot in Israel. He married Feige Devorah, the daughter of R. Yaakov Burak, the Rabbi of Zanz in Toronto, Canada, and became Rebbe in 1974. He collects genealogical data and has a computerized genealogical service. The data were gathered from civil records at the Ozarov city hall in Poland, which provided genealogical information from 1826 to 1857. He further succeeded in obtaining a genealogical tree of the Epstein family from R. Shmuel Eliyahu Halevi, the Neustadter rebbe, who lived on the Lower East Side, New York, copy of which is also available in the Wolfson Museum, Jerusalem. This unique family tree was published in 1984. The youthful Rabbi appears to have the necessary energy to galvanize the dynasty. He maintains a *kollel*, *Esh Dat*, in Tel Aviv.

"His books give us a spiritual uplift," said the late Chief Rabbi Isser Yehuda Untèrman. He was referring to the most prolific writer of the contemporary rebbes, R. Moshe Yehiel Epstein (1890–1971), rebbe of Ozarov. The Ozarov dynasty goes back to R. Yehuda Arye Leib Halevi, known as the "Great Rabbi Leib," who lived at the beginning of the nineteenth century. R. Moshe Yehiel, the previous Ozarov Rebbe (1890–1891), was the son of R. Avraham Shlomo and Reitze Mirel, a granddaughter of R. Hayyim Shmuel of Chentchin, a descendant of R. Yaakov Yitzhak Horowitz, "the Seer of Lublin."

Moshe Yehiel, a child prodigy, received his rabbinical diploma at the age of eighteen and at twenty-four occupied a rabbinic post in Radom, where he succeeded R. Eliezer Yehuda Treisman. He declined an invitation to become *dayan* in the large Jewish community of Lodz, as this would curtail the time he spent in study. On 18 Sivan 1907, he married Hannah, who was known as the *zisse* ("sweet") Hannah, the daughter of R. Emmanuel Weltfreind, the rabbi of Pabianice and Rozprza (south of Lodz), a descendant of R. Yeshayahu of Przedborz. R. Emmanuel's second wife was Havah, the widow of R. Yerahmiel Tzvi Rabinowicz of Siedlice.

R. Moshe Yehiel's wife died on 15 Iyar 1919 at the age of twenty-nine, of typhus, which she caught when looking after people dying from this disease. She was survived by two daughters, Beila Miriam and Hayyah. Two years later, on the death of his father, R. Moshe Yehiel succeeded him as rabbi of Ozarov. During the First World War, he lived in Cologne and was befriended by R. Shalom Moskovitz of Schatz, later rabbi in London.

On *Lag B'Omer* 1920, he married again. His second wife was Keila, the daughter of R. Menahem Mendel Tenenbaum, with whom he had one son and one daughter. He was very active in the Aguda and in 1921 visited Belgium, England, and the United States as a member of the Aguda Delegation, whose other members were: R. Meir Dan Plotzki of Ostrova, the chairman of the Executive Committee of the *Agudat HaRabbanim* in Poland; R. Meier Hildesheimer (1864–1934), preacher at the Berlin Orthodox Congregation *Adat Yisrael*; R. Asher Lemel Spitzer; the philosopher and writer Nathan Birnbaum (1864–1937); and R. Yosef Lew (1884–1951) of Warsaw, who later became rabbi of the Mile End and Bow Synagogue in London.

On returning to Poland, he lived in Otwock near Warsaw for five years, where he wrote a commentary on Psalms *Likkute Orot*, based on the commentaries of R. Shmuel Shmelke Horowitz of Nikolsburg and of his brother R. Pinhas Halevi, rabbi in Frankfurt. On the advice of R. Yaakov Moshe Safrin, the rebbe of Kormarno, he settled on the East Side of New York, where he established a *Bet Hamidrash*.

On 21 Av 1949, his only son, Alter Avraham Shlomo, a graduate of the Yeshivah *Torah V'Daat*, who was spending some time in a summer camp, was drowned at the age of twenty-one. This tragedy took place while his parents were visiting Israel. R. Nahum Mordechai Perlov, the Rebbe of Novominsk, said in his eulogy: "We have to accept God's judgment but we cannot understand it." Only when R. Moshe Yehiel and his wife returned to New York one month later were they told of this tragedy.

After living in the United States for twenty-five years, he settled in Rehov Rothschild 126, Tel Aviv, in 1953. Very soon afterward his wife died on 22 Shevat. In 1954, the Rebbe married his third wife, the widow Sheindel Yocheved Landau (d. 1983), the daughter of R. Moshe David of Brigal, Galicia. The Rebbe often addressed large gatherings, participated in the deliberations of the *Moetzet Gedole HaTorah*, and was very concerned with *Hinuch Atzmai*. He attended and addressed the fifth *Kenesiyah Gedolah* in Av 1960, and personally appealed to the Rebbe of Lubavitch, R. Menahem Mendel Schneerson, for his support of the Aguda List in the forthcoming elections.

The last eighteen years of his life were devoted to his great works, *Esh Dat* (eleven volumes) and *Be'er Moshe*—a twelve-volume commentary on the Pentateuch and Former Prophets, with a total of over ten thousand printed pages. An innovative thinker, a diligent and painstaking writer, his works are a synthesis of traditional Torah thoughts and hasidic lore, full of insights and new ideas. He brought an infectious zest and enthusiasm to all subjects with which he dealt. His publications received the approval of the rebbes of Belz, Ger, Sadagora, Vizhnitz, and other leading halachic authorities.

The first three volumes were published in New York, and the remainder in Israel. Like the first-century *Tanna* Eliezer ben Hyrcanus, he was "a cemented cistern that does not lose a drop." [8] For the last three decades of his life, he was severely handicapped by failing eyesight, yet he persevered in his work with the help of R. Shalom Hayyim Porush. In 1968, the Rebbe was awarded the prestigious Israel Prize for Torah Literature. As a Levite, the Rebbe was usually called up to the reading of the second portion of the Law every Sabbath. On the last Sabbath of his life, he requested to be called up for the last portion (*Aharon*). When he died on 1 Shevat 1971 at the age of eighty-one, he was, on the advice of R. Yisrael Alter of Ger, buried in the Zichron Meir Cemetery in Bene Berak, near the grave of R. Avraham Yeshayahu Karlitz, the Hazon Ish. His grandson R. Tanhum Binyamin Becker succeeded him.

Torah Thoughts

We say in the *Amidah*, "Blessed art Thou, Our Lord, Our God, the God of our Fathers, the God of Abraham, the God of Isaac, and the God of Jacob." Why does the liturgy repeat "God of"? It could have said: "God of Abraham, Isaac and Jacob," but each Patriarch had his own style, and his own way of serving the Almighty (R. Joseph Meir).

"On the coin produced by Abraham, there was a young man on one side, and on the other an old man" (*Bava Kamma* 97b). A young person naturally has the physical stamina to serve the Almighty, but understanding only comes with age. Abraham was blessed with both physical stamina and mature wisdom. Hence,

---

8. *Avot* 2:11; see Aaron Surasky, *Belahavat Esh Dat*, 2 vol. (Tel Aviv: Esh Dat Rabbinical Seminary, 1985); also, Shalom Meir Hakohen Wallach, *Esh Dat* (Tel Aviv: Esh Dat Rabbinical Seminary, 1995).

it says, and "the Lord blessed Abraham in every way" (Genesis 24:1) (The Rebbe of Spinka).

"And the Lord called unto Moses and spoke unto him out of the Tent of Meeting" (Leviticus 1:1). Rashi, commenting on the verse, said: "When God wishes to express affection for a person, he first calls him by his name." Moses was extremely humble but he was fearful that he might not retain this quality forever. He constantly needed the Almighty's reassurance (*Imre Yosef*).

Joseph said: "How then can I do this wicked thing and sin against God" (Genesis 39:9). Potiphar's wife knew that Joseph was a *Zaddik* and that he observed all of God's Commandments. She felt that since he had never committed any sin, he had no opportunity of ever repenting. She wanted him to transgress in order to enable him to repent. Joseph's reaction was that by slandering his brethren (Genesis 37:2), "Joseph brought evil report of them unto their father," accusing them by saying that they "ate limbs torn from a living animal, that they called the sons of the handmaids slaves, and that they were immoral," was far from being totally righteous, and he had enough of which to repent (*idem*).

"And He sanctified the seventh day" (Genesis 2:3). The very first time "sanctifying" is mentioned in the Torah is with reference to the Sabbath, to indicate that the source of all holiness lies in the observance of the Sabbath (R. Moses Yehiel Epstein).

"For all the land which you see, I will give it to you and your descendants for ever" (Genesis 13:15). Rashi points out that "He gave the Land of Israel to the Children of Israel as a gift and not as an inheritance." An inheritance is given irrespective of whether the inheritor is worthy or unworthy. A gift, however, is given only to one who deserves it. The Land of Israel is a gift, and Israel has to prove worthy of it (ibid.).

"Add the Lord said unto him: what is in your hand" and he said: "A rod" and it became a snake (Exodus 4:3). If you put your trust in a human being, you may soon realize how misplaced your trust has been, as he is liable to turn into a snake (*idem*).

15

Cities of the Kabbalah

Safed

Safed, in Upper Galilee, is an enchanted and sacred town, now the home of Israeli artists. In the eighteenth and early nineteenth centuries, many hasidic rebbes settled in Safed, one of the four "Holy Cities" that Kabbalah endows with mystical significance. The kabbalist and biographer R. Hayyim Yosef David Azulai (1724–1806) maintained that the inhabitants of Safed were more fitted to fathom the depths of the Torah and to penetrate its secrets than the inhabitants of any other city in the Holy Land.[1] The kabbalists maintained that the resurrection of the dead will take place there and that the Messiah will reveal himself there.

---

1. Hayyim ben Yaakov Palagi, *Arzot HaHayyim* (Izmir, 1951), chap. 4, p. 3: see David Russoff, *Safed: The Mystical City* (Jerusalem: Shaar Books, 1991).

The numerical value five hundred and seventy of the Hebrew for *Safed* is equivalent to the Hebrew *T'ka*, from the prayer "Sound the great horn for our freedom."

In the sixteenth century, Safed became a center for the manufacture of woolens. In the seventeenth century, the talmudist R. Yaacov Berab, who settled there around 1533, attempted to revive the ordination (*Semichah*) of rabbis according to the ancient procedure so as to "hasten the Redemption." Here, the Codifier R. Yosef Caro (1488–1575) wrote the *Shulhan Aruch*, which today still regulates the daily life of the Jew. It was here that the well-known Hebrew printer Eliezer ben Isaac Ashkenazi produced three books between 1577 and 1580. The six-domed and vaulted synagogue dates back to the sixteenth century.

Safed became the scene of a remarkable renaissance of Kabbalah four hundred years ago. Here lived the men who developed a mystical interpretation of the Bible, the Kabbalah, "workers of miracles" who tried to unravel the mysteries of the universe. By means of self-affliction (*sigufim*), fasts (*taaniyot*), ablutions (*tevilot*), and worship, they strove for closer communion with God. For them, prayer was a means of ascent. Every word, every gesture, every act, every thought was fraught with untold significance. Every blade of grass, every flower, every element of nature was a manifestation of the Creator and His loving concern for man. Foremost among them was the "Holy Lion," the "Ari," R. Yitzhak Luria (1534–1572), who lived and died in Safed. He developed the concept of *Zimtzum*, meaning "contraction" or "withdrawal," which suggests that God initially withdrew a part of Himself to Himself to provide an empty space for Creation.

The Lurian teachings were disseminated by his disciples, known as the "Lion's whelps," especially the kabbalist R. Hayyim Vital (1543–1620), who not only gave form and immortality to his master's doctrines but believed that his master's soul was that of the Messiah, the son of Yosef. Their doctrines were saturated with the theme of national redemption and with preparations for the coming of the Redeemer. Near Vital's resting place is the grave of his master, R. Moshe Ben Yaacov Cordovero (1562–1625), and of his disciple R. Shlomo ben Moshe Halevi Alkabetz (1505–1584), the author of the Sabbath hymn, *Lecha Dodi* (Come, my Beloved), which was incorporated into our prayer books. Surrounded by the breathtaking views of Mount Meron and the Sea of Galilee, the city has inspired James Michener and Leon Uris, even as it inspired the mystics of Kabbalah.

On 9 Heshvan 1759, an earthquake destroyed most of town. One hundred and fifty Jews were killed, and six synagogues in the Jewish Quarter were destroyed. Five years later, in 1764, a number of *hasidim* under R. Nahman of Horodenka and R. Menahem Mendel of Przemyslany came to the Holy Land and settled in Safed. In 1777, three hundred *hasidim* under the leadership of R. Menahem Mendel of Vitebsk, R. Avraham Katz of Kalisk, and the fiery *Maggid* Yisrael ben Perets of Poltusk left Eastern Europe. On 5 Elul the pilgrims arrived in Acre and settled in Safed. For once, the political conditions were favorable for the new settlers. In 1775, the Dher el Amr revolt had been crushed. For more than forty years, Hayyim Farhi of Damascus (d. 1820) used his influence to help his fellow Jews. When R. Menahem Mendel arrived, Safed was still in ruins. The new ruler, Jazzar Pasha, was anxious to attract new settlers and welcomed R. Menahem Mendel and his *hasidim*, granting them tax concessions and permission to rebuild their synagogues and their homes.

They were also welcomed by an unusual display of cordiality on the part of the Sephardim living there. There was even a "mixed" marriage, R. Menahem Mendel's son, R. Moshe, marrying the daughter of a Sephardi family in Jerusalem. The newcomers were aware of the potential of their new country, where they found "houses without inhabitants," the houses having been vacated during the earthquake of 1759–1760. Although the long-term prospects were bright, ignorance of the vernacular and of the local customs hampered their progress. Prices soared, and the funds of the settlers were soon exhausted. R. Menahem Mendel enlisted the support of his followers in Russia, but letters did not produce any immediate results. So he sent R. Yisrael of Poltusk to collect funds in Eastern Europe. He was the forerunner of many hasidic *meshullahim* or *shadarim* (emissaries). Between 1774 and 1846, no less than 136 emissaries were sent to the diaspora.[2]

The funds collected in the diaspora alleviated, but did not solve, the problems of the settlers. The cordiality that had greeted them at first soon gave way to friction, as the differences mounted between the old settlers and the newcomers. The *hasidim* complained that they did not receive an equitable share of the money collected. The Sephardim counterclaimed that the hasidic emissaries were destroying the centralized agencies. A number of Sephardim, moreover, were apprehensive about the Shabbetai Zvi heresy, for the allegations leveled against the *hasidim* in Eastern Europe were repeated in the Holy Land. There were other disagreements: the Sephardim used whetted knives, whereas the *hasidim* used honed knives for animal slaughter. Bringing matters to a head in 1778, Safed was afflicted by a plague of locusts and drought.

In vain did R. Menahem Mendel plead: "Have we not one Father? Hath not one God created us? Why should a man betray his brothers and desecrate the Covenant of our Fathers? All we ask for is peace."[3] To escape dissension, R. Menahem Mendel and seventy-five of his followers left Safed and settled in Tiberias in 1781. A small number of *hasidim* emigrated to Pekiin, a village in Upper Galilee. R. Avraham Katz of Kalisk, however, remained in Safed with twenty-five *hasidim*. Conditions were not much better there, as the local ruler harassed the newcomers. A plague of 1814 was followed by the conquest of Palestine in 1831 by the Egyptian ruler Mohammed Ali, who revolted against the Sultan. His son Ibrahim Pasha inflicted a severe defeat on the Ottoman army. The Egyptians introduced many administrative reforms. The Jews suffered from the revolt of the Druzes against the invaders, who, in Sivan 1834, vandalized the Jewish Quarter and destroyed many religious appurtenances. In 1840, the nine-year benevolent

2. Obed Avissar, *Sefer Tevaria* (Jerusalem: Keter, 1973), pp. 189–192.

3. Y. Barnai, *Hasidic Letters from Eretz Yisrael from the Second Part of the Eighteenth Century and the First Part of the Nineteenth Century*, in Hebrew (Jerusalem, 1980), pp. 64–65.

Egyptian rule came to an end, when the Egyptians left under pressure from the great powers.

On 24 Tevet 1837, an earthquake almost destroyed the community, killing many Jews. Of the fourteen synagogues only three, *Bat Ayin, R. Yossi Bannai,* and *Aboab,* survived. Two years later, in Sivan 1839, Sir Moses Montefiore paid his second visit to the Holy Land and had a census taken in Safed. The *hasidim* then numbered 273—sixty-nine percent of the total Jewish population. R. Shmuel Heller (1796–1884), the Rabbi of Safed, encouraged the settlers to cultivate *etrog* plantations in Kfar Hittim near Tiberias, and they were supported by R. Hayyim Eliezer Waks, the Rabbi of Kalish, the president of the *Kollel Polin* and Kupat R. Meir Baal Hanes, who urged Eastern European Jewry to purchase *etrogim* from the Holy Land in preference to those of Corfu. In 1868 and 1871, R. Yehezkel Shragai Halberstam of Sianiava, the son of R. Hayyim, visited Safed where his relative R. Naftali Hayyim Horowitz, known as *HaZaddik Ha-Pele* (the amazing *Zaddik*) and his son R. Eliezer Nisan Horowitz were the spiritual guides of the *hasidim* of Zanz. Among the other notable *hasidim* was R. Kopel Horowitz (d. 1856), the son of R. Yaakov Yitzhak, the "Seer of Lublin."

In later years Safed's appeal for *hasidim* waned. On 29 August 1920, the Arabs vandalized the Jewish Quarter, killing R. Yishmael Cohen, the Sephardi Rabbi, and his wife. Of the thirty-six synagogues in the Old City of Safed, only ten are hasidic, including *shtieblech* of Czortkov, Vizhnitz, Chernobyl, Zanz (off Meginim Square on David Street, built in 1837). The Radovitzer *Shtiebl* was founded by R. Yosef Alter Hager (d. 1879), and Habad now had a center for *Baale Teshuva.*

Near the tomb of R. Shimon bar Yochai is a small yeshivah that was directed by R. Yohanan Twersky of Jerusalem. For forty years, Safed was the home of R. Aaron Yehiel Leifer, who married the daughter of R. Zeev Tirnoer, a native of Safed. Although the Rabbi of Klausenburg, R. Yekutiel Halberstam, established there a *kollel* and a settlement for thirty families in 1971, he did not erect his *Kirya* is Safed. Apart from Habad House, many Lubavitch students study in the *Zemah Zeddek Kollel* in the Jewish Quarter. They also have a housing complex for two hundred families on Mount Canaan.

"The flame of my soul will burn until the coming of the Messiah," said R. Nahman of Braclav in the first decade of the nineteenth century. "Safed is a town," said R. Avraham Steinhartz (a descendant of R. Nathan of Nemirov), "where one can do much for Judaism." In the last three decades, the *hasidim* of Braclav have been building settlements in Safed. The "toite *hasidim*" (dead *hasidim*), as the followers of R. Nahman are known, are coming to life. The entrepreneurs call themselves the "Society for the Revival of the Religious Settlement of Upper Galilee." In 1968, R. Aaron Gedalia Kenig (1921–1980) acquired land near the Ari Sephardi Synagogue, and despite his early death, homes, schools, welfare institutions, and local printing and diamond industries were established and are providing work for the growing population. This project is endorsed by many rabbis and by the Jewish Agency.

Tiberias

"From Tiberias the Israelites will be redeemed," says the Talmud.[4] "The King Messiah," declared the *Zohar*, "will appear in Tiberias." Here the Palestinian Talmud was produced. This town, on the shores of the Sea of Galilee, seven hundred feet below sea level and founded by Herod Antipas, Tetrarch of Galilee, is now a fashionable health resort. It is the site of the graves of many famous men: Maimonides, R. Yeshayahu Halevi Horowitz, the *Shelo HaKadosh*, and many *Tannaim* and *Amoraim*, especially R. Meir Baal Hanes, the "miracle worker," so called on account of the many miracles ascribed to him in haggadic literature.

During the second half of the sixteenth century, the Turkish Jewish statesman Don Yosef HaNasi (1524–1579) and his mother-in-law, Donna Gracia Mendes (1510–1569), obtained a charter from

---

4. *Rosh Hashanah* 31b.

Suleiman the Magnificent, granting them Tiberias and seven surrounding villages, together with the permission to rebuild the walls of the city and to settle the town and the land with Jews, whether immigrants or natives. Don Yosef planted mulberry trees to encourage a silk industry and imported the finest wools from Spain for weaving. With the death of Don Yosef, the scheme to establish an autonomous Jewish settlement in Tiberias was abandoned. In 1740, Dhaher-el-Amr, then governor of Galilee, rebuilt Tiberias and invited Jews to settle there.

In the eighteenth century, the city attracted the hasidic leaders R. Menahem Mendel of Vitebsk and R. Avraham Katz of Kalisk. A first, the *hasidim* worshiped in a separate section of the Sephardi synagogue, but because of their boisterous and loud prayers, "read aloud," to quote the words of a visitor, "as if they wished to be heard in Jerusalem," [5] they were forced to move their religious services to the second floor of R. Menahem Mendel's three-story house. This building was destroyed in the earthquake of 1837 but was soon rebuilt. It was there that Sir Moses and his wife Judith worshiped. It was eventually taken over by the *hasidim* of Karlin in the middle of the nineteenth century. Visiting his friend in Tiberias, R. Wolf of Zbarazh in 1792, R. Yaakov Samson of Shepetovka saw the rabbi's wife washing linen in a courtyard. When he commiserated with her, she replied proudly: "These clothes are not mine. I am washing them for others, and I am being paid for the task. But I feel no regrets. No sacrifice is too great for the privilege of living in *Eretz Yisrael*."

It is noteworthy that R. Nahman of Braclav, to whom the city of Jerusalem was "the city of the world," never visited Jerusalem but lived for a time in Tiberias. R. Nahman of Horodenka (d. 1780), a disciple of the Besht and the grandfather of R. Nahman of Braclav, also lived there and established a *Bet Hamidrash*. Like the second-century Tanna Nahman of Gimze, R. Nahman accepted every misfortune with *gamzu letova* (that, too, is for the

---

5. L. Wilson, *The Land of the Bible, Visited and Described*, vol. 2 (London, 1847), p. 133.

best). He yearned to meet the kabbalist R. Elazar (Eliezer) ben Shmuel Rokeah, but the meeting never took place. Other notable hasidic leaders were R. Menahem Mendel of Przemyslany, R. Moshe Dov of Stolin (d. 1857), the brother of R. Aaron Perlow of Karlin, R. Zeev Wolf of Stary-Ostrov, and R. Aaron, the son of R. Baruch Mordecai of Karlin. It was in Tiberias that R. Moshe Kliers, who married the daughter of R. Yehuda Leib, a hasid of Kobryn, together with the followers of R. Shmuel Weinberg of Slonim, founded soup kitchens for the needy and established the *Or Torah* Yeshivah beside the tomb of R. Meir Baal Hanes. Now the whole Jewish city of Tiberias, including the Jewish Quarter of Kiryat Shmuel, has relatively few hasidic residents.

Hebron

Hebron, situated in the Judaean mountains southwest of Jerusalem and now the stronghold of the violent Islamic Hamas, is deeply rooted in hasidic lore. The Besht yearned to fulfill the Commandment to live in the Land of Israel and to plant the seeds of Hasidism in the hallowed soil—a fusion that could hasten the messianic age. From the accounts of the Besht's attempts to reach the Holy Land, it is difficult to distinguish fact from fiction. According to tradition, he set out three times for the Holy Land. The Besht would have wept as his ancestors wept at the Western Wall, and he would have visited the city of Hebron. He grieved that he was not successful. However, it was his brother-in-law R. Avraham Gershon of·Kutov who reached the Holy Land.

Accompanied by his second wife and his two sons, R. Hayyim Aaron and R. Yakir, R. Avraham Gershon arrived in Jerusalem on the eve of the New Year 1747. He was warmly greeted by the Sephardim, especially those who had been associated with Judah Hasid. He lived in Hebron for six years. Though the hasidic movement was splintered by now, support for this *Yishuv*, especially for the Holy Cities, was an issue that united the various groups, for the State of Israel unites the most disparate factions of Jewry. The rebbes, who were poles apart in temperament, character, and outlook, found common ground here, and many endorsed the ruling that it was wrong to divert money collected for the poor of the Holy Land to any other charity. Support for the Holy Land and the Holy Cities became one of the unwritten articles of Hasidism.

R. Avraham of Kalisk, like R. Menahem Mendel, repeatedly appealed for help. He urged people to contribute regularly, and he even composed a special blessing for those who make such offerings. His relations with R. Shneur Zalman were at first cordial. But later on, with the publication in 1797 of *Likkute Amarim*, the Bible of Habad Hasidism, their relationship began to deteriorate. R. Avraham believed that R. Shneur Zalman was deviating from the teachings of R. Dov Ber, the Maggid Mezhirech. Theological differences were intensified by a clash of personalities. R. Avraham felt that his permanent residence in the Holy Land entitled him to precedence, and he accused his erstwhile friend of being more concerned with publicity than with the needs of the *Yishuv*. There were undignified exchanges.

Habad has long been associated with Hebron. The Habad settlement there probably goes back to the first decade of the nineteenth century, with the arrival of R. Shimon Shmerling. Repeatedly, R. Shneur Zalman urged his followers to make weekly or at least monthly contributions "to sustain people who are literally without food. They are depending on us, and we must help them." He stressed that God was revealed neither in the Torah nor in prayer, but in charity. "As light springs out of its concealment in dark clouds to flash through the world, so the Divine light emerges through charitable deeds."[6] Not satisfied with exhortations, R. Shneur Zalman traveled far and wide to raise money. At that time, the Holy Land was under Turkish rule, and Russia was at war with Turkey. So R. Shneur Zalman's activities were virtually treason, and he was twice arrested.

R. Dov Ber, the Mittler Rebbe, urged his followers to acquire land in Hebron, the "City of our Patriarchs." In 1819, fifteen fami-

---

6. *Seder Tefilot* (Warsaw, 1867), p. 57; *Likkute Torah Reeh.*

lies moved from Safed to Hebron. In 1823, the Rebbe once again wrote to his followers, emphasizing the holiness of the city. He encouraged R. Shimon Menashe Chaikin to settle there. At this time, in 1834, Ibrahim Pasha's soldiers sacked the Jewish Ghetto, looted the synagogues, tore the Torah Scrolls, and plundered and robbed the community. In 1842, the *hasidim* sent R. Moshe Jaffe to Egypt, Yemen, and India, and R. Uri Orenstein to Eastern countries to collect funds.

Among the newcomers to Hebron was R. Yaakov Slonim, the son-in-law of the Mittler Rebbe. His wife, Menuhah Rachel, was regarded for many years as the "grandmother" of the community. The third rebbe of Lubavitch, R. Menachem Mendel Schneersohn (1789–1866), actively supported the *Yishuv* during his thirty-five years of leadership. In 1855, he sent money to establish the *Avraham Avinu* synagogue. By 1876, the Hebron community numbered four hundred souls, and their spiritual leader was R. Shimon Menashe, who guided the community for more than fifty years. The community had its own *Hevra Kadisha, Hevrat Bikkur Holim* (society for visiting the sick), and *Hachnosat Kallah* (a society that assists the poor and orphaned in their marriage preparations, including providing them with dowries). Sir Moses Montefiore contributed £5 sterling toward the funds of the society.

An interesting group was the *Ole Regalim*, headed by R. Zalman Slonim. It enabled ten members of the community to visit Jerusalem at the Festivals, to pray there for peace on behalf of their brethren in the diaspora. Lots were drawn to select the ten, and each pilgrim received £2 sterling to help defray expenses. There was also the *Hachnosat Orchim* Society, whose function it was to provide hospitality to those who came from afar to pray at the resting place of our holy forefathers. The *Hevra Lina* society sent caretaker to stay with invalids during their illness. The *Gemillat Hasadim* society, under the leadership of R. Binyamin Rivlin, granted loans to the poor in time of need.

R. Shmuel Schneersohn of Lubavitch encouraged his followers to settle in Hebron, and he persuaded R. Shlomo Zalman Klonsky to make his home there. A large edifice, *Bet Rumani* or *Dir Istanbula*, which belonged to Avraham Rumani of Istanbul, was bought by Shimon Hozman, for twenty-two thousand roubles for Habad purposes. The Rebbe's successor, R. Shalom Dov Ber Schneersohn, established a yeshivah, *Torat Emet*, in 1912.[7] This replaced the original yeshivah, *Magen Avraham*, established in 1889. The Rebbe sent seven students from his own yeshivah, *Tomhe Temimim*, to the new yeshivah in Hebron, which was under the guidance of R. Shlomo Zalman Havlin. This yeshivah survived until World War One when the students, who were classified as citizens of an enemy country, had to return to Russia.

After the war, R. Yosef Yitzhak Schneersohn (1880–1950), who was ideologically opposed to both political Zionism and the Aguda, attempted to revive the yeshivah. On 3 Tammuz 1929, the Rebbe, together with his son-in-law R. Shmaryahu Gourary, R. Yaakov Yosef Slonim, R. Eliezer Dan Slonim, and others, visited Hebron, and special permission was given to them to visit the Cave of Machpela. The Rabbi narrowly missed the massacre of 1929, when sixty-seven Jews were murdered and sixty wounded, an event that completely shattered the community. Following the Arab rebellion of 1936, Hebron became *Judenrein*. Very few *hasidim* now live there.

Torah Thoughts

One should fear sin more than the punishment that follows it (R. Menahem Mendel of Vitebsk).

When R. Menahem Mendel was told that there was a rumor that the Messiah had come, he looked out of the window and said: "He has not come. For I cannot see any change in the creation" (*idem*).

---

7. Shlomo Dov Ber Levin, op. cit., pp. 181–184; *Challenge: an encounter with Lubavitch-Chabad in Israel* (London: Lubavitch Foundation of Great Britain, 1973), pp. 13–21; Bezalel Landau, *HaYishuv HaHasidi B'Hevron*, in *Kerem HaHasidut* (Jerusalem, 1985); Mehon Zecher Naftali, vol. 2 (Jerusalem), pp. 183–269.

The Talmud tells us that "the climate of the Holy Land makes one wise" (*Bava Batra* 158b). In the diaspora I did not succeed to recite the prayers in the proper manner. In the Holy Land I manage to recite just "Amen" in the proper manner, and I am more than satisfied there (*idem*).

The object of R. Menahem Mendel's journey to the Holy Land was the same as that of our Patriarch Abraham's: to pave the way for the children of Israel (R. Israel of Ruzhin).

"And these are the words which Moses spoke to all Israel" (Deuteronomy 1:1). In his last discourse, Moses did not admonish or rebuke the Israelites. He merely recounted and recorded the notable events in the wilderness, feeling that through stories he would attract his listeners and convey to them the moral lessons. And this should be a guide for the leaders of Israel: to attract the attention of listeners by stories and fables (*idem*).

"No one has perceived iniquity in Jacob, neither has one seen perverseness in Israel" (Numbers 23:21). Even when a Jew commits iniquities and transgressions, he is never for one moment oblivious of the Divine spark that is in him (*idem*).

"Abide ye every man in his place, and do not go out to gather Manna on the Sabbath" (Exodus 16:29). A person should always cultivate humility, nor should he aim or aspire to heights that he does not deserve, but rather should place himself in a position lower than is really due to him (*idem*).

"Two lambs of the first year without blemish, day by day for a continual offering" (Numbers 28:4). Even today, when there is no Temple and no sacrificial cult, we should still be aware twice every day of the twofold maxims "I have set the Lord always before me" (Psalms 16:8) and "I know my transgression and my sin is ever before me" (Psalms 51:5). The omnipresence of the Almighty and the importance of acknowledging one's guilt should always be with us (*idem*).

"But all the children of Israel had light in their dwellings" (Exodus 10:23). Every Israelite without exception is endowed with a Divine spark, but it surely depends on how one utilizes it. A diamond ring is a personal ornament, but it is not decorative if it is placed in the mud (*idem*).

The general principle is that all a man's Torah and all the precepts he carries out avail him nothing, God forbid, without the *devekut*. It depends on each man's particular circumstances, but it is demanded of man that his attachment to God be of the same order as his attachment to whatever material thing happens to attract him. Man must cleave to God, for this is the whole duty of man. For man's body is called only "the flesh of man." Therefore, that which constitutes his humanity must be directed to the Creator, Blessed be He, Who is eternal, and then his humanity will remain with him for all enternity, even after the death of the body, and he will then be able to make use of all that he has comprehended, and he will delight in the Lord forever (*Peri Ha-Aretz KiTissa*, p. 34).

16

Hasidic Luminaries

Rehovot, a town in central Israel that is twenty-two kilometers from Tel Aviv, is the home of the Levi Eshkol Faculty of Agriculture and the Weizmann Institute of Science, one of the leading research institutions in the world. It is also home of R. Menahem Eliezer Zeev Rosenbaum, the Rebbe of Kretchneff. Born in Jerusalem in 1949, he married the daughter of R. Yoel Ber, the Rebbe of Ratsford. His younger brother R. Yisrael Nisan was the Rebbe in *Kiryat Gat* but has now moved to Sao Paulo.

The biblical verse "Though thy beginning was small, yet thy latter end shall greatly increase,"[1] applies in no small measure to the Rebbe. In a secular and irreligious area, his late father was a religious pioneer in the establishment of many religious *Mosdot*: the Yeshivah *Shaar Eliezer*; the Talmud Torah *Bene Moshe*, the only religious elementary school in the Rehovot area, where hasidic and

---

1. Job 8:8.

other Haredi families send their children for a religious education; *Benot Esther*, a school for two hundred fifty girls; a *kollel, Bet David*; societies for the study of *Mishnah* and Talmud; and welfare agencies. Over one hundred families now live in the *Kirya*. Apartments are sold to the students of the *kollel* at cost price or given entirely free to those who cannot afford the cost. There is also a home for senior citizens.

The Rebbe's grandfather, R. Eliezer, was a descendant of R. Meir of Przemyslany and R. Mordecai Rosenbaum of Nadvorna. R. Eliezer settled in Craciunesti, Romania, which had a Jewish population of nine hundred souls, and became rebbe at the age of seventeen. He married the daughter of R. Tzvi Hirsch Reiman, the son-in-law of R. Avraham Aaron Teitelbaum, and they had sixteen children, of which eight died in his lifetime. "I have eight sons in this world," he would say, "and eight to the world on high." All his surviving children became rabbis in different parts of Romania. In 1919, he moved to Sziget, the capital of Marmaros. His hospitality was renowned. He impressed upon his family that every beggar should be treated with respect. "Who knows," he said, "it is possible that the Prophet Elijah, or even one of the *Lamed Vav* (the thirty-six righteous men who traditionally exist in every generation)[2] may be among them." He had taught himself medicine and specialized in giving medical prescriptions that were accepted by the pharmacists. He perished in Auschwitz on 27 Iyar 1944. His last words were: "I want to make a public declaration that not even for one second have I lost faith in the Almighty."

Sixteen members of his family perished. Only his elder sister, the wife of the present Rebbe of Nadvorna in Bene Berak, and his son R. David Moshe, born in Kretshneff at the end of the Day of Atonement 1922, survived. R. David Moshe's mother, Hayyah Beila, was a descendant of the rebbes of Nadvorna and Przemyslany. The Rebbe survived a number of labor camps and the death camp at Auschwitz. After the war, he returned to Sziget,

---

2. *Sukkah* 45b.

southern Hungary, which, before the war, had a Jewish population of four thousand with many thousands living in the surrounding villages. Half the Jewish population perished in Auschwitz.

In 1948 in Sziget, he married Esther Rachel, the daughter of
the Rabbi Hayyim Mordecai of Nadvorna. Two years later, they
emigrated to Israel and stayed in Jerusalem for a short time. R.
Aaron Rokeah of Belz advised him to settle in Rehovot. Similar
advice was proffered to him by R. Avraham Yeshoyahu Karlitz,
the Hazon Ish: "It is a pleasant town, stay there." R. David Moshe
took their advice and made his home in Rehovot. Israelis who had
never heard of Hasidism, who never knew what a rebbe was,
found in him a friend. There were no visiting hours; he was "at
home" for ten hours each day, from late afternoon to dawn, apart
from Friday and the Sabbath. All were free to consult him, and
most left his presence comforted. "Nobody ever comes to tell me,"
he would say, "that he has won the lottery. But all, without exception, come to tell me their troubles and woes." He interpreted
the verse from the Book of Esther,[3] "Let my life be given me at
my petition and my people at my request" as follows: "As far as
I am concerned, my life's only desire is for spirituality, but as far
as my people is concerned, I pray that God should fulfill not only
their spiritual cravings, but also their material needs."

Daily, he would study four pages of the Talmud by heart. The
Book of Psalms was always at his side. "Even when I was in
Auschwitz," the Rabbi recalled, "no day ever passed without my
reciting a verse or a chapter of the Psalms." In 1966, he exhorted
his followers to vote for the United Religious Block at the municipal elections. Quoting the words of the *Midrash*: "For when
God sought to bless Israel, he found no other vessel that could
comprehend all the blessings, save peace."[4] He pointed out: "Only
through unity shall we be able to strengthen the religious life of
the *Yishuv*." On Friday evening, prior to the inaugural service for
the Sabbath, he recited the forty-five verses from Psalms 107. "Oh,

3. Esther 7:4.
4. *Midrash Rabba*, Deuteronomy, 5:15.

give thanks unto the Lord, for He is good, for His mercy endureth forever"—a custom initiated by R. Yisrael Baal Shem Tov. On Friday, he would salt the fish himself, following the custom of the Babylonian Amora Rabba.[5]

He prayed with such devotion that his *tallit* became soaked with perspiration. Not only did he read the weekly portion of the Torah on the Sabbath, but he also called up as many people as possible to the Reading of the Torah. On the eve of the Day of Atonement, like the High Priest of old, he would immerse himself five times in the ritual bath. Though he would normally prolong services, an exception was made on the Day of Atonement, when he terminated the service the moment the fast ended. "Some of the people here are elderly and sick. One should not harm them unnecessarily."[6]

The Rabbi's father was an accomplished violinist: "I fashioned it (my violin) myself," he said. "It is as sacred as a Scroll of the Law. In case of fire, it must be rescued together with all the other religious objects." The Rabbi followed in his father's footsteps. He played the violin on important occasions: during Hanukkah, on Purim, at the termination of the Day of Atonement, and on Lag B'Omer. He was very reluctant to discuss his wartime experiences: "Hell has no terror for me. I have been to Auschwitz. What can be worse than that?" He died while visiting Eastern Europe to pray at the graves of his ancestors, at Sziget on 15 Tammuz 1969. He was buried in Rehovot, and a sepulcher was erected over his grave. He is survived by seven sons and seven daughters. His discourses are to be found in the work *Arba Arazim*.[7]

Bat Yam

The founding of *Kiryat Zanz* and *Kiryat Vizhnitz* encouraged other hasidic rabbis to establish settlements. It was in Bat Yam, on the

---

5. *Shabbat* 119a.

6. *HaRebbe B'Yisrael*, Rehovot, Shikun Kretchneff, 1971.

7. Bene Berak, 1967.

coast south of Tel Aviv, that R. Shlomo Halberstam of Bobov founded his *Kirya*. The foundation stone of *Kiryat Bobov* was laid on 20 Kislev 1958, and R. Yosef Kahaneman declared: "In my mind I can already envisage *Kiryat Bobov* a traditional Jewish city." Nearly one hundred families are now living in the *Kirya*'s modern apartments. The magnificent Yeshivah *Kedushat Ziyon* and the synagogue *Bet Yehoshua*, the gift of the Rabbi's brother-in-law, the late Osias Freshwater of London, who married Nehama Golda, the daughter of R. Benzion Halberstam of Bobov, were established in 1963. Two-thirds of the students are Israelis, and the rest come from the United States.

The yeshivah is justifiably proud of the excellent accommodations and efficient medical services that are provided for the students. The Talmud Torah *Kol Arye* is named after R. Arye Leib Rubin, the rabbi of Tomaszov, the martyred father of the Rabbi's wife. "The most effective answer to the problem of religion in Israel lies in education," declared the Rebbe. "If we increase Torah *Hinuch* in Israel, if we are able to bring up more and more children to lead a truly traditional life, we shall succeed in our struggle for the national recognition of Torah in Israel's public life."

Forty-eight elderly people live in a pleasant and comfortable home *segula* that was opened in 1963. The Rabbi maintains a flat in the *Kirya* and frequently stays there, accompanied by his son R. Naftali Halberstam. The yeshivah is now under the guidance of the Rabbi's son-in-law R. Yaakov Yisrael Meisels. The *Kirya*'s development has been hindered by technical and financial problems, as it is difficult to create a new settlement by remote control from New York.

Bobov (Bobova in Western Galicia) was next in importance to Belz and Spinka. In prewar Poland, there were forty-three Bobov Yeshivot *Etz Hayyim*, and the rebbes of Bobov were among the first hasidic rebbes to pay special attention to young people, whom they treated with great consideration. The Rebbe's father, R. Benzion; his son R. Moshe Aaron; and his three sons-in-law, R. Yehezkel Shragai Halberstam, R. Moshe Stempel, and R. Shlomo Rubin, were killed in Lvov on 4 Av 1941. R. Benzion met his death dressed in his Sabbath garments and his *streimel*.

R. Shlomo, the present Rebbe of Bobov, a man of vision and ability, was born in Bobov on 1 Kislev 1906. He studied under his father and was ordained by R. Shmuel Fuhrer and R. Alter Yehiel Nebentzahl of Stanislav. At the age of eighteen, R. Shlomo married his cousin, the daughter of R. Hayyim Yaakov Teitelbaum, a descendant of R. Moshe Teitelbaum. At the outbreak of World War Two, he was living with his parents in Lvov, which was under Russian domination. After the German invasion of Russia in June 1941, he and his family returned to Bobov and were soon confined to the labor camp at Bochnia, near Cracow. On one occasion, Rabbi Shlomo's wife and two of their children were caught by the Gestapo. He and his elder son, Naftali, were arrested, but although they had only a small piece of bread to sustain them, he did not despair. His Hungarian citizenship stood him in good stead, and they were permitted to return to Bochnia. His wife and two children, however, were murdered in Auschwitz.

R. Shlomo's narrow escape did not deter him from resuming his rescue operations. He, his mother, and his son first escaped to Grosswardein, and from there to Romania. After the war, he made his way to Italy but could not obtain a permit to enter the Holy Land. He came to London and, in a moving address in the Conway Hall, urged British Jews to rescue the remnants of European Jewry. He settled in New York, first in Manhattan, then in Crown Heights, and eventually in Borough Park, Brooklyn.

In 1947, he married Frieda, the daughter of R. Arye Leibush Rubin of Cieszanov, by whom he had five daughters and one son. He founded a network of educational establishments and, like his father, he pays great attention to young people. The Bobov Holiday Camp gives many children the opportunity of spending the summer in a traditional atmosphere. He does not hesitate to break new ground. He introduced a scheme whereby courses, leading to jobs in industry, are taught in yeshivah trade schools.

The Rabbi is approachable, very lucid, and illustrates his points by rabbinic maxims or parables. When asked why he did not influence his wealthy followers and his millionaire relatives to erect apartments for yeshivah students in Israel, he replied: "There was once a simple villager who had a very small shop in the village.

He was always harassed by his creditors. One day he visited a big city and stood gazing outside a huge store for a long time. 'What are you doing here?' he was asked. 'And what are you thinking?' 'I have a tiny shop in a village,' replied the man, 'and I have many debts. I am wondering how much money the owner of this great store owes to his creditors?' Similarly, said the Rabbi, "I have tremendous problems balancing the budget of my educational establishments, both in the United States and in Israel. It is not easy for me to take up new financial commitments." In 1976, he established educational centers in Jerusalem and Bene Berak.

Kiryat Yismah Moshe

R. Hananya Yom Tov Lipa Teitelbaum was the founder of *Kiryat Yismah Moshe* in Ganei Tikvah and *Kiryat Ono* near Ramat Gan. R. Teitelbaum's father was R. Hanoch Heinoch Rubin of Sasov (1830–1883), a descendant of Belz, Sziget, and R. Hanoch Heinoch Dov of Olesk. On his mother's side, he was a grandson of R. Hananya Yom Tov Lipa Teitelbaum.

The Rebbe was born on the Day of Atonement 1905. He studied under R. Avraham Menahem Steinberg of Brody. At nineteen, in Orshova on 12 Elul 1924, he married Hayyah Rosa, the daughter of R. Yoel Teitelbaum. He later became head of the *Bet Din* of Satmar. He subsequently became rabbi in Samiah, where he was also principal of the yeshivah. During the war, disguised as a beggar and sometimes as a soldier, he escaped to Romania. From 1944 to 1947, he lived in Jerusalem, where he established a yeshivah, *Yitav Lev*, and set up a girls' school, *Or HaHayyim*, in Bene Berak. In 1948, he settled in New York, where he started a Sasov, *Bet Hamidrash*. He visited Israel frequently.

His wife died in 1954, and in Israel he remarried Bluma, the daughter of the principal of the Yeshivah of Satmar. In Adar 1963, he laid the foundation to a new 260-*dunam Kiryah*. "In the diaspora, the dangers of spiritual disintegration and assimilation loom large, even in the main centers of Jewish population," declared the Rabbi. "There is no bulwark against the onslaught of

assimilation. It is my fervent aim and desire, to save these Jews."
His late father-in-law, R. Yoel Teitelbaum, the Rabbi believed that
a Jewish State was an "abomination." To him Zionism was an evil
creed, and to cooperate with Zionists was a major sin. Nationalism was an "imitation of the Gentiles." The precept of *Yishuv
HaAretz* (settling in the Holy Land) applied only to the period of
the Temple and was not binding today. After the Selig Reuben
Bengis in 1953, the Rabbi of Satmar became the spiritual head of
the *Edah Haredit*, which then also comprised the *Neture Karta*, a
group of about two hundred Jews who regard Zionism as a product of false messianism, founded on assimilationist ideologies, and
were convinced that the Holocaust represented Divine retribution
for the aims of Zionism.

R. Hananya Yom Tov Lipa disagreed with the ideology of his
father-in-law, and sought the support of David Ben Gurion and
the Mizrachi leader Shlomo Zalman Shragai for his new project.
"If you want an up-to-date apartment in a pleasant environment,
then come and make your home at *Yismah Moshe*," he urged his
followers in the United States.

"If a man comes here," remarked the Rabbi, "then his heart
will rejoice." Aesthetic considerations were important. He insisted
on flowerbeds and even chose the plants himself. "Whenever a
woman looks out of the window, let the fragrance of the flowers
delight her." He was a perfectionist and amazed the architects with
his knowledge of technical detail. His familiarity with building
matters, his tolerance and readiness to listen to divergent opinions,
his relaxed generosity and courtesy, his vigor and indefatigable
enthusiasm endeared him to many but undermined his health. In
the summer of 1963, he became very ill and was forced to spend
the next eighteen months in the hospital. From his sickbed, he
planned and directed new projects for the *Kirya*. When R. Yoel
Teitelbaum visited him in hospital, the ailing Rabbi summoned
his last ounce of strength to greet him. Both patient and visitor
wept bitterly, knowing that this was probably their last meeting
on earth. The Rabbi died on 12 Adar 1966 and was buried in
Tiberias. He left one daughter and four young sons. After the
funeral, the eldest boy, R. Yosef David, who was born in 1954,

the *Yanuka* of Sasov, was proclaimed Rebbe. He studied at the yeshivah of the Rabbi of Klausenburg and under Rabbi Wozner of Bene Berak. He married the daughter of R. David Moshe Rosenbaum of Kretchnef.

With the death of the Rebbe, the *Kirya* was faced with tremendous financial problems. In August 1972, the late Rabbi's wife sold two hundred *dunams* to the Africa-Israel Investment Company, one of Israel's foremost property and development companies. The company built a new garden suburb, called *Givat Savyon*, which contained thirteen hundred residential units, in addition to shopping facilities and public services, and gave priority to religious settlers. At the time of the sale, there was no hasidic yeshivah in the *Kirya*, because the existing yeshivah had been "lent" to a Lithuanian group. There are now four houses of worship, two kindergartens, and a *Bet Yaakov* school. It is noteworthy that R. Yoel Teitelbaum advised the Rabbi's family not to leave Israel during the Six-Day War but has otherwise shown no interest in the *Kirya*.

Torah Thoughts

"And Abraham went on his journeys" (Genesis 13:3). Despite the fact that Abraham was "rich in cattle, silver and good" (Verse 2), he went "on his journeys." His wealth made no difference to his service of the Almighty (R. Eliezer Tzvi Rosenbaum of Kretchneff).

"Noah was righteous, an upright man, wholehearted, and he walked with God" (Genesis 6:9). Noah lived in an age of depravity. He had no one to model himself on. He was a self-made man (R. Zvi Hirsch of Nadvorna).

"And they stood at the nether part of the mountain" (Exodus 19:17). According to the *Mechilta*, "they were actually beneath the mountain." God elevated the mountain so that the Israelites were under it. Despite the many Divine manifestations that they witnessed in Egypt and at the Red Sea, they still remained "under the mountain," they still remained humble (R. Mordecai of Nadvorna).

In the liturgy for the Additional Service on Sabbath New Moon, we pray: "Inaugurate for us the coming month for happiness and for blessing, for joy and gladness, for deliverance and consolidation, for sustenance and maintenance, for life and peace, for pardon of sin and forgiveness of iniquity." Why do we give precedence to material needs? Surely, we should give priority to the pardoning of sin, and so forth. But how can we truly repent when we are beset continually by financial problems and material privation? Our minds are fully occupied with obtaining our daily bread. Repentance and forgiveness of iniquity are only possible if we are relieved from our material entanglements (R. Benzion Halberstam of Bobov).

We read in the Talmud (*Berachot* 61a) that "the evil inclination resembles a fly." When a sensible man observes a fly approaching, he gets out of reach immediately to avoid any contact. The foolish man, on the other hand, takes no action until the fly actually touches him. Similarly, the moment a sinful idea enters the mind of a wise man, he turns away from it immediately and does not allow himself to become trapped (R. Solomon of Boblov).

Michal, the daughter of Saul, came out to meet David and said: "How glorious was the King of Israel today, who uncovered himself today in the eyes of the handmaids as one of the vain fellows" (2 Samuel 6:20). How could Michal compare David to "one of the vain fellows"? She knew that David "walked humbly with God" (Micah 6:8), that he frowned upon externals but believed in inner awareness. David, in justification, regarded this incident as exceptional. He was bringing back the Ark of the Lord from the House of Obed Edom to Jerusalem. This had to be marked by special rejoicing with dance and song. And this attitude contrasted with the action of Saul, her father (who hid himself among the baggage) (1 Samvel 10:22) and who believed in the "still small voice." (*idem*).

"And I will bring the land into desolation" (Leviticus 26:32). Nahmanides states that Israel's enemies would find no delight in the land. Despite their prodigious efforts to cultivate the soil, their attempts would be unsuccessful, and the land would remain desolate (R. Hayyim Elazar of Munkacz).

"I am the Lord your God Who brought you out of the Land of Egypt, out of the House of Bondage" (Exodus 22:2). The Decalogue states that "God brought the Israelites out of the Land of Egypt" and omits to mention that "God created the Universe." Their delivery from Egypt was a sufficient guarantee to obtain Israel's complete allegiance. Stressing the fact that God brought the Israelites out of Egypt teaches us that the Almighty is involved in the affairs of the world (*idem*).

"And Moses took their case before the Lord" (Numbers 27:5). The five daughters of Zelophehad complained to Moses that because they had no brothers, their families would be left without a share in the Holy Land. Why did not Moses himself adjudicate, choosing instead to refer their claims to God Himself? We read in *Ketubot* (105b) that a man should not act as a judge, either for one whom he loves or for one whom he hates, for no man can see the guilt of one whom he loves or the merit of one whom he hates. Moses could not judge their claim, because the daughters of Zelophehad stated that their father "was not among the company of them that gathered themselves together against the Lord in the company of Korach" (Verse 3). Moses regarded this reference as a kind of "bribe" (*idem*).

"Do whatever the host tells you, except when he tells you to depart" (*Pesahim* 86b). A guest should not outstay his welcome. If, however, the host (the Almighty, the Master of the Universe) tells you to depart from this world, do not be compliant, but pray that He should prolong your days to enable you to study the Torah (*idem*).

"We will go with our young and with our old, with our sons and with our daughters" (Exodus 10:9). A living person is described by the Sages as "walking," that is, continually making progress. The "dead," on the other hand, are considered "stationary" and can no longer advance spiritually. Pharaoh could not understand why Moses wanted the old to participate. "They can no longer 'walk,' they are frail and the evil inclination no longer dominates them." Moses, however, insisted that even the old can often be fallible. The duty of religion devolves upon all alike, irrespective of age (R. Baruch Rabinowicz of Munkacz).

17

The Munkacz Dynasty

Very few Jews now live in the Ukrainian city of Munkacz (Mukachevo), but it was once one of the largest centres of Hasidism in Hungary.

Jews have lived there since the middle of the sixteenth century, and the first synagogue was built in 1741. Jewish settlement was encouraged by the local landlord, the Count of Schonborn-Buchheim. It was the home, for some time, of R. Baruch (d. 1792), the father of R. Shneur Zalman of Liady. Among the first rabbis were R. Leibish (d. 1789), R. Abraham Gottesman (d. 1815), and R. Victor Ashkenazy, R. Hayyim Sofer, a disciple of the *Hatam Sofer*.

Before the Second World War, Munkacz had a Jewish population of 13,488 (42.7 percent of its entire population).[1] It had thirty

---

1. S. Kohn Weingarten, *Arim Ve'Imaot B'Yisrael* (Jerusalem, 1946), *Mosad HaRav Kook*, pp. 345–366.

synagogues, bathhouses, a Jewish hospital (established in 1845), nine *Talmud Torah* Schools, four Hebrew Elementary Schools (founded in 1920), a Hebrew Secondary School (founded in 1925), a flourishing Hebrew press (established in 1871), and four Yiddish newspapers. It was a highly organized *shtetl*, a Jewish townlet, permeated throughout by the spirit of Torah Judaism. For example, before the Sabbath the electricity generator was turned off, and the current was supplied between then and the end of the Sabbath by accumulators.[2]

The Nazis established two Ghettos there, one situated in the Jewish section of the town, and the other at the Sajovits brickyard. To these Ghettos fourteen thousand Jews were brought from the rural communities in Bereg County, including Bardhaza, Ilasva and Szolyvc, and transports to the concentration camps continued until 24 May 1944.

Munkacz was, in first four decades of the twentieth century, the 'Jerusalem of Hasidism.' It was the home of one of the most influential dynasties and the most charismatic rebbes of our generation, who were also Hasidism's greatest intellectual giants. No rebbe inspired so much veneration and so much antagonism as the rebbes of Munkacz, who were generous to a fault, uncompromising in the realm of religion, yet kindly and considerate, while often displaying a sense of humor. Apart from R. Abraham Bornstein of Sochaczev and R. Yitzhak Meir Alter of Ger, no other hasidic dynasty provided Torah scholars of such influence as Munkacz.

The founder of the dynasty was R. Shlomo Shapira (1831-1893), the possessor of a many-sided personality. Zest, vitality, courage and enthusiasm flowed from him. He was born in Rybotycz near Pzemyslany Galicia, on the seventh day of Hanukah 1831, the son of R. Eliezer of Lancut. In his youth, R. Shlomo was betrothed to Frimet, the daughter of R. Yekutiel Shmelke of Sasov. R. Shlomo was a frequent visitor of R. Yisrael of Ruzhin, R. Hirsch

---

2. *Universal Jewish Encyclopedia* (New York: Abraham Fuchs, 1948), vol. 8, p. 39.

of Rymanov and R. Asher of Ropczyce and his son, R. Shimon of Yaroslav. In 1846, he was married in Sasov, where he lived in the home of his inlaws. In Sasov, he befriended R. Nehemia, the rabbi of Sasov, and after his death, R. Shmelke became rabbi of Sasov, whilst R. Shlomo acted as *Dayan*. He received his *Semicha* from R. Yosef Shaul Nathanson of Lvov, and from R. Avraham Teumim, rabbi of Zbarazh, the author of *Hesed L'Avraham* (Lvov, 1837). He was frequently consulted on difficult and complex halachic problems by R. Yoel Ashkenazi of Zloczov.

When his father accepted the position as rabbi of Lancut, R. Shlomo succeeded him as rabbi of Stryzov, where he spent the next twenty-two years. Even tempered and on good terms with all, he could administer a well-deserved rebuke without creating resentment. His lively personality filled his followers with vigour and warmth. He would rarely fail to visit Rabbi Hayyim Halberstam of Zanz, where he spent many Sabbaths and festivals, especially the last two days of Passover.

He also held rabbinical posts in Lancut and Tarnogorod. In 1880, he became rabbi in Munkacz, the place where his grandfather, R. Tzvi Elimelech of Dynov (1783–1841), had also been rabbi. R. Tzvi Elimelech was the author of the classical work, *Bene Yissahar Discourses on the Sabbath, New Moon and Festivals*, first published in Zolkiev in 1846, and since reprinted twenty-one times. He was also the author of twenty-nine other works. Whatever he took up, he carried through with untiring thoroughness. He was utterly fearless in argument, for his position was always based on a full knowledge of factual information, and strong personal convictions. R. Tzvi considered philosophical speculation a waste of time and it is not surprising, therefore, that he censured the philosopher Moses Mendelssohn "for sinning and causing others to sin." He fought against the *Haskalah* maintaining that there was no knowledge in the realm of either science or philosophy that could not be found in the Torah. "I am fully aware," he wrote, "of the presumptuousness of the assimilationists that they respect neither the prophets nor the *Tannaim*. They are descended from the 'mixed multitude'." He established the *Tamhin DeOreitha Hevra* (Czernowitz, 1864), the rules and regulations of which he personally drafted. One of its aims was to provide free tuition for children of poor parents. R. Tzvi Elimelech remained rabbi for four years from 1825–1829. "I have come to Munkacz," the rebbe wrote, "a city that has no parallel among the orthodox communities. They are thirsty for Torah and the Fear of God."

R. Shlomo, his grandson, was concerned about the problems affecting Hungarian Jews, and was active in the work of the Orthodox *Landeskanzelrat*, the administrative headquarters of Hungarian Jewry. He was indefatigable in issuing many volumes of responsa that were so popular that they were often out of print. He wrote a number of books: *Shem Torah, Bet Shlomo* (Jerusalem, 1962), commentaries on the Lesser Tractates of the Talmud, and Psalms, and many responsa to halachic problems.

On *Erev Sukkot*, R. Shlomo's wife passed away, and he instructed his son to recite the phrase "my revered mother" in the *Grace after Meals*, on grounds that the rabbis said that you have "to honour your parents in life and after death." R. Shlomo never remarried. He was a great bibliophile. On one occasion several precious manuscripts were stolen from his library. The rebbe was very distressed. He stopped giving discourses on the following Sabbath. "It seems," he told his *hasidim*, "that my Torah is not desired by Heaven." On the following day, one of his *hasidim*, Moshe Yosef Lewkovitch, came and told him the good tidings that a fisherman had found the stolen manuscripts by the river. The rebbe was overjoyed, and he omitted to say *Tahanun* (supplicatory prayers recited at morning and afternoon services) on that day, regarding it almost as a festival. On the day before his death, he wrote his will. Before his death, he washed his hands, and said "I feel like a Cohen prior to his *Avoda* in the Temple." He died on 21 Sivan 1883. In his will, he instructed that a manuscript which he had not completed should not be published. In this respect, however, his descendants reinterpreted his wishes. He also asked that no eulogies be delivered at his funeral[3] He was survived by two sons, R. Tzvi Hirsch and R. Moshe Leib of Stryzov (1850–1917).

---

3. *Tzavaah* in *Sefer Hamisha Maamarot*, (Jerusalem: Abraham Fuchs, 1962), p. 274.

R. Tzvi Hirsch Shapira

R. Tzvi Hirsch was born in Stryzov on 11 Tammuz 1850, and was one of the greatest halakhic luminaries of Hasidism. His youth was spent under the spiritual guidance of his father and grandfather. His father put him in charge of the *Bet Din* of Munkacz, and he was appointed rabbi on 5 June 1893. In Adar 1865, he married Esther (d. 1929), the daughter of R. Hanina Horowitz of Ulanov. He was a disciple of R. Hayyim Halberstam of Zanz and of his son, R. Ezekiel of Sianiawa. He wrote the *Darke Teshuvah*, a four volume monumental work of more than 1,000 pages, on the 182 sections of *Yoreh Deah*. What R. Yisrael Meir Hakohen (1838–1933), known as the *Hafetz Hayyim*, did for *Mishne Berura* on *Shulhan Aruch Orah Hayyim*, R. Shapira did for *Yoreh Deah*.

The greatest talmudic authorities enthusiastically welcomed his efforts. No problem defied his analysis. The work was based on the perusal of hundreds of published volumes of responsa by both Sephardi and Ashkenazi scholars, as well as on rare and priceless manuscripts. Among those who gave their approbation were R. Yitzhak Elhanan Spector (1817–1896) of Kovno, R. Yitzhak Aaron Ettinger (1827–1891) of Przemysl-Lvov, and R. Shlomo ben Yisrael Moshe Hakohen of Vilna. The work was printed in Vilna by the famous ROM publishing house and in Munkacz (1892–1904). The fifth part was completed by his son and printed in Szlovo in 1912. The work became the *vade mecum* (reference book) of every rabbi and of every student studying for the rabbinical diploma and an indispensable record book of practical halachah.

A staunch champion of tradition, he was prepared to clash headlong with all who opposed him. Possessed of prodigious energy, he was the uncompromising spokesman for Hasidism in Hungary and Galicia. He was the author of Responsa *Tzvi Tiferet* (Munkacz, 1912), *Beer L'Hai Roi*, a commentary on the *Tikkune Zohar* (Munkacz, 1903), and twenty other works. His hasidic works are to be found in his commentary to the Torah, *Tiferet Banim* (Bardiov, 1921), his commentary to the Passover *Haggada* (Munkacz, 1914), and *Darke Emuna* (Munkacz, 1914), 102 discourses on Hanukkah. He died on the second day of Sukkot (16 Tishri) 1914.

In 1846, R. Tzvi Hirsch made a public declaration that the Messiah would not come that year. His views were later endorsed by R. Eliezer of Dzikov, who, in 1860, declared, "I believe with a perfect faith in the coming of the Messiah, but I solemnly affirm that he will not appear this year."

R. Hayyim Elazar Shapira

His son and successor, R. Hayyim Elazar was one of the most colorful and controversial rebbes of the twentieth century, for he was a man who combined considerable intellectual powers with spiritual discernment of a high order. Though capable of love and compassion, he did not flinch from standing up for his principles. A man of outstanding integrity, he was a fighter for the principles in which he believed. The strength of his will impressed even his most implacable opponents.

He was born in Stryzov on 5 Tevet 1872. When R. Hayyim Halberstam of Zanz first met him as a young child, he remarked, "A soul like this is only rarely found on this earth." He had no formal Yeshivah education, as his father preferred him to study with tutors. At the age of sixteen, he was already corresponding with outstanding scholars, among whom were R. Moshe Yehoshua Yehuda Leib Diskin (1817–1898) and R. Hayyim Elazar Waks (1822–1889) of Piotrokov. He was attached to the hasidic rebbe, R. Ezekiel Halberstam (1815–1896) of Sianiawa.

In 1887 he married (in Trzebina) Hayyah Hasia, the daughter of R. Shragai Yair Rabinowicz (1839–1912) of Bialobrzegi, a descendant of the 'Holy Jew' of Przysucha and son-in-law of R. Shmelke Rubin of Sasov. He was the author of *Aron Edut* (Warsaw/Piotrokov, 1916–1922). In 1896, R. Hayyim Elazar became rabbi of Sendiszov, near Munkacz. As the marriage remained childless, he divorced his wife, and, in 1907, he married Rachel Pearl (d. 15 Sivan 1944), the daughter of R. Yaakov Moshe Safrin of Komarno.

R. Hayyim Elazar was an outstanding scholar and prolific writer. His greatest work was the responsa *Minhat Elazar* in five parts (Munkacz, 1902–1920), consisting of 230 responsa, a work that received the approval of R. Mordecai Dov Twersky (1846–1902) of Hornistopl, R. Moses Hirsch Fuchs of Grosswardein and R. Hayyim Hezkiyahu Medini (1833–1905), the author of *Sede Hemed*, an encyclopedic work of eighteen volumes, which dealt with countless talmudic and halachic problems. His own father, R. Tzvi Hirsch, wrote, "A wise son makes a glad father." [4] It is noteworthy that the author in his Responsa deletes the names of his correspondents, with the explanation that mentioning names causes much dissension, but little profit. His masterly responsa reflected Jewish life in all its ramifications, and his work received praise from all quarters. It was a vast quarry of halachic thought.

R. Hayyim Elazar was one of the finest *mohelim* in the country, acting in a dual capacity of *Sandek* (one who holds the baby on his knee) and *Mohel*. To perform the mitzvah of *milah* he would travel any distance. Under his father's guidance, he also became *Av Bet Din* of Munkacz. His *bet din* consisted of R. Aaron Weiss, author of *Midrash Aaron*, R. David Schlussel, author of *Imre David* on the 613 Commandments (Waitzen, 1908), and R. Meir Zeev Zelzer HaKohen. On Rabbi Tzvi Hirsch's death in 1914, R. Hayyim Elazar succeeded him as rabbi, but before his appointment could be confirmed, he was forced to undergo an examination by the civil authorities to prove that he knew Hungarian.

He often interceded with the Hungarian authorities on behalf of Jewry, especially with Count Schonborn. Although not an orator in the traditional manner, he mesmerized and captivated his audience. His thoughts ran ahead of his speech, which, even so, was so fast that people found difficulty in following, whilst his melodious and tuneful prayers were full of tears and sighs. Even non-*hasidim* were drawn to his *bet hamidrash*. He published his father's works on *Hilchot Nida and Mikvaot* (Munkacz, 1921) and was the author of *Ot Hayyim V'Shalom* on the Laws of tefillin and circumcision (Munkacz, 1936), *Olat Tamid*, a commentary on

---

4. *Proverbs*, 15:20.

the Tractate *Tamid* (Bratislava, 1922), and twenty other works.[5] His works are repleat with liturgical items.

After the First World War, Munkacz became part of Czechoslovakia, and the Jews enjoyed twenty years of civic equality. The rebbe was a great bibliophile and had a valuable library in which were incorporated the books of his father and grandfather. It was one of the finest rabbinical collections ever assembled, especially in the realm of responsa and Hasidism. It also included many early and rare sephardic prints, as well as antique silver appurtenances. Most of these works were edited and published by R. Hayyim Elazar himself, but a number of manuscripts appeared posthumously between 1938 and 1944.

The Rebbe's Religious Views

The Rebbe endorsed the view of R. Moses Sofer Schreiber (1786–1839), known as the *Hatam Sofer*, who maintained *Hadash Assur Min HaTorah*—meaning that any innovation, however trivial, is strictly forbidden. This attitude was based on the biblical concept of *hadash* (i.e. new grain that ripens in spring), could not be eaten until a sheaf of the first fruit of the new harvest (*omer*) could be offered by the Priest in the Temple on the second day of Passover. Often the rabbi's language would acquire apocalyptic fire, and he had a mercurial temperament.

The rebbe observed *Tikkun Rachel*, prayers recited at midnight to mourn the destruction of the Temple and the original Jewish State. On occasions when this was not suitable, *Tikkun Leah* was substituted. He wore two pairs of tefillin simultaneously, those of Rashi and Rashi's grandson, R. Yaakov ben Meir Tam (1100–1171), who differed as to the order of the texts in the four parchments. The normal practice is to follow Rashi, but the custom has developed in some pious circles of donning an additional pair of tefillin according to the arrangement of Rabbenu Tam.

5. Yitzhak Alfasi, *Encyclopedia of Hasidism* (in Hebrew) (Jerusalem, *Mosad HaRav Kook*, 1986); pp. 626–644.

He would light four candles on weekdays when he officiated at the reader's desk, and would insist that any officiant (*Sheliah Tzibbur*) would first immerse himself in the ritual bath before leading the prayers. He himself would be called up to the Torah for the sixth portion (*Shishi*), which the *Zohar* regards as the most important *Aliyah*, for the sixth *Sefira* is *Yesod* which is identical with the *Zaddik* who is called the 'foundation of the world'.[6] He was particular not to allow anyone who publicly desecrated the Sabbath to receive any honour in the synagogue, and throughout the High Holy Days he always officiated at the reader's desk. He would read the Law on Sabbaths and weekdays.

He insisted that *mezizah* (suction) in order to remove the blood from the distant parts of the wound during circumcision should be done by mouth, and through a glass tube or by swab. In this he was supported by Rabbi Shaul Elisha Shneur Zalman Ladier and R. Shmuel Salant of Jerusalem. He endorsed the prohibition of R. Hayyim Halberstam of Zanz, forbidding *matzot* produced by machine to be eaten on Passover. Nor would he use *etrogim* (citrons), one of the four species carried and shaken in the Tabernacles synagogue services, emanating from the Holy Land.

He would not permit anyone just to wear a skullcap during prayers or the Reading of the Law, a hat had to be worn. Tombstone inscriptions were not to use the vernacular, nor would he permit postmortem, based on the argument of the inviolability of the body. He insisted that every part of the body had to be interred with the coffin without delay. He would not recognize any marriages that had been performed by the rabbis of the Neolog, and he insisted that a second ceremony be performed. No one should visit the graves of the *zaddikim* without prior immersion in a ritual bath, or would he accept gifts from anyone who desecrated the Sabbath publicly. He did not encourage the display of the Shield of David (*Magen David*) in the synagogue, or engravings of lions on *Sefer Torah* mantles.

---

6. *Proverbs*, 10:25.

Cremation, the disposal of the dead body by burning, was forbidden by Jewish law and a desecration of the dead. He would not allow the ashes of those who had been cremated to be buried in the Jewish cemetery. He permitted, however, the recitation of Memorial Prayers for the Dead (*Mazkir* or *Yizkor*) to be recited during the first year of mourning for such souls. He would not allow *kohanim* (priests) to visit the graves of the *zaddikim*, as they are forbidden to defile themselves by contact with the dead.

In the Middle Ages, the *herem* (excommunication) had been the most powerful weapon the Jewish authorities possessed, as it enabled them to maintain "law and order" within the community; in those days the mere threat of the *herem* would often subdue unruly elements. This weird ceremony, complete with wax candles and a *shofar* was designed to strike terror into the heart, and the words fell on the victim like a sentence of death. The *herem* was widely used and even more widely misused by the Rebbe of Munkacz.

The Rebbe condemned the *Mesifta Yeshivah*, which was established in Warsaw in 1919 under R. Meir Don Plotzki, R. Menachem Zemba and R. Mendel Menachem Kasher, with the active encouragement of R. Abraham Mordecai Alter of Ger. The *Mesifta* was administered by R. Shlomo Yoskovitch and R. Shalom Klepfish. During his first year at the institution, the student would study two hundred forty-five pages of Talmud, and this was progressively increased to three hundred five, three hundred forty-five, four hundred four, and four hundred thirty pages, in the second, third, fourth, and fifth year, so that, in all, a student mastered 1735 pages of Talmud during his time there. The *Mesifta*, nonetheless, devoted two hours each day to Polish language, mathematics, and history. This 'revolutionary' departure did not go unchallenged by the Rebbe of Munkacz who condemned it as 'heresy.'

In 1922, the Rebbe established a Yeshivah *Darke Teshuvah* in memory of his father,[7] which was recognized by the State as an

---

7. Abraham Fuchs, *Hungarian Yeshivot* (in Hebrew), (Jerusalem, privately printed, 1978), p. 500.

academy for training rabbis. In spite of having neither a dormitory, nor adequate kitchen facilities, it attracted two hundred fifty students from Poland, Hungary, Romania, and Yugoslavia. Students ate according to a unique rota system, whereby generous householders would invite them to share their family meals on a specific day of the week. The rebbe was a stimulating teacher. He impressed upon his students the need to be cheerful when expounding a discourse. He was supported by R. David Schlussel, R. Hayyim Schreiber, and R. Nathan Shlomo Schlussel, the author of *Nata Shashuim* (Munkacz, 1925).

The rebbe paid a warm tribute to Schlussel's work "as one whom he loves with his heart and soul, and one who is fully versed in Torah, Talmud, and Codifiers".[8] On Mondays and Thursdays, the rebbe would give a discourse. Although it was still daylight, he insisted on delivering his discourses in front of two lighted candles, following a custom of the Rebbe of Dynov. His discourses used *pilpul*, a dialectical method introduced by the Polish Halachist, R. Jacob Pollak (1470–1522) in which casuistic hair-splitting was used in order to sharpen the acumen of the students. His *shiurim* (discourses) were a pleasure to his listeners, invariably including new insights into talmudical texts. He was always prepared to give his time and encouragement to any student who needed it. This quality of kindness never deserted him. Addressing his students, he called them 'my masters,' which was based on the talmudic saying "Much Torah have I learned from my masters, more from my fellow-students, but from my disciples most of all."[9] His students were enthralled by his stories and *Divre Torah*.

All the students were expected to attend his three Sabbath *tishen* (communal meals at the rabbi's table), and he expected a high standard of behavior from them, as he wanted them to be an example to the community. He used to say that if a student overlooked his master's anger on two occasions, then his love for Torah would

---

8. Preface to *Neta Shoshanim*, (Munkacz, 1925) p. 9a.
9. *Makkot*, 10a.

survive. His students mostly studied in the different *Bate midrashim* (houses) of the community, especially in the *Bet Hamidrash* of R. Joseph Zerah, where there was a valuable library.

The Rebbe and Zionism

As a staunch champion of tradition, the rebbe was prepared to clash with those who opposed him and thus frequently found himself embroiled in controversy. The Jews were represented in the Czech Parliament by Dr. Angelo Goldstein and Dr. Hayyim Kugel. In order to thwart the Zionist-orientated Jewish Party, which had existed since 1919 in Sub-Carpathian Rus, the rebbe and his allies favored electoral arrangements with the Czech parties, in particular, the rebbe favored the Czech Agrarian Party. (There are parallels with the Polish Aguda's alignment with Pilsudski in 1926.) The Rebbe maintained that it was forbidden to associate with the Mizrachi Zionists and put his view forcibly, saying that, "every Jew, young or old, who voices an opinion in favour of the Zionist List for Parliament, is sinning gravely by abetting the criminals. Of the likes of such our Torah says, 'cursed be he, who does not keep the words of the Law.' " [10] The Aguda was also to be condemned for its role in favor of resettling in the Holy Land, and he viewed with great dismay the fact that the Slovakian Aguda held its national convention at the Trene Ianoska Podhradaice in March 1921.

On 2 Tammuz 1922, at a rabbinical conference held in Czap, he signed a declaration against the policies of the Aguda and the Zionists:[11] "Their leaders are blinded. They are completely unaware of the harm they are committing." Strong language, indeed, but the declaration was endorsed by R. Yoel Teitelbaum, R. Abraham Yosef Greenwood, the rabbi of Ungvar, R. Yaakov Moses of

---

10. *Deuteronomy*, 27:6.

11. Yitzhak Alfasi, *Hasidism and the Return to Zion* (in Hebrew) (Tel Aviv: *Sifrit Maariv*, 1986), pp. 130–131.

Safrin-Lvov, R. Yitzhak Tzvi Leibovitch, rabbi of Czap, R. Hayyim, rabbi of Bergesasz, R. Yitzhak Eizig Adler of Seredna, and R. Yonatan Steif of Ungvar. There is a talmudic phrase, "the destruction of Jerusalem came through A. Kamza and Bar Kamza." [12] The Rebbe interpreted this humorously that the Hebrew letters for Bar Kamza stand for 'Bundists, Revisionists, Communists, Mizrachists, Zionists and Agudists.' [13] He maintained that not only was it forbidden to associate with the Mizrachi, but the Aguda was also to be condemned for its vote in favor of resettlement in the Holy Land. [14]

His views on Zionism had a basis in *halacha*. Nachmanides in his Commentary on Numbers, on the verse, "And you shall inherit the Land and dwell there," [15] rules that it is a positive command to live in the Holy Land. The rebbe pointed out that Maimonides, however, did not include the Commandment concerning the dwelling in the Holy Land among the 613 Commandments, and he sided with Maimonides. He had illustrious support from R. Yosef Yitzhak Schneersohn of Lubavitch who wrote to him, "there is no difference between the Zionists and the Agudists, with the exception that the latter have rabbinical approval. . . ."

Few escaped his disapproval. He attacked the performances of the Yiddish theatre in Munkacz, insisting that the Yiddish theatre would lead Jewish youth into immorality. [16] In the parliamentary elections of 1935, he made the following appeal to his supporters: "I am writing to you concerning the elections for Parliament, a subject on which no Jew may remain silent, though many say, either out of ignorance or a desire to deceive, that the voting has nothing to do with the question of Jewish religion. In view of this it is my duty to proclaim that according to our Holy Law it is

---

12. *Gittin*, 55b.
13. Ibid, A. Fuchs, *op cit*, p. 500.
14. Ibid.
15. *Numbers*, 33:51.
16. "The Yiddish Theatre in Czechoslovakia" in *The Jews of Czechoslovakia*, Vol. 2 (Philadelphia and New York: Jewish Publication Society), p. 553.

forbidden to offer the slightest assistance to the Zionist heretics and free thinkers, much less to vote for their candidate, who is a traitor to our Torah and seducer of our young Jewish children in his Hebrew secondary school, that source of heresy and disobedience to our God, Messiah, Torah, and the Holy Faith which we have inherited from our rabbis and forefathers. Every Jew must do this to oppose this danger." [17]

He opposed the network of Hebrew schools as well as the course for cantors and teachers of religion, established by the Supreme Council of the Jewish Religious Communities. In 1934, he issued the following declaration:

> Blessed be the Lord, Munkacz on the eve of the holy Sabbath, portion of Balak 5694, according to our reckoning. The court of justice of the holy community of Mukacevo and the province may the Lord preserve them.
>
> Also our hands will strengthen this noble society, and there is not sufficient space upon this sheet to describe the grave heresy, may the Merciful preserve us, of the Zionist houses of iniquity in all their varieties, and all the heretical books that they teach the young boys of the children of Israel and they actually ensnare them to apostasy, denial of God, may the Merciful one preserve us. And all this we saw with our own eyes and not those of a stranger, and especially since that which is universally known does not need any proof at all.
>
> Therefore we are coming to warn once more our brethren the children of Israel in our community and in the provinces. Watch out and be careful, and whoever will not be cautious in this, God forbid, will loose his religious reliability and will not be appointed to any function of sanctity. And they, the guilty ones will be separated for shame and disgrace, and the one who listens will be delighted and rewarded with all good things forever and we shall be worthy of redemption among all of Israel and the deliverance should soon come, speedily in our own days.

---

17. Aryeh Sole, "Modern Hebrew Education in Subcarpathian Ruthenia," in *Jews of Czechoslovakia*, Vol. 2 (Philadelphia: Hebrew Publication Society), p. 148.

On the eve of the holy Sabbath, portion of Balak 5684, Munkacz, may the Lord protect it Amen[18]

The rebbe forbade all aid and comfort "to the representatives of the Zionist heretics (*minim*) and atheists," and vilified the Zionist-run modern high schools (from which he claimed issued heresy and atheism) in the city. All those who voted for the Zionists were regarded as criminals. He called immigration certificates to Palestine 'a passage to apostasy.' He issued another proclamation:

> To all Jewish parents, may the Lord keep them and preserve them, who believe in the holy Torah and in the words of our Sages of blessed memory. We are turning to every father and mother and warning them in the name of God and His Torah not to fall into the harmful path of the Zionist school or gymnasium, which has been prohibited by world-renowned rabbis, because it is a place from which come out heretics pure and simple who deny the Torah and deride all the commandments of the Lord, may He be blessed. They make a mockery of the words of our Sages of blessed memory and poison the Jewish heart with disbelief, may the Merciful preserve us (masquerades, balls, mixed excursions, etc). The parents will never be able to defend themselves in this world and in the world to come for the grave sin that they have committed against the innocent children by having torn them away from the Torah and belief and having cut them off from the Jewish religion. . . .
>
> We have already once pointed out the great loss that the Jewish home suffers when you allow the children to study in such schools and public institutions that are not under the compulsory education law, because they bring the innocent child to the desecration of the holy Sabbath and heresy, God forbid. And how many have already forsaken the Jewish home and caused anguish to their parents, may you be preserved from that, with shame and disgrace, God preserve us. Therefore consider carefully now when

---

18. Aryeh Sole, "Modern Hebrew Education in Subcarpathian Ruthenia," in *Jews of Czechoslovakia*, Vol. 2 (Philadelphia: Hebrew Publication Society), p. 247.

there is still a little time—later, there will be no use in regretting—
lead the little children in the path of our fathers and mothers, and
by this merit the Lord, may He be praised, will help us see joy
in our children until the coming of the Redeemer, speedily in our
own days, Amen.[19]

Every Jew, young or old, who voices an opinion in favor of
the Zionist list for Parliament, is sinning gravely by abetting the
criminals. . . . But the main thing is to vote! We all know that our
Torah commands us to promote the peace wherever we live, and
since the governor of this province (Subcarpathian Ruthenia), the
honorable Antonin Rozsypal, has declared his support for List
No. 1 in the elections for Parliament and Senate on the 19th of
May, I request that you all comply with his wishes, especially so
that the distinguished government and its minister for the interior, Josef Cerny may, with God's help, favour our Jewish con-
gregations in all matters of debts and loans. . . . And may the Lord
strengthen them and incline them to deal kindly with us and our
Torah. . . : And whoever acts in accordance with this appeal, may
he be blessed with all good." [20]

Now regarding the election of deputies for the state, that everyone is duty bound to consider carefully, many will take it
lightly, and will be of the opinion either wilfully or inadvertently,
that it does not concern at all the faith of Judaism.

Therefore I find myself compelled to let my voice be heard
publicly that according to the religion of our holy Torah it is
forbidden to assist in any way the representatives of the Zionist
heretics; and an Israelite unbeliever is even more lawless, since they
have nominated as their candidate a rebellious son who forsakes
the way of the Torah, who denies the faith, seduces and leads
astray the young children of Israel in the Hebrew gymnasium
from which emanates, as is well known, heresy and disbelief
against God and His Messiah and against our holy Torah and
faith . . ., which we inherited from our forefathers and our masters, may their merit protect us. It is, therefore, the duty of everyone to stand up against this breach and protest with self-sacri-
ficing efforts.[21]

---

19. *op cit*, Vol. 2, p. 426.
20. Aryeh Sole, Vol. 1, p. 148.
21. *op cit*, Vol. 2, p. 429.

The rebbe's personality included traits that might have appeared to be irreconcilable opposites. Despite his uncompromising political policies, his manner was cordial, winning him friends in many quarters. His kindness and consideration for the underprivileged knew no bounds. 'A man of war who soweth righteousness' is the phrase that the *hasidim* of Munkacz applied to their rebbe. In private he was a loving and thoughtful father. Nothing was too small or inconsequential to escape his notice.

The Rebbe of Munkacz and the Rebbes of Zydaczov of Belz

The rebbe had cordial relations with R. Yissahar Berish Eichenstein (1848–1924 of Zydaczov), a refugee rabbi who even went to hear the recitation of the *kiddush* by the rebbe and stated that 'he was a *zaddik* of his generation and that half of the world survives in his merit.'

During the First World War, refugees from the war zone of Galicia found shelter in Carpathia, especially in Munkacz. Among the refugee rabbis were R. Pinhas Rokeach of Dolino, the son of R. Moshe of Karov and R. Yitzhak Isaac Weiss (1875–1944) of Spinka, who lived in Munkacz for twelve years, and in 1930 moved to Nagyzsulla. The most prominent rabbi, R. Yissahar Dov Rokeach, left Belz and lived for a time in Ratsford (Usefehto), where he resided from 1914 to 1918. In 1918, he moved to Munkacz, where he stayed for three years. Yiri Langer (1894–1943), the Czech poet, describes the Rebbe of Belz as a patriarchal figure, who wore a *kaftan* of fine silk and a *spodek* even during prayer.

The rebbe of Belz revived the *Mahzike Hadas*, founded by his father, and participated in the social and political life of Galicia, yet outside Belz, he never intervened in communal matters and believed that silence was the best answer to calumny. Nonetheless he aroused the enmity of the rebbe of Munkacz. The animosity was more the result of different temperaments than of conflicting religious or communal opinions held by the two rivals. "He and

I," said the rebbe of Munkacz, "cannot live in the same town."
This was a clash of two forceful personalities. They were both
difficult and dogmatic and neither was of a conciliatory disposi-
tion, and as a result of this conflict the rebbe of Belz found it poli-
tic to move to Halicz near Yaroslav.[22]

22. Shlomo Hakohen Weingarten, "Pulmus, Munkacz V'Belz," in
Encyclopedia of Jewish Diaspora (in Hebrew) (Jerusalem, 1959), Vol. 7,
pp. 226–232; George Fleischman, "The Religious Congregation, 1918–
1938, Jews in Czechoslovakia, Vol. 2, p. 292.

18

Abdication of a Rabbi

Petah Tikvah, a city on the coastal plain, northeast of Tel Aviv, was established in 1878 by a group of Hungarian Jews. It is the home of R. Avraham Alter Pollak, the stepson of R. Aaron Rokeah of Belz and a descendant of R. Yosef Meir of Spinka, and the hasidic Yeshivah *Miscolc* under R. Shalom Berger. In Rehov Hanesiim 30 in Kfar Ganim, until recently, lived R. Baruch Yehoshua Yerahmiel Rabinowicz. For a rebbe to abdicate in the prime of his life in favor of his sons, is a rare phenomenon in Hasidism, yet this is the story of perhaps the most versatile of the hasidic personalities in the Holy Land. The rebbe gave up the leadership of the turbulent hasidic movement of Munkacz for the equally demanding and less rewarding office of being, for a time, a rabbi in Holon, then a community of over 70,000 people not known for their religious fervor. Many *hasidim* were aggrieved that he did not revive the Munkacz dynasty in Israel. They disapproved of his strong leanings towards Mizrachi, his discourses in fluent modern Hebrew, his modernity (he drove his own car), and above all things, his marriage to a "commoner."

R. Baruch Yehoshua Yerahmiel

Baruch was born in Parczev, Poland, on 6 Tishri 1914, the third son of R. Nathan David Rabinowicz, the author of *V'ele Hadvarim Sheneumru L'David*. He was the son of R. Yaakov Yitzhak (d. 1906) of Biala, a descendant of the Yehudi, "the Holy Jew" of Przysucha. The four sons of R. Yaakov Yitzhak, like their counterparts in the twentieth century, established their own courts in different parts of Poland: R. Avraham Yehoshua Heschel (1875–1933) in Lublin; R. Meir Shlomo Yehuda (1868–1942) in Miedzyrzec; the youngest, R. Yerahmiel Tzvi, who was the most gifted of all, in Siedlice. R. Yerahmiel Tzvi excelled as a reader. Once, when he was ill, his anxious mother urged his father to dissuade him from officiating at the reader's desk, but his father refused to interfere. "The entire heavenly host wants to hear the prayer of my son, how dare I stop it!" R. Tzvi became rebbe on 8 Iyar, but he was rebbe for merely six months—he died on 7 Heshvan 1906, on the anniversary of the death of his grandfather, R. Nathan David. His death, at the age of twenty-six, robbed Hasidism of a towering genius.

The eldest son, R. Nathan David (1868–1930) of Parczev, married Leah Reizel, the daughter of R. Yehuda Yaakov Hofstein of Kozienice, a descendant of R. Hayyim Halberstam of Zanz. They had two daughters and one son. On Leah's death, he married Yitta Shapira Horowitz, the widowed daughter of R. Moshe Yehuda Leib Shapira of Sasov-Stryzov, the son-in-law of R. Baruch of Gorlice. They had seven children, three daughters and four sons. At the outbreak of the First World War, the rebbe left Parczev for Retziz, and from 1919 onwards he lived in Siedlice, where his widowed sister-in-law lived with her five children. He was still known as the rebbe of Parczev. He died on 7 Shevat 1930, when his son Baruch was sixteen years old. The rebbe, like his ancestors, left an ethical will, which was published in Warsaw in 1930.

He instructed his family to notify his ancestors, who are buried in Przysucha, Szydlowiec, Biala, and Warsaw, of his demise, so that they would intervene on his behalf. He instructed that a space of four cubits be left around his grave, where no one was to be buried. He expressed a wish that his heirs should purchase a plot of land in Hebron and establish a *bet hamidrash* bearing his name.

After the rebbe's death, his widow, her five daughters and three sons moved to Gensia 7a, Warsaw. Baruch studied in the *Mesifta* Yeshiva in Warsaw, and, at the age of fifteen, obtained his rabbinical diploma from R. Tzvi Yehezkel Michelson, "the Plonsker Rav" of Warsaw, R. Yehiel Meir Blumenfeld, head of the Mizrachi Rabbinic Seminary *Tachkemoni* of Warsaw, as well as from R. Yosef Elimelech Grunwald of Ungvar, and R. Yonathan Steif of Budapest. He was exceptionally gifted and known as an *Illui*. His relative, R. Hayyim Elazar, came especially to Siedlice, where he subjected his twelve-year-old future son-in-law to a searching examination in talmudics. When the boy passed the test, the rabbi declared in the words of the Psalms: "Thou art my son. This day I have begotten you." [1]

At the tender age of twelve, on 2 Sivan 1926, at Rzeszov, he became engaged to Hayyah Frimet Rebecca, born on 19 March 1915, the only daughter of the second marriage of R. Hayyim Elazar Shapira, the rebbe of Munkacz. Four years later, in 1930, the sixteen-year old Baruch accompanied his future father-in-law to a visit to the Holy Land. The rebbe left Munkacz on Sunday, the eve of Rosh Hodesh Iyar 1930, and traveled via Vienna, Trieste, and Alexandria. As Baruch was a Polish citizen, he could not obtain an Egyptian visa, and had to make his own way to Jaffa.

The rebbe was accompanied by fourteen followers, among them: R. Benzion Wiesel, Rabbi of Tardo, R. Yitzhak Tzvi Leibovitch of Czap, R. Hillel Weinberger and R. Shlomo Zucker, as well as by his assistant Hayyim Dov Grunfeld, and his chronicler, Moshe Goldstein. The Rebbe was motivated to undertake this journey because of his desire to see the kabbalist R. Shlomo Eliezer

---

1. Psalm 2:7.

ben Yaacov Alfandari (1829–1930)—known as *Mercado* or
Maharasha, and also as the *Saba Kadisha* (the 'holy grandfather')—
with whom he had corresponded, and who, at long last, withdrew
his objection to this visit.

R. Alfandari was a native of Istanbul, where he was for many
years the head of a yeshivah that produced many distinguished
Sephardi rabbis, among whom were R. Ezekiel Medini, and R.
Yitzhak Arkis, the author of *Kiryat Arba*. R. Alfandari's personal
life was beset by tragedy. His only son died in the prime of life.
This was followed by his wife's death. He never remarried. R.
Alfandari then became rabbi of Damascus, and from 1904 until
1914, rabbi of Safed. In Adar 1921, he settled in the Old City of
Jerusalem. His Responsa were published in the periodical *Torah
Mi-Zion* and in *Kenaf Avraham* by Abraham Hai Amozag ben Isaac
Nissim in *Sheelot U'Teshuvot Maharsha* (1932). He also wrote a
learned responsum on the religious status of the Karaites.[2] He
strongly supported the educational institutions established by R.
Yosef Hayyim Sonnenfeld.

The rebbe of Munkacz found in him a soulmate. Like him, he
was antagonistic to all political parties, and like him, he did not
differentiate between the Agudists, Mizrachists, and Zionists. They
were all anathema to him. He was moreover highly critical of the
rabbinical establishment in the Holy Land, whom he regarded as
'Zionist tools,' even refusing to receive any visitor who had been
seen by R. Abraham Isaac Kook (1865–1931), the first Ashkenazi
Chief Rabbi of Eretz Yisrael.

The rebbe was welcomed in Alexandria by the wealthy David
Ezra Anzarat, a friend of R. Alfandari, and prayed in the 'Elijah
the Prophet' Synagogue in Alexandria. From Alexandria, he traveled by train to Cantara through the Sinai Desert to Lud, where
he was welcomed by R. Hayyim Shaul Davich Hakohen of the
Yeshivot *Bet El* and *Rehovot Ha-Nahor*, which was in Bukhara
district. The Rabbi was blind for twenty years, but he knew by
heart all the writings of R. Hayyim Vital. He was also the author

---

2. Shalom Eliezer Margulies, *Gedole Eretz Yisrael*, Jerusalem, 1975.

of *Eifa Shelema*, and the Rebbe described him as a personality who had not been reincarnated from an earlier generation—an untarnished soul.

He was also welcomed by R. Yaakov Hayyim Sofer (1870–1939), who was in charge of a kabbalistic yeshivah and by R. Shalom ben Yosef Halevi Alsheikh (1859–1944), chief rabbi of the Yemenite community of Jerusalem, and one of the leaders of the Yeshivah *Rehovot Ha-Nahor*. He there received a welcoming note from R. Alfandari, who was 'lovesick for him.'[3]

He arrived in Jerusalem on 10 Iyar, where his first task was to visit the Western Wall: Here he took off his shoes, as had already cut *keriya* (rending of clothes) and uttered the blessing, *"Baruch Dayan Ha-Emet"* (Blessed be the righteous Judge) on arrival in Jerusalem.

The memorable and long-awaited encounter between the rebbe and R. Alfandari who lived in *Shehunat Rehama* took place, and it was noteworthy that the latter shook the rabbi's hand, for it was not his custom to salute anyone by handshaking, which he regarded as a social convention, emanating from Europe and introduced by the irreligious element. He would not, however, let him kiss his hand. The rebbe recited the *She-heheyanu* ('Who has kept us alive'), a blessing of thanksgiving when enjoying something for the first time, and asked R. Alfandari for a blessing that his future son-in-law might arrive safely. He told him that he would not be able to stay for Shavuot (Pentecost), as he had to observe the Second Day of Yomtov, as in the diaspora—despite the view of R. Tzvi Hirsch Ashkenazi, known as the Haham Tzvi (1660–1718) who maintained that there was no need for visitors to the Holy Land to observe the Second Day of the Festival.

The rebbe then visited R. Yosef Hayyim Sonnenfeld (1849–1933), the rabbi of the Separated Orthodox Community in Jerusalem, who, too, strongly opposed Zionism. He stayed in *Bate Munkacz*. Apart from the itinerary of R. Yosef Yitzhak Schneersohn (1880–1950) of Lubavitch, written by Shimon Glatzenstein, (Tammuz/Av 1929), no journey has been so graphi-

---

3. *Song of Songs*, 2:5.

cally described by the *hasidim*, as that of the Rebbe of Munkacz. He was indefatigable in visiting the holy places.

On Friday he visited the tomb of the fourth-century BCE scholar and High Priest, R. Simeon Hazaddik (the Just) near Mount Scopus Road and the massive monument in the Kidron Valley of the ninth-century Prophet Zecharia, located off the Mount of Olives. He then visited the Mount of Olives, the holiest Jewish cemetery in the world, where the grave of R. Moshe Biederman (d. 1851) of Lelov is located. R. Moshe spent seventy-four days in the Holy Land and died in his seventy-fourth year. He was the father-in-law of the 'Holy Jew' of Przysucha, whose last wish was to be interred next to the grave of the Prophet Zacharia. He also visited the grave of R. Hayyim ben Moshe Ibn Attar (1696–1743), the author of *Or Hahayyim* on the Pentateuch (Venice, 1742), who was known among the *hasidim* as the *Or Hahayyim Hakadosh*. He is buried with his wife and two levirite wives. When R. Hayyim died, the Besht proclaimed: "The western light has been extinguished."

He paid tribute to the memory of the Turkish rabbi, R. Solomon ben Abraham Algazi (1610–1683), who excommunicated the false messiah, Shabbetai Tzvi, and also attended the grave of R. Hezkia ben David de Silva (1659–1695), author of *Pri Hadash* (Amsterdam, 1706), a work on the *Shulhan Aruch*. The rabbi searched in vain for the resting place of R. Avraham Gershon of Kutov (d. 1761), the brother-in-law of R. Yisrael Baal Shem (whose grave was only discovered after the Six-Day War) and of R. Moshe Galanti (1620–1689). The rabbi expressed his concern that so many tombs of famous personalities were not clearly marked or preserved, and had hence disappeared into oblivion.

On the same day and on Sabbath, he re-visited R. Alfandari, with whom he discussed the halachic problem as to whether priests (*kohanim*) are permitted to visit the grave of Rachel. To everyone's amazement, the scholarly and frail octogenarian recalled that this subject has already been dealt with in the rebbe's responsa.[4] In all,

---

4. *Minhat Elazar*, Responsa Bratislava 1922 Part 3, 64

the Rabbi had a busy schedule, not only with his indefatigable tours of the graves, but also because of intensive meetings with officials of the Kollel Munkacz to plan building extensions, which were intended to accommodate four additional hasidic families. He was also invited by Sefphardi families to officiate at circumcisions in Yemenite synagogues.

In the old Jewish Quarter, the south end of the Old City, he visited the synagogues of R. Yohanan ben Zakkai, the first-century sage, as well as *Bet El*, the kabbalistic center of R. Shalom Sharabi (1720–1777), and then the traditional site of the tomb of King David on Mount Zion. It is noteworthy to mention that he did not visit the impressive Hurva Synagogue of R. Juda Hasid, which had stood in ruins for nearly 150 years, and was dedicated in 1864, nor the Tiferet Yisrael Synagogue, named in honor of R. Israel Friedman of Ruzhin, which was also known as Bet Hakneset Nisan Bak (Nisan's Shul). Opened in 1870, it was the largest and most attractive synagogue in Jerusalem until 1948, when it was destroyed by Arabs. It is significant that he did not meet any of the hasidic rebbes such as R. Shimon Nathan Nata Biderman (1870–1930), nor R. Yehuda Leib Halevi Ashlag (1886–1955), the kabbalistic lion of the twentieth century. Neither did he visit the Yeshiva of Ger *Sefat Emet*, established in 1925, after the visit of R. Abraham Mordecai Alter of Ger in 1924, nor the Habad Synagogue in the Old City.

On 16 Iyar he visited the traditional burial place of the matriarch Rachel at the northern entrance to Bethlehem on the Jerusalem road, five kilometers south of Jerusalem. This grave symbolizes Jewish motherhood throughout the ages: "Rachel," in the words of the Prophet,[5] "weeps for her children." The rebbe there cried out, "Two million Jews in Soviet Russia are under threat of apostasy. There is no one to help them. In the Holy Land, too, your children are murdered without pity. . . . How long will you sleep in peace? Please intercede on behalf of your children." He praised Sir Moses Montefiore for his work on Rachel's sepulcher.

---

5. *Jeremiah*, 5:17.

Prior to leaving Jerusalem, on the way to Safed, he once again
visited R. Alfandari. On arriving in Safed, which has special mys-
tical significance for the kabbalists, he visited the graves of R. Yosef
Caro (1488–1575), the author of the *magnum opus*, which regulates the daily life of the observant Jew, the *Shulhan Aruch*, completed in 1536. He also visited other graves, including those of R.
Moshe ben Yaakov Cordovero (1522–1570), the author of *Pardes
Rimonim* (Cracow, 1591), and his brother-in-law, R. Shlomo
Alkabetz (1505–1584), the author of the Sabbath hymn *Lecha Dodi*
("Come My Beloved"), and that of the key figure in Jewish mysticism, R. Yitzhak ben Shlomo Luria Ashkenazi (1534–1572),
known as *Ha-Ari* (the Holy Lion), who had established the Lurian
system of Kabbalah.

He prayed at the most famous of all Safed synagogues, the Ari
and the Abohav, the latter named after the fifteenth century
scholar, R. Isaac Abohav, whose ancient Torah scroll is only used
on the High Holy Days. The rebbe was permitted to read a few
sentences from this ancient scroll, and he spoke highly of R. Shalom ben Moshe Butago (1700–1760), the Moroccan kabbalist who
settled in England and wrote a commentary on the Zohar *Mikdash
Melech* (Amsterdam, 1750), and of R. Joseph ben Moses Trani, the
Mahbit (1568–1639) whose graves have not been traced. He visited the graves of the *Tanna*, R. Yohanan Ha-Sandelar (the 'shoemaker'), first half of the second-century and pupil of R. Akiva,
who maintained that "dwelling in Eretz Yisrael is equal to all the
precepts of the Torah." [6]

He regularly visited the *bet hamidrash* of R. Ezekiel Shragai
Halberstam (1815–1898) of Sianiawa where he, too, performed
hadlaka (bonfire) on Lag B'Omer (the thirty-third day of the
Omer), as he did not go to Meron in Upper Galilee that night,
where there were large mixed gatherings of men and women,
young and old, Ashkenazim, Sephardim, Sabras and Yemenites,
especially irreligious *halutzim*. A day later, he went to the sepulcher of R. Shimon ben Yochai and his son R. Eliezer, and there

---

6. *Sifri, Deuteronomy*, 80.

he beheld the traditional ceremony of three-year-old children having their first haircut.

He visited the burial places of the first-century scholar Hillel, and his opponent and contemporary, Shammai, who is buried in the massive sarcophagus next to the hill facing Hillel's tomb.

On the outskirts between Meron and Safed, the Rebbe visited the graves of R. Yehuda ben Ilai, the second-century Palestinian *Amora*, who was called "the Chief Spokesman," and of R. Pinhas ben Yair, he second-century Tanna, best known for his ability to perform miracles. At one grave, he stated, that this was the tomb of the second-century *Tanna*, a disciple of R. Yohanan ben Zakkai, R. Joshua ben Hanania, and not that of Joshua ben Beeri, the eighth-century pre-Common Era prophet, who prophesied in the reign of Hezekiah, King of Juda, and of Jereboam, King of Israel.[7]

On 20 Iyar, he went to Tiberias, one of the four holy cities in Eretz Yisrael, for there were the graves of so many immortals. He saw the twelfth-century grave of Moses Maimonides, and he was greatly distressed that on one of the stones were engraved in the vernacular the words, "Born 13 March 1135 to 13 December 1204." He particularly resented the fact that the common era date was recorded. He intervened with the authorities in both Tiberias and Jerusalem, and they promised to erase the offending inscription. Near the grave of Maimonides and R. Yohanan ben Zakkai is the resting place of R. Isaiah Horowitz, the *Shelah* (1565–1630), author of *Shne Luhot HaBrit*, who is known among the *hasidim* as the *Shelah Hakadosh*. He was the spiritual leader of Jewry, of both Ashkenazim and Sephardim, in the Holy Land from 1621 to 1626. He was also the author of a kabbalistic commentary to prayerbook, called *Shaar HaShamayim* (Amsterdam, 1717). The rebbe remarked that on his mother's side he was the grandson of R. Naftali Tzvi Horowitz (1760–1827) of Ropczyce, who was the third son of the Rebbe of Dzikov, a descendant of R. Isaiah Horowitz.[8]

---

7. Moshe Goldstein, *Sefer Masaot Yerushalayim*, (Munkacz: Grafia 1931), pp. 61–63.

8. *op cit*, p. 61a.

He also visited the graves of R. Yohanan ben Zakkai, the first-century *Tanna* who is buried with his five disciples as ennumerated in *Ethics of the Fathers*,[9] R. Eliezer ben Hyrcanos, R. Joshua ben Hanania, R. Yosi the Priest, R. Shimon ben Nethanel and R. Eleazar ben Arach. The rebbe, however, remarked that, according to the Talmud,[10] R. Eleazar's coffin was carried from Caesaria to Lydda. He then, of course, saw the graves of R. Akiva (c 40- c 135), the outstanding *Tanna* and martyr and R. Hiyya, also called 'Rabba the Great,' a *Tanna* of the second century, who was responsible for the collection of *Beraitot*, contained in the *Tosefta*.

He then paid a visit to the burial place of R. Meir Baal Hanes on the shore of Lake Kinneret and his Yeshivah *Or Torah*. The identity of R. Meir has baffled scholars throughout the ages. He is identified as one of the second-century teachers of the Talmud, who died in Asia Minor, but ordered that his coffin be taken to the Holy Land. Others identify him as R. Meir Kazin or R. Meir ben Yaakov who emigrated to the Holy Land with R. Yehiel of Paris or that R. Meir, the author of *Akdamot* (a poem recited in the Ashkenazi synagogue on the morning of Shavuot). Miraculous deeds have been connected with the tomb. Many Jewish homes had a 'Meir Baal Hanes' charity box into which contributions were dropped regularly by householders, especially before the kindling of the Sabbath lights. In Tiberias, too, he visited the home and the synagogue of R. Menahem Mendel of Vitebsk, the disciple of the Besht, and one of the early pioneers of Hasidism in the Holy Land.

He subsequently visited the grave of R. Yirmiyahu bar Abba, the fourth-century Babylonian Amora who instructed, "clothe me in a white garment, put stockings on my feet, and a staff in my hand, and lay me on my side so when the Messiah comes, I will be ready." [11] Bar Abba also asked that his staff be buried with him,

---

9. *Avot* 2:10.

10. *Sanhedrin*, 68a. See Goldstein, *op cit*, p. 61. See also H. E. Shap, *Divre Torah Madura Tenira* (Munkacz, 1936), p. 654. See also *Shaar Hagilgulim* of the Ari who does not mention Elazar ben Arach.

11. *Yerushalmi Kilayim*, 9:4.

again, so that he could readily welcome the Messiah. In Tiberias itself, the old cemetery had a great fascination for him, for there were the graves of the disciples of the Besht, R. Menahem Mendel of Vitebsk (d. 1788), R. Menahem Mendel Przemyslany (d. 1744), R. Avraham of Kalisk (d. 1810), R. Yaakov Samson[12] of Shepetovka (d. 1801), R. Nahman of Horodenka (d. 1780), and R. Zeev Wolf of Czsarni-Ostrog (d. 1823), as well as that of R. Abraham Yehoshua Heschel of Opatov (d. 1825), who was actually buried in Medziborz, but to whom legend gives an additional resting place in Tiberias.

He returned to Jerusalem on 21 Iyar where R. Alfandari gave him a letter of approval of his work. The aged R. Alfandari, however, became very ill and contracted pneumonia. He died on 22 Iyar 1930, aged 100. The rebbe rent his garments, and inconsolably heartbroken, participated in the funeral, which took place on the Mount of Olives. He lamented, "No one is fit enough to deliver the eulogy that he deserved." He himself was too grief-stricken to pay the eulogy. On the way home via Jaffa, the rebbe passed through Tel Aviv, and once again expressed his sorrow that so many people desecrated the Sabbath there. He arrived home on 2 Sivan and said, in the words of Naomi: "I went out full, and the Lord has brought me back empty," [13] referring, of course, to the death of R. Alfandari. Alfandari's responsa on *Shulhan Aruch* in three volumes was published posthumously.[14]

The *hasidim* of Munkacz devoted a special section in the publication *Masot Yerushalayim* in praise of Alfandari. "Believe me," the Rebbe wrote,[15] "I truly love the Holy Land, especially all those who are zealous for the Lord and His Torah." A twenty-nine-page detailed account of his journey to the Holy Land was printed by

---

12. Goldstein in *op cit*, p. 60, calls him Simon, his name was Samson.

13. *Ruth*, 1–21.

14. First published in 1974, and reprinted in 1990, in Jerusalem, with a letter by R. Hayyim Elazar.

15. Abraham Fuchs, *op cit*, p. 506.

Moses Goldstein under the title *Masot Yerushalayim* (Munkacz, 1931). The rebbe spent thirteen days in the Holy Land, intentionally corresponding to the thirteen years that R. Shimon Bar Yochai spent in the cave composing the Zohar.[16]

The rebbe, like his father, was in charge of fundraising for the poor of the Holy Land and was also the president of *Kollel Munkacz V'Aaseret Gelilot*. Even during the First World War, he was able to transmit money to the Holy Land. Like R. Menahem Mendel Morgenstern of Kotsk, he believed in truth. His motto was the verse in Psalms[17]: "Thy word is true from the beginning and everyone of your righteous judgments endures for ever." He could not conceive of how a Jew could ever tell a lie. He hated hypocrisy and deceit, and those "who dressed like *hasidim* and were dishonest like Laban." He expected a high standard from his students, and he wanted them to be an example to others. He refused to accept donations from anyone who desecrated the Sabbath.

The Next Generation

The marriage of the Rebbe's eighteen-year-old daughter, Frimet, took place in Munkacz on 17 Adar 1933. It was regarded by the *hasidim* as the "wedding of the year." Triumphal arches were erected in the city, and six white horses drove the bridegroom to the wedding ceremony. The frontiers of Czechoslovakia and Hungary were opened to enable *hasidim* to attend the wedding without visas. Rebbes from all over Galicia attended the festivities, including R. Shalom Eliezer Halberstam (1862–1944) of Ratzford, whilst R. Nehemia Shapira (1874–1942) of Sasov officiated.

---

16. *Shabbat* 33b.
17. Psalm 119:60.

This alliance made R. Baruch the heir apparent of Munkacz. His "Last Will and Testament," [18] which he wrote at the age of fifty-seven in 1928, consisted of twenty-six paragraphs, R. Hayyim Elazar said: "I am not sorry that I cannot bequeath you material possessions. Wealth by itself does not bring happiness. We have to follow the path of our fathers, and we must not associate ourselves with any organization." He requested that a scholar be engaged to recite *kaddish* in his memory. His coffin was to be made from the table on which he studied in the *bet hamidrash*. He permitted his heirs to sell his books and even his phylacteries to pay any debts he may have incurred. He even composed the wording for his tombstone, "He studied the Torah in spite of great pain." His tombstone was to be erected, if possible, at the end of the *shiva* (seven days of mourning), and his disciples were to study at least three chapters of the Mishnah in his memory.

He begged his family not to wear modern garments, not even wigs, but rather that his daughter Frimet was to wear a kerchief, (*Sterentiechel*) as his mother had worn. A scholar should be hired to recite *kaddish* in his memory for eleven months. His coffin was not to be carried through streets where there was a church. No eulogies should be paid to him, especially they should not say that he was a *Zaddik*, a *hasid*, or a *Gaon*, which he was not. He instructed that all his unpublished manuscripts be published as soon as possible.

The rebbe suffered ill health for many years, and he regularly visited physicians in Prague, Vienna, Italy, and Budapest. When he died on 2 Sivan 1937 at the age of sixty-five, the *London Jewish Chronicle* stated that he "held extreme orthodox views on the sacredness of the Hebrew language." [19] R. Baruch became rebbe at the age of twenty-three, and was later elected as Rabbi of Munkacz.

---

18. *Tzavaah*, published in *Hamisha Mamarot* (Jerusalem: Tzvi Moskovitch, 1962) pp. 282–287.

19. *Jewish Chronicle*, 21 May 1937, p. 12, which stated that he died in Prague.

He received six hundred six votes, out of a total electorate of six hundred seventy. He was ably supported by R. Nata Shlomo Schlussel and R. Berish Klitshniver. R. Baruch expanded the Yeshivah *Darke Teshuvah* which soon had over 300 students, and thus eclipsed the Yeshivot of Kormarno, Presov and Kosice. R. Baruch delivered daily *Shiurim*. In opposition to the *Judische Stimme*, the *Zionist Weekly*, and the *UJSZO* (*New World*), the *Munkaczev Humorist*, edited by Zelig Weiss, of the Hebrew Monthly *Hakohov* (The Star), which was a monthly Torah periodical, edited by Isaac Shterenheim. The Rebbe patronised the *Yiddishe Zeitung*, known as "The Rebbe's Newspaper", which was edited by Elimelech Kalus, and appeared between 1927 and 1928.

He often intervened with the Supreme Council of the Religious Communities that was headed by R. Yosef Popper, the Chief Rabbi of Prague, and also worked with the authorities in Slovakia and Carpatho-Russia where the salaries of the rabbis were augmented by Kongrau, a government fund for the upkeep of religious life.

By the Vienna Award of 2 November 1938, imposed on Czechoslovakia by Germany and Italy, Hungary acquired Felvidek upper provinces which included the cities of Kassa (Kosice), Ungvar and Munkacz. Parts of Slovakia and Carpathian Russia, with a Jewish population of 80,000 were ceded to Hungary. Seventy-eight thousand Jews were affected by the restrictive anti-Jewish laws of 1938, and during the war 15,000 Jews of Munkacz were confined to Ghettos from 14 April 1940.

At the outbreak of the Second World War, R. Baruch and his wife and their four children moved to Budapest, where they stayed for some time. He was in constant touch with R. Michael Dov Weissmandel (1903–1956), one of the leaders of the *Pracovna Skupina* (Working Group), a Jewish Underground Organization in Slovakia, whose object was to smuggle Jews from Slovakia to Hungary. Many Jews from Austria and Poland were sheltered in his home and in the *Bet Hamidrash Polin*, through which many were saved from certain death. He was also instrumental in helping R. Aaron Rokeach, the Rebbe of Belz and his brother, R. Mordecai, to evade the Nazis.

The Hungarian government adopted anti-Jewish laws and a discriminatory system that enforced labor service for Jews of military age. Shortly after Hungary declared war on the Soviet Union on 27 June 1941, a plan was devised to 'resettle' the Jews. The Hungarian authorities began to deport not only recently arrived Polish and Russian Jews, but also Hungarian Jews who could not prove their citizenship, simply because their papers were not immediately available in the Hungarian-administered parts of liberated Galicia. The Rebbe and his son, Tzvi Nathan David, born on 14 February 1934, together with eight thousand other Jews, were packed into freight wagons and taken to Korosmezo, near the Polish border, to Kolomya, and finally to Kamenets Podolski. Between 27 and 29 August, 11,000 Jews were murdered in an area between the Dnieper and Burg Rivers, known as Transnistria.

The rebbe escaped to Yagolnice, near Czortkov, the very town where one of his great-grandfathers, R. Shmuel Shmelke of Sasov, was buried.[20] With the help of the local priest and the local rabbi, R. Rossenzweig, and above all through R. Avraham Mann, the son of R. Baruch whom the Bet Din of Munkacz permitted that he may even work on the Sabbath to rescue the Rebbe. The Rebbe and his son were able to cross the Dnjester and make their way to Kolomya and then to Munkacz, and eventually to Budapest, where they sheltered in the Jewish Old Age Home. His sister, Havah Tovah and his brother-in-law, R. Yerahmiel Yisrael Yosef Danziger (son of the Rebbe of Alexander), his sister, Feige, and her husband, R. Aaron Perlow of Stolin, his brother, R. Moshe Yehiel Elimelech, the rabbi of Lubartov and his uncle, R. Meir Shlomo Yehuda Rabinowicz, the rebbe of Miedzyrzec all perished together with their families in the Holocaust. A doctor induced a temporary hip displacement which made the rabbi appear to be lame. He was thus able to avoid being sent to a more rigorous labor camp. "My leg falters, your kindness, O God, supports me,"[21] he quoted. He befriended a Hungarian countess named

---

20. B. Rabinowicz, *Binat Nevonim*, (privately printed, 1996), p. 3.

21. Psalm 94:18; Peska Friedman, *Going Forward* (New York: *Mesorah Publications*, 1994) pp. 150–160.

Safra who was living in Buda, who had contact with foreign dip-
lomats, which enabled him to obtain visas to Australia and Brazil
for many Jews. The Nazis regarded him as 'Enemy Number One'.
Through the intervention of his brother-in-law, Jacob Landau,
a grandson of R. Avraham of *Chechanov*, who was the director of
the Poale Agudat Yisrael, and R. Hayyim Moshe Shapira, then a
member of the Executive of the Jewish Agency, nine certificates
were issued to his family to permit them to enter the Holy Land.
On the way the family stopped in Istanbul, where the Rebbe supplied information to the Jewish authorities about the state of the
Jews in Eastern Europe. Here his wife gave birth to a daughter.
They then settled in Tel Aviv. He succeeded in transferring the
entire library of his father-in-law and his own personal possessions
to Israel. His wife died in a sanatorium in Hadera on 27 Nisan
1945 and was buried on the Mount of Olives. She left him with
five young children. The Rebbe often appeared on public plat-
forms, protesting against the policies of the British Foreign Secretary, Ernest Bevin, and the *White Paper* of 1939, which restricted
Jewish immigration to seventy-five thousand over five years.

In 1946, the rebbe was a candidate for the Chief Rabbinate of
Tel Aviv. Dr. Hayyim Kugel (1879–1953), the former principal
of the Hebrew High School in Munkacz, the representative of the
Zionist Movement in the Czech Parliament and later Mayor of
Holon, launched a ferocious media attack against him, under the
heading "Is It Possible?" [22] accusing him of anti-Zionism and of
following the traditions of Munkacz. He pointed out that in September 1938, at the time of Munich, the Rebbe accused the Zionists of undermining the Czech Republic by sending funds to Palestine. His splendid gifts and accomplishments were devalued by
his opponents. Owing to this campaign, the position went to R.
Isser Yehuda Unterman, who later became Chief Rabbi of Israel.
The rebbe negotiated with R. Yehezkel Abramski (d. 1966), the
head of the London *beth din* for a suitable rabbinic post in London. In 1947, R. Baruch married Yehudit, the daughter of Asher
Walhoiz, originally a merchant in Regensburg, Germany, who

22. *Dvar*, 30 May 1946.

later lived in Raanana. This marriage caused great controversy among Munkacz *hasidim*, but his new wife brought much love and devotion to his children. The Rebbe spent many months in New York and visited *hasidim* in Chicago, Los Angeles, and Montreal, but he decided to move to Sao Paulo Brazil, where he received from the University degree of Master of Philosophy for a thesis on "The Conflict between contradictory Ethical Principles." He stayed there for fifteen years, while his children were educated in the United States, where they eventually married. He had his own *shtiebl* and was in charge of the local *kashrut* and *shehita* facilities, which enabled meat to be exported to Israel. He was also in great demand as a *Mohel*, in which capacity he travelled long distances. He developed there the full range of his abilities and threw himself into many communal activities.

R. Baruch became Chief Rabbi of Holon in 1964, and lived at 14 Feierberg. He faced the dual challenge of eliciting the cooperation of the civic authorities and overcoming the hostility of the local rabbis. The Rebbe was not easily intimidated, and never evaded troublesome issues. He was a man of determination and forthright views. While his scholarship was outstanding, his diplomacy was less so. His adherence to the Mizrachi alienated the ultra-orthodox factions.

In 1968, R. Baruch founded the *Darke Teshuvah* the short-lived Institute for Rabbinic Education and Training in Tel Aviv. It accepted students who had completed the basic yeshivah education, and were ready for a three-year course in advanced theoretical and practical rabbinics. "There is a dearth of trained experienced rabbis," said Rabbi Baruch. "Everyday life in the State of Israel confronts the rabbinate with new problems." He also wanted to establish a genealogical chart tracing back his own pedigree to King David.

The rabbi had a library of over 5,000 books, which he had inherited from his father-in-law, who was an exceptional connoisseur with an encyclopedic knowledge of places and dates of Hebrew publications. The library's star item was an incunabulum of R. Moshe ben Yaakov of Coucy's work *Sefer Mitzvot Gadol* (known as the *Semag*), printed at Soncino in 1488. His collection also included many other sixteenth century rarities. He possessed a Scroll of the Law said to have belonged to R. Yisrael Baal Shem Tov and to have been written by his scribe Hirsch Sofer, but he also had a *Sefer Torah* of R. Moshe Leib of Sasov (1745–1807). He owned a pair of phylacteries that had belonged to R. Elimelech of Lejask (1717–1786), a circumcision knife, once the property of his forebears, and *tefillin* of the *Bene Yissahar*.

He possessed a set of Rashi's *tefillin*, previously owned by R. Shlomo Shapira, sets of Rashi and Rabbenu Tam *tefillin*, prayerbooks according to the liturgy of R. Yitzhak Luria, festival prayerbooks, the *Zohar*, and *Tikkune Zohar*. He owned complete sets of early editions of the Babylonian Talmud and the Palestinian Talmud, all originally the property of the late R. Tzvi Hirsch Shapira. Among his proud possessions was the volume of *Bene Yissahar* by R. Tzvi Elimelech Shapira of Dynov, first published in Zolkiev in 1846 (a volume that both R. Tzvi Hirsch and R. Hayyim Elazar cherished), a Scroll of Esther that had belonged to R. Tzvi Elemelech of Dynov, a set of R. Moshe Leib of Sasov's *tefillin*, versions of the manuscripts *Yeriot Shlomo*, and *Tiv Gittin*, and holographs of R. Shlomo Shapira, as well as a *hanukiah* and silver utensils used by the past rebbes of Munkacz.

In 1977, he succeeded in removing his father's remains from Siedlice to be re-interred in Petah Tikvah. He lived in a beautiful apartment in Petah Tikvah, above his *bet hamidrash* and a banqueting hall. His eclectic taste led him to acquire many fine pictures, drawings, and ritual silver. He retained many historic items, including a chair that had belonged to R. Yaakov Yitzhak, the "Holy Jew," a table cover used by his grandfather, R. Yaakov Yitzhak of Biala, and a watch, originally the possession of R. Yehoshua of Ostrova (1829–1873), whose only daughter, Rachel Leviah, married R. Yaakov Yitzhak of Biala.

In 1995, the rebbe suffered a stroke, which paralyzed his right side, after which his health declined, but the vigor of his mind and the range of his astonishing memory remained unclouded. He published a three-volume work *Binat Nevonim*,[23] containing dis-

---

23. He was helped by his grandson, Asher Grossman.

courses mainly on the Holocaust. Whoever visited him, could have no doubt that his second marriage was the solid foundation that had enabled him to perform his manifold duties.

After blessing the third Hanukah candle, he died of a heart-attack on 27 Kislev 1997,[24] the day of the *yahrzeit* of his step-brother, R. Hayyim Shlomo Horowitz. The rebbe was buried next to his father in the cemetery *Segula* in Petah Tikvah the very next day. R. Shmuel Alexander Unsdorfer and R. Hayyim Leib Deutsch, the rabbis of Petah Tikvah, as well as his sons, Hayyim Elazar and Meir Bezalel Yair, delivered eulogies.

He was survived by five children from his first marriage (Tzvi Nathan David, Hayyim Elazar, R. Moshe Yehuda Leib, R. Yitzhak Yaakov, and one daughter Yitta, the wife of R. Tzvi Williaminsky, and by the two children of his second marriage, a son, Meir Bezalel Yair, and a daughter, who is married to R. Hayyim Leib Grossman, as well as by his grandchildren. His son, who is now an attorney, was a judge in the army. His surviving sisters are Devorah Landau of Tel Aviv and Peska Friedman of New York, the author of *Going Forward*, which deals with her life in Europe.[25]

Two of his sons, R. Moshe Yehuda Leib of Borough Park, and R. Yitzhak Yaakov of Flatbush, who were educated in the Yeshivot of Cleveland, Ohio, became rebbes of Munkacz and Dynov respectively. They established great *yeshivot*, *Darke Teshuva*, and *Minhat Elazar*, and a Kollel *Nahlat Yisrael*, and thus revived the glory of the Munkacz dynasty. R. Moshe Yehuda Leib has great spiritual affinity with the ideology of Satmar and was closely befriended by the late Rebbe of Satmar, R. Yoel Teitelbaum. R. Moshe Yehuda Leib also set up the *Minhat Elazar* Center in Bene Berak, a Kollel *Tiferet Tzvi* in Mea Shearim, *Bate Munkacz* in Mea Shearim, a *Bet Hamidrash* in Rehov Yoel and *Shtieblech* in Montreal, Canada, Los Angeles and North London.

---

24. *Der Yid*, New York, 2 January 1998, p. 39; *Hamodia*, 29 Kislev 1998, p. 2; *Jewish Tribune*, London, 8 January 1998.
25. See Peska Friedman, Note 21.

He also has a girls' school and a high school, named *Bet Frimet.* One of the most popular Bikkur Holim organizations in New York under the name of *Mazkeret Frimet.*

It is sad that R. Baruch—a man of phenomenal vigor and intelligence, a splendid orator, a great linguist, an innovator, a colorful personality who often aroused controversy—failed to obtain the allegiance of the *hasidim* of Munkacz. He was the only rebbe in the history of Hasidism who has ever abdicated his position.

The Land of Israel is particularly precious to the kabbalists and the *hasidim.* The adoption of *Nusah Aari* (the liturgy of Luria) by the *hasidim,* forged another link with the Holy Land. Many *hasidim* yearned for a more personal attachment and sought to settle there. "If I forget thee, O Jerusalem, let my right hand forget her cunning," [26] wept the Jews by the alien waters of Babylon. Throughout their long and bitter exile, the Jews kept alive the memory of their ancient homeland. The passionate love of the *hasidim* for the Holy Land today, finds creative and tangible expression. Now that the re-establishment of the State of Israel is a miraculous *fait accompli,* most of the *hasidim* are among its staunchest supporters, working as well as praying for its welfare and security.

---

26. Psalms 137:5.

Glossary

Adar: Twelfth month of the Hebrew calendar, preceding the spring month of Nisan, approximating to February–March.

Adar sheni: Additional month, generally corresponding to March, occurring in the Hebrew calendar in a leap year. There are seven leap years in every nineteen years in the Hebrew calendar.

Additional prayer: See Musaf.

Aggadah (pl., Aggadot): Lit., "narration"—the nonlegal part of rabbinic literature; homiletic sections of rabbinic literature.

Aliya: Lit., "going up"—term used in connection with being called up to the Torah in the synagogue; also used in connection with immigration to the Holy Land.

Amida: The name by which the prayer of the eighteen blessings is known.

Amora (pl., Amoraim): Lit., "speaker," "interpreter"—title given to the Jewish scholars of Palestine and especially of Babylon in the third to the sixth centuries, whose work and thought is recorded in the Gemarah (see also Talmud).

Arba Minim: Lit., "Four Species"—that is, palm branch, citron, willow, and myrtle, used for the Festival of Tabernacles.

Ashkenazim: Term applied to the Jews of Germany or of Western, Central, or Eastern Europe.

Av: Month in the lunar Jewish calendar, generally corresponding to August.

Beadle (Shamash): Attendant to the rabbi.

Bet Din: Lit., "House of Law"—assembly of three or more learned men acting as a Jewish court of law.

Bet Hamidrash: Lit., "House of Study," used for study and prayer.

Bimah: Platform.

Codes: Systematic compilation of talmudic law and later decisions of rabbinic authorities composed at various periods.

Dayan: A judge, a member of a rabbinical court.

Elul: Sixth month of the Hebrew calendar, corresponding to September–October.

Etrog: Citron, "the fruit of the goodly tree"; one of the Four Species used during the Festival of Tabernacles.

Gabba: Overseer or secretary.

Gaon (pl., Geonim): Title of the head of the Babylonian academies from the end of the sixth to the eleventh centuries; also given to outstanding talmudic scholars.

Gemarah: Discussions and ruling of the Amoraim commenting on the Mishnah and forming part of the Babylonian and Palestinian Talmuds.

Haggadah: Lit., "telling"—the Haggadah is the book that tells the story of the Exodus from Egypt; it is read at the family table on the first two nights of Passover.

Hakafot: Lit., "circuits"—processions with the Torah round the Bimah on Simhat Torah.

Halachah (pl., Halachot): Lit., "walking"—term used for guidance, law, traditional practice, in contradistinction to Aggadah, which includes ethical teachings and everything in rabbinic literature not of a legal nature.

Halukah: Lit., "division"—relief system for distribution of funds in Holy Land; each of the halukah organizations in the Holy Land was called a kollel.

Hanukah: The Festival of Lights—holiday celebrating the victory of the Maccabees in 165 B.C.E.; celebrated for eight days, beginning 25 Kislev.

Haskalah: The Jewish Enlightenment Movement originating in late eighteenth-century Germany, to break away from the narrow limits of Jewish life and acquire the culture and customs of the outside world; an adherent was called a *Maskil*.

Havdalah: Lit., "division"—prayer recited at the conclusion of the Sabbath and Festivals, signifying that the Sabbath or Festival is over.

Herem: Decree of excommunication; Jewish authorities frequently punished certain misdeeds with excommunication and social ostracism.

Heshvan: Seventh month of the Hebrew calendar, corresponding to October–November.

Hevra Kaddisha: Lit., "sacred society"—title applied to a group formed for burying the dead and supervising burial arrangements.

Hol Hamoed: The intermediate days of the festivals of Passover and Tabernacles, on which only essential work may be carried out.

Hoshanah Rabbah: The seventh day of Sukkot is called "the great Hoshanah" because of the seven processions formed around the synagogue. It is a day on which, according to tradition, the ultimate fate of each Jew is decided in the Heavenly Court.

Illui: Title given to an exceptionally brilliant student of the Talmud.

Iyar: Second month of the Hebrew calendar, approximating to April–May.

Kaddish: Lit., "sanctification"—a prayer that marks the end of a unit of the service and refers to the doxology recited in the synagogue; also, a prayer recited in memory of a dead person.

Kaftan: Long coat.

Kapote: Long black coat, formerly common among Jews of Eastern Europe.

Kashrut: Jewish dietary laws.

Kiddush: Benediction recited to inaugurate the Sabbath and festivals, usually over a cup of wine before the meal.

Kiddush HaShem: Sanctification of the Divine Name; the extreme form of this is self-sacrifice for Judaism.

Kirya: A town or suburb.

Kislev: Eighth month of the Hebrew calendar, usually coinciding with November–December.

Kittle: White robe worn by officials on special occasions.

Knesset: The Assembly (the Israel Parliament).

Kol Nidre: The evening service of the Day of Atonement is preceded by the chanting of the *Kol Nidre* (lit., "All Vows").

Lag Ba-Omer: Thirty-third day of the counting of the Omer, corresponding to the eighteenth day of the month of Iyar; observed as a minor holiday.

Lulav: A palm branch.

Maariv: Evening prayer.

Maggid (pl., Maggidim): A popular preacher.

Maskil (pl., maskilim): Follower of the Haskalah movement.

Matzah Shmurah: Lit., "guarded matzah," baked from flour that has been carefully kept from the time of the cutting of the wheat so that no moisture should touch it.

Megillah: The book of Esther, read on the eve and the day of Purim.

Melaveh Malkah: Lit., "escorting the Queen"—applied to the meal after the termination of the Sabbath; accompanied by community singing and often by a discourse from the Rabbi.

Meshulah: Lit., "messenger"—emissary sent to collect funds for religious and charitable institutions.

Mezuzah: Small parchment inscribed with the first two paragraphs of the *Shema* (Deuteronomy 6:4-9, 11, 13-21) that is attached to the right-hand doorpost of an Orthodox Jewish home.

Mikveh: Indoor ritual bath or pool required for Jewish ritual purification.

Minhah: The afternoon prayer.

Minyan (pl., minyanim): Required quorum of ten Jews above the age of thirteen for communal prayer.

Mishnah: Lit., "repetition"—collection of the oral law and rabbinic teachings compiled by Rabbi Judah Ha-Nasi during the early part of the third century that, with the Gemarah, forms the text of the Talmud.

Minagged (pl., Mitnaggedim): Lit., "opponent"—that is, opponent of Hasidism in Eastern Europe.

Mitzvah (pl., mitzvot): Religious precept; also applied to a good and charitable deed.

Moezet Gedole HaTorah: Council of sages.

Mohel: Religious functionary who performs circumcisions.

Mosdot: Institutions.

Moshav: Settlement.

Musaf: The additional *Amida* recited in the morning on the Sabbath, Rosh Hodesh, and Festivals; corresponding to the additional offering sacrificed in the Temple.

Musar: Ethical literature; study of topics on admonition and repentance.

Nigun (pl., nigunim): Lit., "melody".

Ninth Av: Anniversary of the destruction of the First and Second Temples.

Nisan: First month of the Hebrew calendar, generally corresponding to March–April.

Nusah: Lit., "pattern"—term applied to distinguish different liturgical rites.

Orah Hayyim: A code dealing with the ritual obligations of daily life.

Phylacteries: See *tefillin*.

Pidyon: Lit., "redemption"—money followers give to their Rebbe when visiting him.

Pikuah Nefesh: The sacred duty of saving life.

Purim: Lit., "lots"—festival celebrated on 14 Adar in commemoration of the deliverance of the Jews of Persia from the hands of Haman, as recorded in the Book of Esther.

Qvittel: Petition given to a Rebbe.

Rebbe: Religious leader of the hasidic community, as distinct from the rabbi proper or the rav, who discharges the rabbinic functions as spiritual leader of the whole community; occassionally combined in one person.

Responsa: Written replies given to questions on all aspects of Jewish law by qualified rabbinic authorities.

Rosh Hashanah: New Year, the first and second day of Tishri.

Rosh Hodesh: New moon; the first day(s) of the Hebrew month.

Rosh Yeshivah: Head of the talmudical college.

Sabra: Hebrew term applied to a person born in Israel.

Sandak: The person who holds the child during circumcision.

Seder: Lit., "order"—the order of the festive meal at home on the first and second nights of Passover.

Selihot: Penitential prayers recited on certain days of the Jewish calendar.

Semicha: Conferring of the title of "rabbi."

Sephardim: Jews of Spanish, Portuguese, or Middle Eastern extraction.

Sefer Torah: Scroll of the Law.

Seudah: Lit., "meal".

Shadhan: Professional marriage-broker.

Shaharit: Morning service.

Shaitl: Wig worn by Orthodox Jewish women after marriage.

Shalosh Seudot: Third meal, eaten after the afternoon service on the Sabbath, accompanied by community singing and discourses.

Shaatnez: Mingling of fabrics. Garments containing mixed wool and linen are forbidden.

Shavuot: Pentecost or the Feast of Weeks, celebrated on 6 and 7 Sivan, commemorating the Giving of the Torah and the ingathering of the firstfruits.

Shema: "Hear, O Israel" (Deuteronomy 6:4)—the Jewish profession of faith recited during morning and evening prayers.

Shemini Atzeret: Eighth day of Assembly, the concluding day of Sukkot, regarded as a separate festival.

Shemitah: Term used in connection with a sabbatical year; comes from a verb that means "to detach" or "to drop." Hence, the year of *Shemitah* denotes the year of relaxation of debts, the sabbatical years during which the land was to lie fallow and be withdrawn from cultivation.

Shevat: Ninth month of the Hebrew calendar, corresponding to January–February.

Shikkun: Colony of settlement.

Shirayim: Remains of the Rebbe's meal, shared by his followers.

Shofar: The ram's horn blown on the new year.

Shohet: Ritual slaughterer of animals for food, using the method of *Shechitah*.

Shtetel: Yiddish term denoting a small town or village, especially in Eastern Europe before 1914.

Shtiebl (Yiddish, "small room"): Hasidic term for a place of worship (also "klaus").

Shulhan Aruch: Lit., "set table"—standard code of Jewish Law compiled by R. Joseph Caro (1488–1575), in four parts: Orah Hayyim, Yoreh Deah, Even Ha-Ezer, and Hoshen Mishpat.

Shushan Purim: Day succeeding Purim (15 Adar), regarded as a minor holiday.

Simhat Torah: Lit., "Rejoicing of the Law"—name given by the diaspora to the second day of Shemini Atzeret, when the reading of the Pentateuch is completed.

Simhot: Joyous occasions.

Sivan: Third month of the Hebrew calendar, corresponding to May–June.

Siyyum: Lit., "completion"—celebration marking completion of a course of a study.

Streimel: A fur-trimmed hat worn by the hasidim, especially by those from Poland and Galicia.

Sukkah: Festive booth for Tabernacles; wooden hut with a roof of leaves and branches, in which all meals are taken during the festival.

Sukkot: Festival commemorating the wanderings of the children of Israel in the wilderness, observed from 15 to 23 Tishri.

Takkanah: Regulation or ordinance.

Tallit: Lit., "cloak"—commonly used designation for a prayer-shawl with fringes at four corners worn by males in synagogue at Morning Service (Numbers 15:38).

Talmud: Title applied to the two great compilations distinguished as the Babylonian Talmud (*Bavli*) and Palestinian Talmud (*Yerushalmi*), in which the records of academic discussions and of judicial administration of postbiblical Jewish law are assembled. Both Talmuds also contain *Aggadah* or nonlegal material. The Palestinian Talmud was edited in the fourth century C.E. and the Babylonian in about 500 C.E.

Talmud Torah: A school devoted to Jewish religious learning.

Tammuz: Fourth month of the Hebrew calendar, approximating to June–July.

Tanna (pl., Tannaim): Teacher mentioned in the *Mishnah* or in the literature contemporaneous with the *Mishnah*, living during the first two centuries C.E.

Tanya: Philosophical work by R. Shneur Zalman, expanding the principles of Habad; the name is derived from the initial word of the work; also called *Likkute Amarim* ("Collected Sayings").

Tefillin: Lit., "phylacteries"—two black leather boxes fastened to leather straps, worn on the arm and head by an adult male Jew during the weekday morning prayer; the boxes contain four portions of the Pentateuch (Exodus 3:1–10, 11–16; Deuteronomy 6:4–9, 9:13–21), written on parchment.

Tevet: Tenth month of the Hebrew calendar, approximating to September–October.

Tish: Table of the Rebbe.

Tishri: Month of the lunar Hebrew calendar, generally corresponding to October.

Torah: Word variously used for the Pentateuch, the entire Scripture, or the Oral Tradition, as well as for the whole body of religious truth, study, and practice.

Tosaphists: Scholars who wrote novellas on the Talmud.

Yahrzeit: Anniversary of a death.

Yeshivah: Academy of Jewish studies.

Yeshivah Ketanah: Academy for young students.

Yevsektzia: The Jewish branch of the Russian Communist Party, 1918–1930, which was responsible for the destruction of Jewish institutions.

Yiddishkeit: Torah Judaism.

Yom Kippur: The Day of Atonement.

Yoreh Deah: A code dealing with dietary and ritual laws.

Zaddik (pl., Zaddikim): A totally righteous person, a leader of a hasidic group.

Zohar: Lit., "brightness"—chief work of the Kabbalah; commentary on sections of the Pentateuch and parts of the Hagiographa, traditionally ascribed to the Tanna Shimon bar Yochai (second century C.E.), "discovered" by the Spanish kabbalist R. Moses de Leon at the end of the thirteenth century.

Select Bibliography

Selected Bibliography

Alfasi, Yitzhak. *Sefer Haadmorim*. Tel Aviv: Ariel, 1961.

——— *Hahasidut*. Tel Aviv: Hotzat Zion, 1969.

——— *Bisde Hahasidut*. Tel Aviv: Ariel, 1986.

——— *Entziklopedia Lehasidut*, vol. 1. Jerusalem: Mosad Harav Kook, 1986.

——— *Hahasidut V'Shivat Zion*. Tel Aviv: Sifrit Maariv, 1986.

——— *Tiferet Shebetiferet, Bet Gur*. Tel Aviv: Sinai, 1993.

Benayahu, M. "The printing press of R. Israel Bak is Safed," vol. 4 (Hebrew). Jerusalem: Areshet, Mosad Harav Kook, 1966, pp. 271–295.

Birnbaum, Meyer. *Lieutenant Birnbaum*. Brooklyn: Mesorah Publications, 1993.

Federbush, Simon. *Hahasidut Vezion*, Jerusalem: Mosad Harav Kook, 1963.

Geshuri, Meir Shimon. *Haniggun Veharikud Bahasidut*, 3 vols. Tel Aviv: Netzah, 1954–1959.

Halahmi, Meir. *Toldot Hahasidut B'Eretz Yisrael*, vol. 1. Jerusalem: Bamah, 1996.

Halevi, Shoshana. *The Printed Hebrew Book in Jerusalem during the First Half Century (1841–1891)*. Jerusalem: Mechon Ben Zevi, 1963.

Halper, Jeff. *Between Redemption and Revival*. San Francisco: Westview Press, 1991.

Hoffman, Edward. *Despite All Odds*, New York: Simon & Schuster, 1991.

Landau, David. *Piety and Power*, London: Secker & Warburg, 1993.

Lewin, Isaac, ed. *Ele Ezkerah*, 6 vols. New York: Research Institute of Religious Jewry, 1956–1965.

Meijers, Daniel. *Ascetic Hasidism in Jerusalem*. Leiden: E. J. Brill, 1992.

Mintz, Jerome R. *Hasidic People*. Cambridge, Mass.: Harvard University Press, 1992.

Parfitt, Tudor. *The Jews in Palestine (1800–1882)*. Boydell: The Royal Historical Society Press, 1897.

Porush, Shalom Hayyim. *Encyclopedia L'Hasidut*, vol. 1. Jerusalem: Mosad Harav Kook, 1980.

Prager, Moshe. *Ele Shelo Nichneu*, 2 vols. Bene Berak: Netzah, 1963.

Rabinowicz, Harry. *A Guide to Hasidism*. London: Thomas Yoseloff, 1960.

——— *The World of Hasidism*. London: Vallentine Mitchell, 1970.

——— *Hasidism and the State of Israel*. Rutherford: The Littman Library of Jewish Civilization, 1982.

——— *Hasidism, the Movement and Its Masters*. New Jersey: Jason Aronson, 1988.

——— *Hasidic Rebbes*. Israel: Targum/Feldheim, 1989.

——— *A World Apart*. London: Vallentine Mitchell, 1997.

Rabinowicz, Tzvi M. ed. *The Encyclopedia of Hasidism*. New Jersey: Jason Aronson, 1996.

Rabinowitsch, Wolf Zeev. *Hahasidut Halitait*. Jerusalem: Mosad Bialik, 1961.

——— *Lithuanian Hasidism*. London: Vallentine Mitchell, 1970.

Roseman, Moshe. *Founder of Hasidism*. Berkeley: University of California Press, 1966.

Teller, Hanoch. *The Bostoner*. Jerusalem and New York: Feldheim, 1990.

Schindler, Pesach. *Hasidic Responses to the Holocaust in the Light of Hasidic Thought*. New Jersey: Ktav Publishing House, 1990.

Suraski, Aaron. *Rosh Golat Ariel*, vol. 1. Jerusalem: Mechon Amudei Esh, 1993; vol. 2., 1995.

——— *Blavat Esh*, vol. 1. Tel Aviv: Esh Dat Rabbinical Seminary, 1996.

Unger, Menashe. *Sefer Kedoshim*. New York: Shulzinger, 1967.

Werfel (Raphael), Yitzhak. *Hahasidut V'Eretz Yisrael*. Jerusalem: Hotzaat Sefarim, 1940.

Wolpin, Nisson, ed. *Torah Luminaries*. Brooklyn: Mesorah Publications, 1994.

——— *Torah Lives*. Brooklyn: Mesorah Publications, 1995.

Wunder, Meir. *Meore Galicia*, vols. 1-4. Jerusalem: Mechon L'hanzeah Yehudit Galicia, 1978-1990.

Yehezke'eli, Moshe. *Hazalat Harebe Mebelz Megay Haharegah*. Jerusalem: Yeshurun, 1962.

Newspapers and Periodicals

Israeli Daily Newspapers, *Hamodia* and *Hatzofe*
Yated Neeman (weekly), *Hamahane Haharedi* (weekly), *Jewish Tribune, London* (weekly)

Index

About the Author

Dr. Tzvi Rabinowicz, a descendant of famous hasidic families in Poland, was the regional rabbi of Cricklewood, Willesden and Brondesbury Synagogues in London. He obtained a bachelor's degree from the University of London, where he was also awarded a Ph.D. for his thesis entitled, "The Life and Times of Rabbi Joseph Colon (1420-1480)," a study of Italian Jewry during the Renaissance. He received a Rabbinical Diploma from Jews' College, London. Dr. Rabinowicz was a recipient of the Sir Robert Waley-Cohen Memorial Scholarship and of a Fellowship of the Memorial Foundation for Jewish Culture. A noted historian and writer, he has lectured extensively for the Extra-mural Department of the University of London and the United States. He was recently shortlisted by the London Times as best preacher for 1998. Dr. Rabinowicz's love for Hasidism is made evident by his constant researches into its history; by his many articles on this subject; and by his previously published works, including: *The World of Hasidism, Hasidism and the State of Israel, Hasidism: The Movement and Its Masters, Hasidic Rebbes*, and *A World Apart*. He has also edited *The Encyclopedia of Hasidism*.